JAZZ MASTERS
of the 20s

7/16

JAZZ MASTERS
of the 20s

RICHARD HADLOCK

New introduction by the author

A DA CAPO PAPERBACK

Library of Congress Cataloging in Publication Data

Hadlock, Richard.
  Jazz masters of the 20s / by Richard Hadlock: new introduction by the author.
    (A Da Capo paperback)
  Reprint. Originally published: New York: Macmillan,
1972.
  Includes bibliographies, discographies, and indexes.
  1. Jazz musicians — United States — Biography. 2. Jazz
music — United States. 3. Jazz music — United States — Discog-
raphy. I. Title. II. Title: Jazz masters of the twenties.
[ML394.H33   1988]
785.42'092'2 — dc19
[B]   88-15963
ISBN 0-306-80328-3 (pbk.)

Excerpt from *Jazz: Its Evolution and Essence* by Andre Hodeir, Translated by David Noakes, copyright © 1956 by the Grove Press. Used by
permission.

Excerpt from *Really the Blues* by Mezz Mezzrow and Bernard Wolfe, copyright © 1946 by Random House, Inc. Reprinted by permission of the
Harold Matson Company.

Excerpt from Tom Davin's "Conversation with James P. Johnson" in *Jazz
Panorama*, edited by Martin Williams, copyright © 1964, The Macmillan
Company.

"Jail House Blues" by Bessie Smith and Clarence Williams, © copyright
MXMXXIII by Pickwick Music Corporation, New York, N.Y. Copyright
renewed MCML and assigned to Pickwick Music Corporation, 322 West
48th Street, New York, New York. Used by permission. All rights reserved.

Excerpts from *Jazz: Hot and Hybrid* by Winthrop Sargeant (E. P. Dutton,
1946). Used by permission of the author.

This Da Capo Press paperback edition of *Jazz Masters of the
20s* is an unabridged republication of the edition published
in New York in 1972, here supplemented with a new
introduction and index. It is reprinted by arrangement with
Macmillan Publishing Co.

Published by Da Capo Press, Inc.
A Subsidiary of Plenum Publishing Corporation
233 Spring Street, New York, N.Y. 10013

CONTENTS

INTRODUCTION TO THE
DA CAPO PAPERBACK EDITION

So young is America's best-known music that close to one-third of
its recorded history has passed since this book was originally
published in 1965. At the time I undertook research for *Jazz
Masters of the '20s* virtually all the significant books ever written
about jazz could be stored in a dozen orange crates. Today the
documents and literature of jazz would fill rooms, not just boxes.
In 1965 many of the pioneer players represented in this book were
still performing. Pianist Earl Hines was actually *beginning* the
most prolific and musically exciting phase of his long recording
career. With rare exceptions — saxophonists Benny Carter and
Bud Freeman are two — the talented people considered here are
retired or gone now.

I have conversed with several young jazz musicians of the '80s
who think that John Coltrane was an "early" jazzman. Others I
have met do know about "oldtimers" Charlie Parker and Dizzy
Gillespie, but it is an uncommon initiate who is familiar with the
contributions of James P. Johnson or Don Redman. That is, I suggest, a pity. There is still much to learn from the early masters. A
jazz pianist who hasn't studied Fats Waller, a jazz trumpet player
who missed hearing Louis Armstrong's best recordings, are people
not properly grounded in their own music. However, I see some
hopeful signs of change in young attitudes, as in the historical
awareness of youthful trumpeter Wynton Marsalis. His roots lie
deep in New Orleans, a city that has erected a statue of its own
Louis Armstrong, and Wynton is proud of his lineage.

In recent years stage productions built around the compositions
of "Fats" Waller, Duke Ellington, Eubie Blake, Scott Joplin and
Ma Rainey have helped to remind young Americans of their
musical heritage. Jazz, often presented as "nostalgia," is widely
heard on radio these days and there is a proliferation of repertory
jazz bands making the rounds of clubs, concert halls, and festivals
all over the world. One should mention also, the rather eclectic
outlook of most jazz schools, which are a relatively recent

development in this country. All these activities may encourage new generations to treat older jazz with increased respect.

My own perspective on the '20s remains pretty much what it was in 1965, but there are details I might add today. For example, it is now clear that the wonderful swing brought out of New Orleans by Louis Armstrong was already known to some in the North (and even abroad) by way of reedman Sidney Bechet. Bechet was affecting younger players such as Benny Carter, Johnny Hodges, and Coleman Hawkins in the Northeast before Armstrong was well known.

Today there is such an outpouring of reissue recordings by the early masters that a comprehensive list would take more space than this book could provide. And, too, the list would be outdated before it could be printed. With the arrival of compact discs, all predictions of availability are in question. The best course for the beginning collector is to visit a jazz record shop and look for important artists' names. Most of the finest work of Armstrong, Jelly Roll Morton, Ellington, Bessie Smith, Beiderbecke, Benny Goodman, Hines, Jack Teagarden, and Waller is available, although finding it all may require some searching. The original reference lists found here are old indeed, but they cover the same music now available under dozens of labels from many countries.

The more we listen to (and read about) the great jazz musicians of the '20s and beyond the more they come to life and continue to help shape the music of today and tomorrow. They are the founders of America's own classical music — jazz — and their names should not be filed away in a bottom drawer with faded photographs. For this listener, at least, every playing of a record by Armstrong, Beiderbecke, Smith, or Waller is a free and fruitful music lesson. I hope that each reader of this book may discover a comparable sense of pleasure and satisfaction from listening to these masters.

A final word of thanks is due to Judy Kopanic, who gave generously of her time to compile the index, which is new with this edition of *Jazz Masters of the '20s*.

— RICHARD B. HADLOCK
Berkeley, California
April, 1988

INTRODUCTION

A FEW WORDS are in order on what this book is and what it is not, along with some general remarks about jazz in the twenties.

The book deals with the music of a select group of gifted jazz musicians who played in the twenties. It is not a treatise on the social, economic, or psychological conditions surrounding jazz at the time, although there are fleeting glimpses of some of these outside pressures. Many books already describe in detail the non-musical vagaries of the twenties, and I have elected to bypass those aspects of the period in an attempt to trace the *musical* changes this decade brought to jazz in America.

It should be remembered, however, that the musicians dealt with here were subjected variously to many stresses and inequities brought about by Prohibition, avarice and callousness in the music business, race prejudice, two economic depressions, and public apathy toward honest jazz. Few of these men were able to earn livings as jazzmen exclusively during the twenties, although their gifts for improvisation were frequently exploited by leaders and promoters.

Despite public indifference to its aims, jazz underwent extensive change and development between 1920 and 1930. At the beginning of the decade, the handful of jazz records produced was devoted largely to an agitated novelty music, dominated by vaudevillians, trick-effect artists, and musicians looking for profitable trends. Except for the Original Dixieland Jazz Band (and even this group relied partly on musical eccentricity for its success), virtually no significant jazzmen recorded until 1923. (An obscure 1922 Kid Ory date is of little importance in the larger picture.) But by 1929, most of the period's major contributors, embracing a wide variety of artistically valid styles, were making records, notwithstanding the fact that much of their product had to be marketed as dance, novelty, or "race" music.

In the twenties, most of those who listened at all regarded jazz as merely an energetic background for dancers; the few who sought more profound values in the music tended to accept Paul

Whiteman's concert productions (*Rhapsody in Blue*, etc.) as the only jazz worth taking seriously. Again, magazines ran long pieces on jazz without having much idea what it was all about. One, called *The Dance*, bubbled over the music with articles such as "Beyond Jazz" and "Blame It on Jazz" around 1927, but the writers turned out to be concerned only with the Charleston and the fox trot, not with the musical worth of individual improvisations. In reviewing current "dance" records, the same magazine lumped together releases by Sam Lanin, Miff Mole, Fred Waring, Jelly Roll Morton, Ben Bernie, and the Dixieland Jug Blowers, without much regard for purpose, originality, or profundity.

This mass misunderstanding, occurring in even large segments of the music and entertainment worlds, resulted in the development of a spirit of "underground" comradeship among jazz musicians. It was a spirit that permitted a free exchange of ideas across traditionally forbidding economic, racial, musical, and geographic barriers, but it also bred clannishness and the tendency to set up a closed society-within-a-society. Some musicians never recovered from this period of disengagement from the world around them. Bix Beiderbecke is the classic example. Beiderbecke was actually not widely known outside musician circles in his own lifetime. Paul Whiteman's most celebrated soloist in 1928 was not Bix, but nonjazz trumpeter Henry Busse, who drew $350 a week, or $150 more than Beiderbecke. Most jazz musicians, including many who were to achieve international fame a few years later, despaired of finding recognition in the twenties.

When immersed in the story of these jazzmen, then, it is useful to remember that their world occupied an almost unacknowledged corner of the entertainment industry throughout the so-called Jazz Age. Much of the best jazz of the decade was doubtless played in private sessions after regular jobs. That any worthwhile jazz at all was recorded and preserved is a wonder, owing in part to the dedication and determination of the musicians and in part to the help of a few recording executives sympathetic to jazz.

The choice of musicians to represent the decade is basically my own. However, it will be noted that some important names are conspicuously absent: Coleman Hawkins, Duke Ellington, King Oliver, Baby Dodds, and Sidney Bechet are examples. The reason for these omissions is that additional volumes in the series of which this book is a part will cover New Orleans jazzmen and jazzmen important during the thirties, some of whom happened to be active and influential also in the twenties. I have, however, made numerous references to several of these men throughout the book.

I have regarded each man's music in two ways. First, I've looked at the individual's work for its own value—how the music grew, at what point it reached its apex, and, if necessary, why it declined. Second, a good deal of emphasis is placed upon each subject's historical function as a bridge from what came before him to what grew in part out of his own ideas. Indeed, the jazz masters described in this book were selected to some extent on the basis of their influence over other musicians.

In the nine chapters, then, will be found more than just the biographies of nine key jazz figures of the twenties. The chapter about Bessie Smith, for example, also touches on the valuable contributions of Ma Rainey and Ethel Waters. The story of Fletcher Henderson cannot be divorced from the early career of Don Redman. To understand the positions of Jack Teagarden and Fats Waller in jazz history, it is desirable to know something of Miff Mole and James P. Johnson.

The Chicagoans almost always have been treated as a group, and it struck me as logical to do so again. The story revolves around those whom I felt to be the most creative in their approach to jazz. These eight individualists (Goodman, Stacy, Sullivan, Teschemacher, Freeman, Krupa, Tough, and, though not a true Chicagoan, Russell) had a kind of collective effect on jazz, but it was a significant effect nonetheless. (Goodman, of course, exerted a wide personal influence over several areas of jazz as well, but his largest contributions were made in the thirties.)

The book is not comprehensive in its coverage of all these players. The Armstrong chapter, for example, picks up the trumpet player upon his departure from King Oliver's band and leaves him in the early thirties. So long and all-pervasive is this man's career that distinct segments of it turn up in separate volumes of the series.

Most of these biographies carry through the entire lives of the subjects, although the focus is always on the twenties. This leads to at least one unfortunate implication. It may seem that, say, the

Chicagoans were at their individual creative peaks in the twenties. Actually, they were at their best in the thirties and forties, although their initial (and most important) collective impact was made in the twenties. For that reason, their recorded music (excepting Goodman's) is followed down to recent times. The approach is similar for Earl Hines, Jack Teagarden, and Fats Waller, but I have given in less detail the events after 1930.

This is not a set of bio-discographies. It happens, though, that records are the only real evidence of just what any musician was playing at a given time. Therefore, I have relied largely upon recorded performances in describing and judging each subject's music. It should be remembered that records are only a guide and may not always present a complete picture of jazz at a particular period. This is especially true of the twenties, a decade that was not really very interested in jazz for its own sake.

The lists of books and LP records following each chapter are not meant to be complete biblio-discographies. They are, in the main, currently available reference material, but I have also included a number of out-of-print books and hard-to-find records for those who would like to dig deeper into the subject through libraries or stores dealing in collectors' records.

I am indebted to the following persons, who gave time and/or material assistance to me in connection with this book: Jimmy Archey, Louis Armstrong, Charles Beiderbecke, Harry Brooks, Paul A. Brown, Garvin Bushell, Ralph Collins, Edd Dickerman, Eddie Duran, Roy Eldridge, Phil Elwood, Phil Evans, Pops Foster, Bud Freeman, Russell Glynn, Marty Grosz, Ruth Hadlock, Tony Hagert, Al Hall, Jim Hall, Horace Henderson, Earl Hines, Virginia Hodes, Darnell Howard, Lonnie Johnson, Peck Kelley, Charles Lindsley, Jackie Mabley, Paul Miller, Grover Mitchell, Red Nichols, Jerome Pasquall, Norman Pierce, Leon Radsliff, Kenneth Rexroth, Rocky Rockenstein, Joe Rushton, Pee Wee Russell, Arthur Schutt, George Shearing, Muggsy Spanier, John Steiner, Jack Stratford, Joe Sullivan, Ralph Sutton, Jack Teagarden, Norma Teagarden, Joe Venuti, Martin Williams, Mary Lou Williams, and Estella Yancey.

LOUIS ARMSTRONG
FROM 1924 TO 1931

JULIAN "CANNONBALL" ADDERLEY, an outstanding jazz saxophonist yet unborn when Louis Armstrong was beginning to receive international acclaim in the twenties, once asked an older musician friend for the real facts about Armstrong. "I know Louis was good and got all the fame," began Adderley, "but who was *really* the top man on trumpet in the old days?"

The answer was swift and unequivocal: "Louis Armstrong was head and shoulders above them all."

To a young musician of the late fifties like Adderley, Armstrong the pacesetting trumpeter seemed more legend than fact, for Louis had long since settled into a routinized presentation of his talents that offered only fleeting hints of his earlier creative powers.

The physical aspects of Armstrong's playing equipment have, however, withstood the years remarkably well. It was his good fortune to be born with an almost perfect physiological trumpet-playing mechanism, and it was mostly in the twenties that Louis put it to best use. From the beginning, the trumpeter enjoyed the physical assets of ideal lip size, extraordinarily relaxed and open throat muscles, a broad and powerful diaphragm, good strong teeth, and a robust, sinewy frame. Large lips allowed him maximum compression for high notes without losing the use of soft flesh for tone quality. Louis' open throat and loose vocal cords were in his favor because the increased tension of high-note playing did not constrict these passages, and as a result, his tone remained full and clear in the highest register. His diaphragm furnished the push for the air that produced the Armstrong trumpet sound, and his fine physical condition accounted for the remarkable Armstrong stamina that continues to amaze his colleagues to this day. In short, Louis Armstrong was (and is) a natural trumpet player in every physical way. Happily, he also possessed a fine musical mind.

This was the man whom Joe Oliver sent "down home" for in 1922. Louis, already considered the best trumpeter in New Orleans, had timorously turned down an offer from Fletcher Henderson the year before, but Oliver was an old friend and mentor who played the familiar New Orleans style. Louis felt secure enough to accept, and he promptly left for Chicago. He spent two important years with King Oliver's popular band—making records, touring, playing shows, and learning a great deal about music and life in the world outside New Orleans.

Actually, Armstrong had traveled away from home before, in Mississippi riverboat orchestras. These bands, though, were made up largely of New Orleans musicians, and the effect was that of working in a floating New Orleans ballroom. Armstrong learned more reading on the boats than he had in previous hometown jobs, which had consisted largely in playing for picnics. marching in parades, and entertaining in noisy cabarets or second-class dance halls. The trumpeter had worked often for Kid Ory, sitting in the trumpet chair held by Joe Oliver until 1918. Louis was more than content to follow in Oliver's footsteps and, of course, felt honored when he received the call from Chicago.

"I guess Joe decided to have two [cornets] because he figured I could blend with him, because he liked me and wanted me to be with him," Louis recalled in 1950. "He probably wouldn't have sent for anyone else. . . . He must have remembered the way I played, the things we'd talked about. I must have proved it to him *some* way before he left [New Orleans] in 1918."

Armstrong, fresh out of the waifs' home at 14, had met Oliver and had spent nearly four years studying his style. On the basis of this experience, Oliver decided he could use the youngster in 1922. Joe got more than he had bargained for.

The young second trumpeter developed a quick ear for harmony in the semi-improvising Oliver ensemble. He learned, too, the value of discretion and restraint in an organization dedicated to building a *band* sound rather than a showcase for individual soloists. From Oliver himself, Louis picked up valuable secrets of rhythmic phrasing, of good blues playing, and of establishing a sure, driving lead melody line.

"He's the one that stopped me playin' all those variations—what they call bebop today," Louis recalled in 1949. " 'You get yourself a lead [melody] and you stick to it,' Papa Joe told me, and I always do."

The Oliver band was an ideal school of higher learning for the already advanced Armstrong, as it provided for him a logical bridge from the conservative New Orleans outlook to the more advanced musical ideas of the bustling entertainment world of Chicago. By the time Louis left Oliver in the summer of 1924, he had married pianist Lil Hardin, a non-New Orleanian and perhaps the most sophisticated member of Oliver's band, and had begun to lose his provincial New Orleans ways.

As the old New Orleans gang (clarinetist Johnny Dodds, drummer Baby Dodds, trombonist Honoré Dutrey) departed from the Oliver band, to be replaced by more-schooled players, such as clarinetist Buster Bailey, Louis began to broaden his interests, musical and otherwise. He developed his range, tone, articulation, and reading ability to new levels. Shortly after leaving Oliver, he studied embouchure with a German teacher in Chicago. (Other New Orleans jazzmen, such as Jimmy Noone and Tommy Ladnier, also studied with Chicago teachers in an attempt to refine their "down home" playing styles.)

Lil Armstrong was as aggressive as her husband was conservative, and it was largely her prodding that finally forced Louis to seek a more suitable setting for his rapidly expanding abilities. He was more than ready for a job playing first trumpet.

"I never did try to overblow Joe at any time when I played with him," Armstrong recalled many years after. "It wasn't any show-off thing like a youngster probably would do today. He still played whatever part he had played, and I always played 'pretty' under him. Until I left Joe, I never did tear out. Finally, I thought it was about time to move along, and he thought so, too. He couldn't keep me any longer. But things were always very good between us—that *never* did cease."

One of Armstrong's last recordings with the Oliver band, *Krooked Blues*, demonstrates how ready for independence Louis was, even in late 1923. Under the leader's attractive muted lead can be heard a distant, full-toned cornet playing a "pretty" countermelody. The second cornetist seems to be attempting ideas of more interest than those of Oliver himself.

After an unsuccessful application to join Sammy Stewart's

highly rated band, Louis went with Ollie Powers at the Dreamland as a first trumpet player. It was a significant initial step in the right direction. With Lil supplying encouragement, Louis gained confidence and a sense of showmanship quickly. He stayed with Powers about three months, until September, 1924, when Fletcher Henderson offered him the third chair in his new three-man trumpet section. Henderson's was considered by many to be the best band in the country at that time, and Louis, who had not yet gained full confidence, accepted somewhat diffidently. He received only $55 a week—$20 less than he had earned with Oliver a few months before—but this was to be an important final phase of Louis' basic training. In Henderson's eleven-man organization, he found high ensemble discipline and contact with a wide variety of musical materials that extended well beyond even the ambitious arrangements Louis had played in riverboat orchestras several years earlier.

The 24-year-old trumpeter was uncomfortable at first, but he unwound within a couple of weeks, especially after his old friend from the Oliver band, Buster Bailey, joined the reed section. (It was Armstrong who had recommended Bailey to Henderson.) Fletcher began to feature Louis as a soloist and vocalist after only three weeks. It was a demanding job—always working on new arrangements; playing opposite leading dance orchestras of the period, such as Vincent Lopez and Sam Lanin; and keeping up with other superior instrumentalists in the band, such as tenor saxophonist Coleman Hawkins, trombonist Charlie Green, and alto saxophonist Don Redman—but Louis saw it through and emerged a much improved musician for his experience.

Henderson was headquartered in New York, and this meant exposure to a wholly new set of influences for Armstrong. Chicago had imported so many New Orleans jazzmen that it was almost like home for them, but New York had its own traditions and its own jazz stars. As Louis exchanged information with instrumentalists like Red Nichols and Miff Mole, he was as impressed by their technical command and polish as they were by his extraordinary power and blues feeling. Armstrong also admired the straight section work of trumpeters who played in opposing bands at New York's Roseland Ballroom.

"Vincent Lopez came in there as guest one time," Louis has

recalled. "B. A. Rolfe was with him, and he would play a tune called *Shadowland* an octave higher than it was written. I observed that, and it inspired me to make *When You're Smiling*. [Louis recorded this tune in 1929.] The way I look at it, that's the way a trumpet *should* play. If something's supposed to be played high, you play it that way, or you play it in whatever register it should be. But I don't dig that skating around a note just because it's high."

Louis had further praise for Vic D'Ippolito, first trumpeter with Sam Lanin's dance band, who "just naturally didn't play as high as B. A. Rolfe, but when it was time to hit the high notes, he hit 'em."

Henderson allowed Louis' natural showmanship to blossom at this time as well. Thursday nights at the Roseland were set aside for visiting acts, and Louis joined the parade of singers and dancers with his raw-throated vocals and showstopping trumpet solos. A great favorite on such occasions was *Everybody Loves My Baby*, which Henderson soon recorded, complete with "scat" (meaningless syllables) vocal breaks by Louis. It was his first recording as a singer, but it went largely unnoticed at the time.

Armstrong was still not known outside a small circle of musicians in 1925, but he was always successful with patrons as an entertainer who could sing, mug, dance, and play incredibly good cornet. On one occasion, he appeared as a special guest at Harlem's Savoy Ballroom and brought the house down. It was dramatic evidence to the still-humble New Orleans youth that he had something of real value as an entertainer and that people responded to him alone, regardless of what setting he worked within.

Louis' musical position at this juncture can be ascertained by the Henderson recordings on which he soloed. Fletcher's arrangements of *Words, Copenhagen, Shanghai Shuffle, When You Do What You Do, How Come You Do Me Like You Do?, Why Couldn't It Be Poor Little Me?*, and *Mandy, Make Up Your Mind* are superior period pieces—but period pieces nonetheless—that suddenly become transformed into stirring jazz vehicles when Armstrong solos. Even the exceptional tenor saxophone solos by young Coleman Hawkins sound stilted and bloodless alongside Armstrong's authoritative statements.

There were several factors leading to Louis' preeminence in the Henderson band. One was his deep identification with the blues, which allowed him to turn the most cloying popular tune into a heartfelt and moving musical declaration. Another was his *singing* approach to the horn, stemming from common New Orleans musical practices and his own vocal experiences. Regardless of tempo, Louis always *completed* each phrase and carried each sustained tone out to its fullest value, creating the illusion of unhurried ease even in the most turbulent arrangement. New York musicians aimed for just the opposite effect; they clipped their notes short and skipped from one choppy phrase to another in an attempt to play ever "hotter" solos. Ironically, it is Louis who still sounds "hot" on these vintage recordings, while most of the New York jazzmen appear painfully dated and about as hot as yesterday's dishwater.

Still another factor that set Armstrong apart from his Henderson colleagues was his superb sense of time and syncopation. On *Shanghai Shuffle,* for example, he plays eight bars of his solo on one note, but there is no sense of repetition or boredom; rather, this one note becomes a vibrant thematic unit because Louis selected the ideal spots to place it for maximum rhythmic impact. It was a deceptively simple-sounding device that the trumpeter was to use to good effect many times in later years.

Finally, Louis stood out because he possessed the already mentioned physical attributes for playing more trumpet than anyone else in jazz had been able to before. These attributes, combined with his New Orleans spirit, were regarded as natural phenomena by other musicians. In addition, he was a competent third-chair section man who could handle difficult Henderson parts ("After he made one mistake," said Henderson drummer Kaiser Marshall years later, "he didn't make it again") and a reliable sideman who took his music seriously, was easy to get along with, appeared on time, and saved his money. Henderson was thoroughly pleased with young Armstrong.

While working in New York in 1924 and 1925, Louis collaborated with pianist Clarence Williams and clarinetist-saxophonist Sidney Bechet on a set of remarkable recordings in the New Orleans small-band style. Bechet, a fellow New Orleanian, was probably the only jazzman in New York at the time who could match Armstrong's brilliance in every way. When the two men improvised together, each prodding the other to more daring flights, they usually finished in a dead heat. The best of the series is *Cake Walkin' Babies,* recorded for the Okeh label in early 1925. Like many of Louis' recordings of the period, this one documents his large debt to Joe Oliver, particularly in the passages where Louis leads the collectively improvising ensemble.

Despite Armstrong's authority and inventiveness on most of the Clarence Williams dates, it was the more experienced Bechet who initially set the pace and tone of each performance. A recording like *I'm a Little Blackbird* is virtually Sidney's show. Yet Armstrong was the perfect foil for the amazing Bechet talent, for Sidney responded positively to Louis' proper New Orleans ensemble manners. Looking back on these sessions and an unsuccessful 1940 re-creation of them, Bechet commented in his book *Treat It Gentle:*

> That's why anyone who knows about jazz music can feel those [1940] records weren't what they should have been. You can have every tub on its own bottom all right, but that don't make real music. What I know is, those other records we'd made back in the 'twenties were talked about much more than those we made at this session in 'forty. The 2:19 *Blues,* we'd put that out again, and *Down in Honky Tonk Town.* But there was nothing missing from those first ones; they were something you could listen to and not have to do any waiting for the music to arrive, because it *was* arriving. They had that feeling right there. In the old days there wasn't no one so anxious to take someone else's run. We were working together. Each person, he was the other person's music: You could feel that really running through the band, making itself up and coming out so new and strong. We played as a group then.

Louis Armstrong was far removed from the lessons of Joe Oliver by 1940.

Other classic performances recorded by Bechet and Armstrong in the mid-twenties were *Nobody Knows the Way I Feel This Mornin', Mandy, Make Up Your Mind, Coal Cart Blues, Texas Moaner Blues, Papa De-Da-Da, Santa Claus Blues,* and another version of *Cake Walkin' Babies* for the Gennett label. It is interesting to note that the first session in this Clarence Williams series was recorded at the time Louis joined Henderson and the last just before he left to return to Chicago. On the final Bechet-Armstrong date in October, 1925, the soprano saxophonist was no longer able to determine the musical direction of each performance, for Louis had increased his stature in the preceding year and was now the dominant force in the group.

He had begun, too, to move away from Oliver and to reach into his own bag of ideas. Less and less did he utilize the plunger mute, an old Oliver trademark. Louis' breaks were now more involved, and his ensemble lead lines were becoming distinctly his own rather than those of "Papa Joe." On one occasion, Louis even played in a New York "Dixieland" framework not unlike that of the Memphis Five—on *Terrible Blues* and *Santa Claus Blues,* recorded with Buster Bailey and Lil Armstrong under the name of the Red Onion Jazz Babies.

If Louis proved musically and commercially successful under the widely differing circumstances of the Henderson and Williams recording sessions, he demonstrated an even more moving and salable side of his musical personality in a series of New York recordings with leading blues singers of the day. A solid market for urban female blues shouters had recently grown to large proportions, and Louis, as an associate of pianist Henderson (a veteran blues accompanist), found his earthy blues playing much in demand. Some dates included Henderson and members of his band, while others were handled by Clarence Williams, but what made most of these sessions special events were Armstrong's moving countermelodies—melodies much like those he had often played beneath Joe Oliver's singing lead cornet a year before.

Louis' blues performances seemed to vary with his mood and the spirit of the individual singer with whom he worked. On Trixie Smith's *Railroad Blues,* he returns to an almost pure Joe Oliver style, but *The World's Jazz Crazy,* recorded the same day, finds Armstrong playing Armstrong, if on an elemental level. Again, behind Ma Rainey's great dark voice, Louis reverts to Oliver and the plunger mute on *Countin' the Blues* but matches the stately singer in a more personal way on *See, See Rider.* (A small Henderson group, including clarinetist Bailey, worked this date with Rainey and Armstrong, but their abortive attempts to play convincing blues serves only to underline the superiority of Louis' contributions.)

The most dramatic matching of talents on record during this period was that of Armstrong and Bessie Smith, whose monumental voice reduced all ordinary players on her recordings to mere background kibitzers. Bessie's mixed training in Southern country blues singing and Northern showmanship paralleled Louis' own experience, and the musical exchanges between these two major performers are of considerable interest. The first date, held only a few months after Armstrong's arrival in New York, was marked by a good deal of straightforward Oliver-like cornet playing. *Cold in Hand Blues, Reckless Blues,* and *You've Been a Good Old Wagon* features fundamental understated plunger-muted cornet counterstatements that might easily have been the work of Oliver at his best—complete to wa-wa-mute effects. On *Good Old Wagon,* Armstrong even attempts the highly personal Oliver "cry," although the result is not especially convincing, and Louis seldom, if ever, attempted this again. (Incidentally, Clyde McCoy's Oliver-inspired *Sugar Blues* might demonstrate how far this "crying" device can be carried in unmusical directions.) In Bessie's version of *St. Louis Blues,* Louis seems more inclined to play his own way, with mixed results. His own expansive style sets up a highly competitive force that tends to intrude upon rather than complement the whole vocal performance. The cornetist obeys the rules, all right (play when the singer breathes, answer her statements with logical phrases, provide a provocative lead-in note as a springboard for the singer's next statement); the problem is simply that Armstrong commands so much attention himself that the listener might momentarily lose touch with the continuity of the blues song as interpreted by Bessie Smith.

Bessie undoubtedly noted this tendency herself, for she seldom used Armstrong after that. Two more dates in May, 1925, producing four titles, ended their association on records. On this occasion, Louis had left Oliver still further behind and was operating more completely within his own style. He is very much the soloist on *Careless Love Blues,* even to running notes into Bessie's words and attempting ideas not necessarily related to the song material as Bessie understood it. The final title may have expressed Bessie's feeling about the collaboration—*I Ain't Gonna Play No Second Fiddle.*

While in New York, Louis also recorded with singers Clara

Smith, Sippie Wallace, Alberta Hunter, Maggie Jones, and others. On Maggie Jones's *Screamin' the Blues* and *Good Time Flat Blues,* he again demonstrates his ambiguous musical posture of the time. The first title shows Louis in a highly cooperative blues-accompanist frame of mind, while the second, *Good Time Flat,* serves only as a stepping-off place for Armstrong the virtuoso cornetist. In this instance, his backing is busy, self-contained, and more musically advanced than the setting calls for. However, the recording is of value precisely because it *is* a fine example of early Armstrong bravura playing, and Miss Jones indeed *is* playing "second fiddle."

Louis spent the summer of 1925 touring with Henderson, who had lined up a long string of one-night engagements in New England and Pennsylvania. This tour brought the sound of Armstrong's horn to many musicians in small cities who had never heard him before, beginning the spiral of influence that eventually affected every jazz trumpeter in the country and beyond. Henderson frequently met other reputable bands in music "battles," and these contests again did much to bring Louis to the attention of musicians and, naturally, of the dancing public as well. It was during this period, too, that Louis discovered the commercial value of his natural broad range on the horn. He began catering to demands for higher notes by performing stunts, such as blowing more than 250 high C's in a row and topping them off with a high F.

Lil Armstrong felt that her husband belonged with her in Chicago, so she talked the owner of the Dreamland, Bill Bottoms, into offering Louis $75 a week to play for him. At the same time, Okeh Records offered a recording contract for a series of small-band dates to be conducted in the older New Orleans style. Chicago had the men Louis wanted for these dates, and the job with Lil was secure, so Louis gave his notice to Henderson. Young Rex Stewart of Elmer Snowden's band was selected as Louis' replacement, but Rex balked at even attempting to fill his idol's chair. It was several months before he finally worked up the courage to join Fletcher.

By the time Louis left Henderson, the band had become the finest "hot" band in the country, and Fletcher's arrangements, deeply influenced by Armstrong's phrasing, were moving rapidly toward a modern four-to-the-bar swing idiom. The ensemble performances were no longer stilted and static, but rather free-flowing and as impelling as the improvised solos. A special attraction was *Sugar Foot Stomp,* which Fletcher borrowed from Oliver (who called it *Dippermouth Blues*) and used as a show-case for Armstrong. Louis' recording of *Sugar Foot Stomp* with the Henderson band makes it clear that his break with Oliver was now complete. Though his melodic lines adhere to the classic Oliver version, Louis discarded the plunger mute and swung into his solo with a distinctly modern 4/4 manner of phrasing.

A couple of final New York recording sessions left no doubt that Louis was fully prepared for his own important upcoming Okeh dates. With singer Eva Taylor, he made *You Can't Shush Katie,* contributing a magnificent solo that briefly changes the musical level of the recording from dull to inspired. Days before leaving New York, Louis recorded with James P. Johnson, Don Redman, and others in a session that included another *I Ain't Gonna Play No Second Fiddle.* This appears to be Armstrong's first recorded effort on the trumpet, for in place of his characteristic rounded cornet tone, there is the penetrating, edgy sound of the longer in-strument. If it is indeed a new and different horn, it seems admi-rably suited to Armstrong; his playing on these casual November, 1925, recordings ranks with his finest early work and—perhaps due to the incisive trumpet tone—is enhanced by an even more authoritative air than had prevailed on earlier recordings.

Immediately upon his return to Chicago, Louis plunged into an around-the-clock schedule of record dates and club work. Veteran New Orleans trombonist Kid Ory had come in from California (at Louis' request) to make records and to work with the Armstrongs at the Dreamland. Soon Erskine Tate, a popular orchestra con-ductor who specialized in movie theater work, convinced Louis he could play for him and still have time to handle the Dreamland job later in the evening. Working (on trumpet) with Tate brought a new audience to Armstrong—an audience of young people, conservative middle-class fans, and musicians who couldn't afford the Prohibition prices of after-hours nightclubs.

Okeh Records knew it had a valuable property in this amazing young trumpeter and put Armstrong to work again as a blues ac-companist. In the first year of his contract with the label, Louis recorded more sides with blues singers than with his own Hot Five. The blues sessions were deliberately earthy and calculated to appeal essentially to Southern migrants living in the North. A few of the blues songs had genuine folk roots, but many were hastily contrived pieces designed to delight listeners who craved uninhibited lyrics. To Louis, it was all blues, and his performances rode on his own creative moods rather than on the quality of the song materials. On Chippie Hill's *Trouble in Mind*, for example, Louis seems to lose interest somewhere along the way and even misses a couple of obvious cues. But Chippie's *Pratt City Blues*, recorded later in 1926, has superb mature Armstrong. On *Pratt City*, Louis accompanies tastefully and works in his own modern ideas as well, making full use of his speed and range rather than hewing to simple, folksy counterstatements. By this time, he seemed virtually unable to be other than what he really was—a blossoming virtuoso trumpet player. Louis' best-selling blues records were turned out with singers Hociel Thomas, Sippie Wallace, and, of course, Bertha "Chippie" Hill.

In the course of his stint at the Dreamland, Louis put the finishing touches on his musicianship, his creative outlook, and his reputation as the best jazz trumpet player in the land. The declining though still friendly Joe "King" Oliver knew better than to challenge Armstrong, but others tried it from time to time. Freddy Keppard, once top trumpeter in New Orleans, attempted to cut down the younger lion, without success. Johnny Dunn, an Easterner, also met defeat in a contest at the Dreamland. Louis' description of the encounter reveals something, too, about the kind of thoroughgoing musician he had become:

"I was playing an act at the Dreamland in Chicago one time, and I was playing something in *seven* sharps for the act—so help me! Well, Johnny Dunn was the big thing in New York then, with that *jive* he was playing. He was tearing up New York, playing the Palace and everything. (Of course, a lot of those people who went for him, they hadn't even heard of Joe Oliver.) He came out to Chicago with one of those big shows, and he came up on the bandstand where I was playing and says, 'Give me some of that.' I gave him that trumpet, and every valve he touched was wrong. Those sharps just about ate him up. So he gave me back my horn, *directly*, and finally when I looked around, he done just *eased* away."

The first recordings by Louis Armstrong and his Hot Five were cut for Okeh in November, 1925, a few days after Louis' return to Chicago. Lil and trombonist Ory, who shared the Dreamland bandstand with Louis, had no trouble fitting into the group. Clarinetist Johnny Dodds and banjoist Johnny St. Cyr were fellow Oliver alumni and New Orleanians who understood exactly what the musical situation demanded. There were almost no adjustments to be made and not even much need for rehearsals. Each member of the group contributed ideas or melodies a few days or hours before each session, then simply walked into the studio and played. Drawing on a common fund of experience and attitudes, these five musicians, who never operated as a going group outside the Okeh studios, turned out a series of records of remarkable consistency and high average musical quality.

Although the Hot Five recordings do not present an accurate picture of Armstrong's musical activities between late 1925 and late 1927, they do reflect his musical growth during that period. There are many Louis Armstrongs on the various Hot Five sessions, almost all of them worth attention.

Despite the appeal of the rather dated New Orleans Dixieland format (Louis at first bowed to tradition and played cornet on these occasions), the winning blues styles of the individual players, and Armstrong's own brilliant horn, it was probably the leader's gruff vocals that accounted for the commercial success of these records. Okeh furnished dealers with pictures of the cornetist to be given away with the records, and this, too, helped sales. It also helped Armstrong's reputation.

Louis was little more than a "novelty" singer in 1926, but his public loved his shouts and garbled lyrics. Only later did he become a sensitive jazz singer and a significant influence over others in this field. The introduction of the electric microphone around 1926 helped to bring Louis' voice down to a decibel rating suitable for good music, but it was some time before the important quality of tenderness came into his vocal work.

The group's first date was a rewarding one. The initial tune, *My Heart,* is Lil's, and it is a thoroughly charming melodic-harmonic vehicle. Louis seems in a sunny mood and plays with an easy kind of swing rather rarely heard on records in 1925. On the second title, *Yes, I'm in the Barrel,* the 25-year-old cornetist pays another tribute to Joe Oliver with some traditional plunger work. The third selection, *Gut Bucket Blues,* is a common blues, with sales appeal added by way of spoken introductions of the individual players.

In February, 1926, the Hot Five turned out seven outstanding recordings, one of which—*Heebie Jeebies*—put Louis in the best-seller category. The novel touch that sold the performance was an apparently impromptu scat vocal by Armstrong. It is unlikely that, as the story goes, this event took place without plan because Armstrong happened to drop his copy of the song's lyric. It occurs in the *second* vocal chorus; had Louis planned a straight reading, there would have been no reason to do it twice. Scat singing was not new, but *Heebies Jeebies* became a hit.

The other six titles recorded that month were: *Georgia Grind,* an entertaining minor performance; *Oriental Strut,* a St. Cyr tune that Louis carries almost single-handedly; *Muskat Ramble,* an old theme credited to Ory and featuring splendid New Orleans lead cornet; Lil's *Your Next,* carrying intimations of the majestic style Armstrong developed more fully later; *Cornet Chop Suey,* a tour de force exposition of Louis' ever-expanding musical imagination.

Cornet Chop Suey was the first of many recordings that were to be Armstrong showpieces from start to finish. The supporting players are of little importance; they seem merely to be along for the ride as Louis introduces his composition, states the verse, then tears into the principal theme and its variations. Constructing his solo (and his entire performance is really one long solo) with seemingly simple eighth- and quarter-note patterns, the cornetist displays a superb sense of melodic balance and restraint. Each note falls into place with almost discomforting rightness and inevitability, yet with a bubbling spontaneity that could come only from on-the-spot improvisation. *Cornet Chop Suey* combines the finest expression of the simple New Orleans outlook with the most advanced 1925 concepts of swing phrasing, many of which stemmed from Armstrong himself, of course. In addition to its importance as a piece of music, it was a triumph for Louis as a tactical solution to his Hot Five dilemma: how to remain a true New Orleans musician while upholding his position in the advance guard of young trumpet players.

New Orleans jazzmen have always been sensitive to ensemble

effects, and it is likely that Ory and Dodds, while in awe of Armstrong's abilities, were not always pleased with his soaring digressions. One need but listen to the stirring ensemble passages of the New Orleans Wanderers and Bootblacks, recording groups almost identical to Armstrong's, save for George Mitchell playing a "proper" New Orleans-style lead cornet, to discover how much of the all-out New Orleans ensemble spirit was missing from the Hot Five dates. Interestingly, the Wanderers-Bootblacks sessions took place at the time of the Hot Five's greatest popularity.

The Hot Five ensemble work was good enough for most listeners, however, and Louis gained still more prestige in the world of show business. He became the prime drawing card in the Tate orchestra at the Vendome Theater. After the inevitable overture, the trumpeter would jump out of the pit and onto the stage to perform a special number such as *Heebie Jeebies,* recreating his scat vocal through a megaphone. Some patrons attended the theater to hear Armstrong and left without even finding out what film was being shown.

Early in 1926, Lil and her group decided to demand more money from the Dreamland. It was refused, and the band quit. Louis' problem was not one of finding work (he continued to play with Tate), but rather of which offers to accept. He considered rejoining Oliver, who now fronted an enlarged band with three saxophones, but that would have meant going back to the second cornet chair and to the built-in restrictions of Oliver's modified New Orleans style. Kid Ory, for whom Oliver had once worked in New Orleans, had no reservations about joining Joe's band, but he represented the older generation of Louisiana jazzmen. Finally, partly owing to the urging of Earl Hines to "come over to us young guys," Louis joined Carroll Dickerson's Sunset Café orchestra. There he worked with well-trained musicians like pianist Hines, saxophonist Stump Evans, bassist Pete Briggs, and trumpeter Shirley Clay. To lend a touch of home, there were also New Orleanians Honoré Dutrey on trombone and Tubby Hall at the drums.

The Sunset was one of Chicago's most popular clubs, and in the course of his year-and-a-half stay there, Louis made secure his position as the world's leading jazz trumpeter. His records were selling briskly, tourists paid well to see him perform, and musicians flocked to the Sunset to study his style. Like other Chicago clubs, the Sunset served then illegal liquors openly and was never raided. A floor show, complete with dancers and a chorus line, was the main attraction. Armstrong, of course, was regarded as an entertainer as well as a sideman in the band. Young jazzmen like Jess Stacy, Joe Sullivan, Frank Teschemacher, and Bud Freeman, whom proprietor Joe Glaser permitted to skip the door charge, especially enjoyed the moments of pure music that came with the dancing between shows or in occasional Armstrong features.

Eventually Glaser, whose eye was on the dollar, saw Armstrong as a potentially more successful leader than Dickerson and offered Louis the job. The trumpeter accepted and turned over responsibility for the band to Earl Hines. (Armstrong, in fact, has managed to avoid such duties throughout his career, preferring to delegate them to better organizers so that he might concentrate on his own playing.) As Louis Armstrong and His Stompers, the band (Dickerson sidemen Briggs, Dutrey, and Hall also stayed on) became a front-rank Chicago attraction during 1927.

"Besides the band, we had twelve chorus girls, twelve show girls, and big-name acts," Glaser has recalled. "The place sat about six hundred people, and we had a high-class trade—not like some of the other joints—the best people. There were lines for every show, and, mind you, we charged admission just to get in —from a dollar twenty to two-fifty or so, depending on how business was."

Fronting a show band, playing eight or nine hours a night, attempting to juggle a failing marriage and a budding romance, Louis somehow continued to find time for varied recording assignments. He had used the trumpet more often on records the year before, most impressively on a pair of titles by the Erskine Tate orchestra. With this highly disciplined unit, Louis adopted a fast, showy style quite unlike his Hot Five cornet approach. Tate's *Stomp Off, Let's Go* and *Static Strut* are wild, virtuoso performances that probably came closer to the Armstrong theater and club patrons knew than all the rest of Louis' recorded work in 1926. It does not follow, however, that the Hot Five sessions were musically invalid. On the contrary, the rigid rules of New Orleans playing probably put a useful brake on Armstrong's natural inclination to exploit his abilities exhibitionistically. Although he had begun to sound almost ill at ease with the less brilliant-sounding cornet (there were many poorly articulated notes on the Hot Five sessions), he worked creatively within the offhand gutbucket atmosphere of the Hot Five dates.

In 1926, the quintet turned out more than a dozen sides. A few are marred by roughhewn commercialism (*Don't Forget to Mess Around, I'm Gonna Gitcha, Droppin' Shucks, Big Fat Ma*), but most are enormously appealing compounds of magnificent cornet solos, New Orleans playing, competent collective improvisation, and a pinch of country hokum. *King of the Zulus* is, like *Cornet Chop Suey*, an extended Armstrong solo of striking emotional depth that leaves Louis' colleagues far behind. *Who's It?* features a novel slide-whistle chorus by Armstrong, some fumbling Johnny Dodds (the clarinetist tried to turn every tune into a blues), and a superb, flamboyant cornet finale. *Sweet Little Papa*, which seems to borrow from the melodic structure of *Cornet Chop Suey*, introduced several arranged passages to tie independent phrases together, a practice that became more usual with each successive session.

Records like *Jazz Lips* reveal that by late 1926, Louis had completely outgrown his old New Orleans friends. Only Johnny Dodds stood a chance of coming close to Louis' sheer drive and power, but even he was a poor second. *Jazz Lips* is, like most of the Hot Five performances, marked by simplicity and restraint; yet there is a flippant ease coupled with, paradoxically, an increased degree of tension that represents a new phase for Louis. To a few New Orleans old-timers, it may have stood for a further departure from the mother style, but to young jazzmen, *Jazz Lips* carried exciting implications of a new kind of improvisatory freedom.

Louis was in top form the day he made *Jazz Lips*, and the same session produced some outstanding ensemble playing in *Sunset Café Stomp*, an elegant blues called *Skid-Dat-De-Dat*, in which the trumpeter makes bad notes into good ones by way of some very agile thinking, and a catchy tune named *Big Butter and Egg Man from the West*, which features one of Armstrong's very best solos of this period. The *Big Butter and Egg Man* chorus, which was widely copied by other musicians in subsequent years, is ecstatically described by critic André Hodeir in *Jazz: Its Evolution and Essence:*

> In this record, Armstrong manages to transfigure completely a theme whose vulgarity might well have overwhelmed him; and yet his chorus is only a paraphrase. The theme is not forgotten for a moment; it can always be found there, just as it was originally conceived by its little-known composer, Venable. Taking off melodically from the principal note of the first phrase, the soloist begins with a triple call that disguises, behind its apparent symmetry, subtle differences in rhythm and expressive intensity. This entry by itself is a masterpiece; it is impossible to imagine anything more sober and balanced. During the next eight bars, the paraphrase spreads out, becoming freer and livelier. Armstrong continues to cling to the essential notes of the theme, but he leaves more of its contour to the imagination. At times he gives it an inner animation by means of intelligent syncopated repetitions, as in the case of the first note of the bridge. From measures 20 to 23, the melody bends in a chromatic descent that converges toward the theme while at the same time giving a felicitous interpretation of the underlying harmonic progression. This brings us to the culminating point of the work. Striding over the traditional pause of measures 24–25, Armstrong connects the bridge to the final section by using a short, admirably inventive phrase. Its rhythmic construction of dotted eighths and sixteenths forms a contrast with the more static context in which it is placed, and in both conception and execution it is a miracle of swing. During this brief moment, Louis seems to have foreseen what modern conceptions of rhythm would be like. In phrasing, accentuation, and the way the short note is increasingly curtailed until finally it is merely suggested (measure 25), how far removed all this is from New Orleans rhythm!

A few days later, the Hot Five recorded two more titles. *Irish Black Bottom* is a weak commercial song damaged by Ory's wrong notes, Lil's unbending keyboard style, and an uninspired Armstrong vocal; *You Made Me Love You* (not the later popular song) is, on the other hand, a brilliant performance featuring Dodds at his slashing, bluesy best and Armstrong in peak form. Although the Hot Five made more recordings in later months, *You Made Me Love You* signaled the end of this period for Armstrong; hereafter, his full-blown improvised masterworks were to set a blistering pace for those who ventured to accompany him, relegating almost all of his associates, including Dodds, to positions as mere pawns in Armstrong's musical games.

In April, 1927, Louis recorded a batch of tunes for the competing Vocalion label. Four were unusual quartet sessions with washboard player Jimmy Bertrand in which Armstrong attempted to hold back his command, power, and inventiveness. This was probably done to avoid detection by the Okeh people, but it also served to prove that Louis was a highly flexible player and *could,* if he wished to, still play a simple New Orleans lead.

More stimulating was a series made with Johnny Dodds and, in his initial appearance on records with Louis, Earl Hines. Again the New Orleans spirit prevailed, despite the time given over to solo playing. Louis' thirty-two-bar solo on *Wild Man Blues,* though subdued, is nonetheless a fine example of sustained melodic improvisation at slow tempo. Using a fundamental embellishment approach to the melody, the trumpeter maintains continuity and holds the listener's interest with notes and phrases that cross bar lines, as well as with anticipations up to two beats ahead of upcoming melodic statements. Melrose Brothers, publishers of *Wild Man Blues,* transcribed the solo and published it as part of their commercial orchestration of the tune. To make matters easier for average dance-band trumpeters, Louis' single excursion into the upper register (above concert F on the top line of the staff) was lowered a full octave in the stock arrangement.

Because Armstrong and Hines were kept under wraps, the Dodds recordings only suggested the possibilities that could grow out of this association. It was to be more than a year before the pianist and trumpeter could record some of their specialities together.

The full sound of seven men on the Dodds session may have jogged Okeh into permitting Armstrong to use a similar instrumentation. However it came about, Louis turned out eleven classic recordings in less than a month after his date with Dodds. He used the regular Hot Five plus tuba player Pete Briggs of the Dickerson band and his old New Orleans friend, drummer Baby Dodds. Not surprisingly, the group cut a new *Wild Man Blues* on the very first day. The other ten tunes are not, in themselves, especially distinguished; two had been featured on the prior Dodds session (*Melancholy, Weary Blues*), and the rest were blueslike Armstrong originals (*Keyhole Blues, That's When I'll Come Back to You, Potato Head Blues, S.O.L. Blues,* and *Gully Low Blues*) or simple structures already familiar to the participants (*Twelfth Street Rag, Willie the Weeper, Alligator Crawl*).

With a full rhythm section driving him, Armstrong now pulled out most of the stops, although his essentially New Orleans band continued to exert a slightly sobering influence over him. The second *Wild Man Blues* is, of course, a more expansive affair, full of fast runs and high-note ornamentations, but the basic approach is not unlike the earlier version. (Superior electrical recording quality on these Okeh records made all of Louis' work sound much better than it had before, incidentally.) On the second *Melancholy,* Armstrong improves the attractive written melody without really changing it very much. *Twelfth Street Rag,* a difficult composition to play seriously, emerges as a slow stomp, which Johnny Dodds characteristically plays as a blues and which Louis finally transforms into a moving concerto.

S.O.L. Blues and *Gully Low Blues* are the same tune with altered lyrics. It is of interest to observe here that Armstrong's solo improvisations are improved in the latter version. The first four bars of each solo are identical, suggesting a carefully worked out advance sketch, but *Gully Low* makes more intelligent use of dramatic pauses, allowing deeper penetration into the lower register for contrast to the sustained high A-flat that introduces each two-bar phrase. Incidentally, *S.O.L. Blues,* recorded the day before, was not issued until collectors became interested in it many years later.

Keyhole Blues is a superb blues with a charming scat vocal by Armstrong and some deeply felt trumpet playing. As in many of his best recordings, Louis jumps into improvised situations here that require great skill and inventiveness to resolve gracefully. This penchant for trying the impossible and somehow escaping with honor fascinated other jazzmen as much as did the technical aspects of Louis' playing. After Armstrong, there was much more individual experimentation of this kind in jazz.

The Hot Seven sessions were one more step removed from New Orleans jazz than the Hot Five records had been. Drummer Baby Dodds, a conservative New Orleanian, once recalled the impression these dates made upon him: "With Louis' recording outfit, we used four beats to the measure. That was different from the older days in New Orleans, when we always used two. King Oliver used two also. And Louis used a tuba instead of a string bass. I had started playing with a bass viol and always felt closer to it than to a tuba."

One of Armstrong's enduringly classic solos in his Hot Seven series is *Potato Head Blues*. Using basic phrases made of simple eighth- and quarter-note patterns, a few dotted eighths, and some triplets, Louis organizes his musical thoughts in a truly remarkable way. His solo is a triumph of subtle syncopation and rhythmic enlightenment; strong accents on weak beats and whole phrases placed *against* rather than *on* the pulse create delightful tension. This tension is then suddenly released with an incisive on-the-beat figure, which in turn leads into more tension-building devices. Thus does Armstrong build the emotional pitch of the solo over a full chorus.

While listening to such well-conceived musical essays, one has the feeling that Louis might have gone on building for several more choruses had he not been restricted by the three-minute limit on recorded performances at that time. The trumpeter undoubtedly played longer solos in his nightclub and ballroom appearances, and he did, indeed, frequently record logical solos of two or more choruses a couple of years after making *Potato Head Blues.*

With this new lot of electrically recorded Armstrong performances, the attention of jazzmen everywhere was directed to Chicago and the next Okeh releases. Bix Beiderbecke was turning out his finest recorded work for the same label at the same time, and there were endless discussions as to who was the greater hornman. One musician who was active in both Chicago and New York about this time, saxophonist Jerome Pasquall, put it this way in a taped interview:

"Bix was at the Roseland while I was with Smack [Fletcher Henderson]. He was a wonderful cornetist with a marvelous ear and had many, many followers. There was a big dispute around then whether Bix or Louis was greater. Well, nowadays [1953] almost everybody agrees that Louis is tops, though I imagine there are still a lot of diehards who say Bix is King. When Bix played, it was almost perfect, everything clean and neat, as though he didn't want to make any mistakes; whereas Louis was playing so much that he would occasionally drop a blue note, but, my Lord, the things he was doing, Bix wouldn't even have attempted."

There was, of course, one large difference between the two heroes after 1927: Bix began to disintegrate, while Louis grew better and better—by 1931, Beiderbecke was dead, Armstrong at the peak of his powers.

Not only records and in-person appearances were responsible for the spread of Armstrong's influence in 1927; Melrose Brothers, a jazz-minded music-publishing house, added to the cumulative impact by incorporating more of Louis' ideas in its orchestrations. The publishers also issued a book of *50 Hot Choruses for Cornet* by Louis that sold widely throughout the country. These choruses were recorded by Melrose, transcribed, and published in such a way as to permit any horn player to insert an Armstrong solo in his part of an orchestration. It's anybody's guess how many fledgling jazzmen struggled through Louis' beautifully conceived thirty-two-bar solo on *Someday Sweetheart*, with its dramatic climax on trumpet high D, or what number of competent sidemen fell apart in the middle of Louis' superb version of *Some of These Days* (in concert G), but it may be assumed that many musicians learned from this remarkable collection. From it, too, comes the realization that Louis Armstrong drew from a seemingly bottomless well of ideas; on or off records, the trumpeter played at a remarkably consistent creative level. Few of his fifty solos recorded for Melrose were less than excellent, and several ranked with his very best work. Unfortunately, the recordings from which they were transcribed have vanished.

Of special interest is a single recording made between two Hot Seven sessions in May, 1927. It is *Chicago Breakdown* (a Melrose property also included in *50 Hot Choruses*), the only surviving recorded document of the Sunset Café band. Included on this date were Boyd Atkins and Stump Evans (saxes), Honoré Dutrey, and Earl Hines. The ten-piece band suited Louis' big tone very well, and in Hines there was a player who could parry and thrust on Armstrong's own musical level. It was a stimulating session and a harbinger of recordings to come, but this single side was not issued at the time.

In the summer of 1927, Louis' band met Fletcher Henderson's in a contest at the Sunset Café. Fletcher tried, without success, to hire Armstrong back, but by this time the trumpeter was earning more money and fame than even Henderson could offer. Ironically, at the end of summer, Joe Glaser decided it was time to change his show, and the Stompers were out. Armstrong had switched his theater work from Tate at the Vendome to Clarence Jones at the Metropolitan, but it was not enough for him to play only a few hours in a pit band each night. He thrived on playing in nightclub shows.

Louis, Earl, Lil, and drummer Zutty Singleton (an old New Orleans friend who had been playing at the Café de Paris during the summer) hatched a scheme to present their own show in their own club. Lil rented a ballroom called Warwick Hall, and the new partners called their room the Usonia. They planned a Thanksgiving opening, but the new and elaborate Savoy Ballroom opened nearby at the same time, and the Usonia went almost unnoticed. By December, the Hot Six (Armstrong, Hines, Singleton, George Jones, Charlie Lawson, and William Hall) were without work and unsure of the future, despite their leader's enormous popularity. Louis, Earl, and Zutty were close companions and frequently attended parties or jam sessions together during this slack period. They continued to be much in demand at informal social and musical gatherings.

Carroll Dickerson, by now fronting the band at the new Savoy Ballroom, invited Louis and Zutty to join him, and in April, 1928, the two jazzmen became part of the show that had, a few months earlier, put them out of business. Hines went his own way, joining Jimmy Noone about the same time. The three friends maintained their close ties, however, as can be heard in a series of superlative Okeh recordings made under Armstrong's name later that year.

Show business is intrinsically a risky, up-and-down life, and in looking back at Armstrong's high tide of success in 1927, it seems likely that his popularity at the Sunset was of the ephemeral variety so common to musical revues. During this peak, the trumpeter's Hot Seven recordings reflected his own will to a greater extent than any he had made before. With the collapse of the Sunset engagement, Louis returned to (or possibly was *told* to re-

turn to) the Hot Five formula. By this time, however, the old routines had become anachronistic and less suitable than ever for
Louis' sweeping improvisations. The banjo-piano combination,
good enough for the limited range of preelectrical recordings, now
seems pitifully thin and inadequate as an Armstrong rhythm section. Ory's antique *dut-dut* style and Dodds's lack of harmonic
sophistication also seem to be holding Louis back. Armstrong himself, who has long believed in playing his very best regardless of
surrounding circumstances, is as brilliant as ever on these Hot Five
records, from the quaint, New Orleans-style *Ory's Creole Trombone* to the highly informal *Put 'Em Down Blues*. He breaks
through the conservative barriers on *The Last Time* and even has
Dodds abandoning his traditional ensemble parts on *Got No Blues*,
recorded at a later session. *Struttin' with Some Barbecue*, recorded
in December, is a radiant experiment in the construction of long
lines without sacrifice of melodic simplicity and rhythmic momentum. Dodds's subdued solo here and the arranged ending of *Barbecue* suggest that even the New Orleans gang was now beginning to sense the decline of the Dixieland approach.

On December 10 and 13, 1927, the Hot Five held its last recording sessions, with guitarist Lonnie Johnson added to fill out the
undernourished rhythm section. The New Orleans ensemble pattern was weakened still further. On these records, Dodds and
Ory fill out the background harmony unobtrusively and join
Armstrong in elemental riff patterns along lines fairly typical of
the period. The result of these shifts of emphasis is a more inspired Armstrong than ever. Four titles were made, all containing
good examples of Louis near the apex of his musical career.

Once in a While, notable for its dazzling cornet solo set against
a syncopated stop-time backdrop, is otherwise rendered in the
New Orleans manner, but *Savoy Blues* is a low-key blues carried
out with riffs and an easy tempo that give Louis lots of room to try
his more advanced ideas. *I'm Not Rough* is a curious mixture of
country blues and an apparent attempt to capitalize on the double-time device that was helping to sell a couple of Okeh records
by other artists at that time (*A Good Man Is Hard to Find* by
Frank Trumbauer and *Since My Best Gal Turned Me Down* by
Bix Beiderbecke). *Hotter Than That*, closely related to *Tiger Rag*
in structure, is a fitting tour de force climax to the extended Hot

Five series of recordings. It contains many of Louis' most commonly used phrases, even to a string of repeated high C's, but it is an outstanding accomplishment as an ordered progression of lively ideas that seem to form but a single musical thought. Only the necessity for breathing appears to have prevented Armstrong, in performances like *Hotter Than That,* from executing whole choruses at a time as long, unbroken single statements.

In mid-1928, Louis, Earl Hines, and Zutty Singleton finally got together on records. They recorded nine selections as Louis Armstrong and His Hot Five (actually, it was a sextet; clarinetist Jimmy Strong, guitarist-banjoist Mancy Cara, and trombonist Fred Robinson, all from the Carroll Dickerson band, were the other members). But from the very first note, it was obvious that this was a group totally unlike the old Hot Five. Now Louis was permitted to make records in his own name that accurately reflected the sort of music he had been playing for a living for some two years. Armstrong and Hines, dipping into their recent experiences at the Sunset for material and ideas, established new standards for jazzmen everywhere with these nine performances.

The series began, fittingly, with a piece called *Fireworks,* a display number pieced together from Dickerson specialties and *Tiger Rag.* It is, like many of the Hines-Armstrong sessions, a kind of miniature big-band arrangement, complete with pyramid chords, rapid-fire exchanges among the participants, and complex ensemble maneuvers. In a tune called *Skip the Gutter,* Louis and Earl challenge each other's imagination and agility in "chase" passages of pure whimsy and antithematic improvisation. Double-time effects such as had been used on *I'm Not Rough* had now become commonplace, and the new Hot Five made the most of them. *Two Deuces* is another excursion in advanced jazz playing that bristles with harmonic alterations, double-time routines, and all-out improvisations. *Don't Jive Me,* probably taken from show material used in Sunset or Savoy productions, tests Armstrong's musicianship as well as his ability to think fast in a musical game of high order. The trumpeter and pianist constantly challenge themselves by starting phrases that cannot possibly fit the arrangement, then squirming out of them just in time to save the performance. It was breathtakingly daring music that set a terrifying pace for young jazzmen.

There was another, more far-reaching aspect of Armstrong's playing that emerged on records at this time. It came as a synthesis of his earlier restrained melodic invention and the advanced technical displays just described. Now, in 1928, Armstrong was able to put the best features of both styles to work for him and evolve a modern melodic approach that would serve as the foundation for jazz trumpet developments in the thirties and forties. The new Armstrong outlook can be heard on three titles made with the revised Hot Five—*Squeeze Me, A Monday Date,* and *West End Blues.*

Squeeze Me was the first of many Fats Waller balladlike songs recorded by Louis. It is a thoroughly "modern" performance that includes a vocal without instrumental support and a high-tension trumpet break incorporating a fragment of *High Society.* (This phrase was later worn thin by modern jazzmen of the forties and fifties.) It is in Louis' solo phrasing, however, that something then new and different happens. With solid four-to-the-bar backing, the trumpeter somehow creates the impression of more space between pulses and improvises accordingly. His ideas come faster and in more tightly packed bundles now; rather than conceiving his solos as single chorus-length ideas, he begins constructing a chain of four-bar and even two-bar thematic units, each a miniature chorus unto itself but an essential link to the next unit and a logical part of the whole solo as well. It was a startling effect, even in its early stages.

Monday Date is a good example of the rhythmic freedom that came with the addition of a good drummer like Zutty. No longer required to establish the beat as well as the melody, Louis seems to float over the tune. His use of quarter-note triplets here was doubtless related to this new rhythmic independence. Again there is the "unit" rather than the chorus method of solo construction.

West End Blues, perhaps Armstrong's finest recorded performance of his career, also came from this mid-1928 Okeh session. It has everything: big-toned bravura trumpet playing; effective contrast of expressive simplicity and instrumental complexity; logical development of mood and theme from beginning to end; a heartwarming, tender scat vocal refrain; a perfect balance of all historical aspects of the Armstrong musical personality. *West End* was written by Joe Oliver and Clarence Williams, both of whom were connected with Armstrong's earlier development.

West End begins with a magnificent trumpet cadenza in 2/4 that builds in intensity as it moves from quarter notes to eighth-note triplets to sixteenths to sixteenth-note triplets over twelve bars of brilliant unaccompanied playing. The two blues choruses Armstrong plays after this (and they are not consecutive) are put together in exactly the same way as the overturelike cadenza. The first chorus moves from initial simplicity to a set of ingenious triplet figures. The final chorus picks up the thread again and moves into dramatic sixteenth-note passages and sixteenth-note triplets that correspond exactly to the final part of the opening cadenza. Furthermore, throughout this astonishing set of improvisations, Louis plays a deeply moving blues that never flags in emotional pitch. *West End Blues,* an intuitive improvised composition-performance created by a 27-year-old trumpet player from New Orleans, is a milestone in the history of jazz.

In December, 1928, ten more excellent sides were recorded by Armstrong and Hines. Louis' success at the Savoy prompted Okeh officials to release these under the name Louis Armstrong and His Savoy Ballroom Five. The same men participated, but saxophonist-arranger Don Redman was brought in to give the group a bigger orchestral sound. It was obviously time for Louis to record with a big band, but Okeh seemed reluctant to take the step.

The December sessions were, on the whole, even more advanced than those held six months before. Drummer Singleton was much improved, and the addition of Redman hastened the complete departure from the old Hot Five sound. Louis' trumpet solos, freer than ever, are marked by swift legato passages, thirty-second-note runs, and audacious ideas that only pianist Hines comes close to matching. On selections like *No One Else But You* and *Beau Koo Jack,* there seems to be no limit to Armstrong's imagination or to his ability to play as fast as he can think. Again, the trumpeter was building logically upon his own past, for the support provided by Redman's arrangements was a natural link to Louis' experience in Henderson's band, of which Redman was also a member.

Weather Bird Rag, a tune Louis had played with Joe Oliver, is a monumental duet performance by Hines and Armstrong. It is, too, a symbol of the trumpeter's complete abandonment of the Oliver style, for this display piece is improvisation for improvisation's sake, and the New Orleans old guard had little use for that outlook. Still, with all its wild volleying of modern ideas, *Weather Bird* retains a strand of melodic continuity and thematic unity. With his solid New Orleans training, Louis seemed virtually incapable of losing a melody entirely.

Save It, Pretty Mama and *Hear Me Talkin' to Ya* are touched with a distinct Eastern flavor, due to Redman's arrangements and Trumbauer-like alto saxophone playing. Louis seems to have picked up the idea; his work on *Hear Me Talkin'* is as close to Bix Beiderbecke as Armstrong ever came. *Muggles* is a fascinating essay on rhythm, much of it built around a single tonic note, in which the trumpeter displays his extraordinary sense of time. In the course of thirty-six bars, Louis explores some thirty different ways of rhythmically phrasing a single measure of music. Despite its outward simplicity, *Muggles* was a new kind of Armstrong triumph.

Basin Street Blues is an extension of the exceptionally free melodic style noted in *Squeeze Me*. *St. James Infirmary* left no doubts about the desirability of the smooth, even 4/4 rhythm that was then sweeping Chicago as it already had New York. Finally, there is a colossal trumpet solo called *Tight Like This*, which is actually little more than a series of double-time arpeggiolike embellishments on a minor blues theme. Here is a fine demonstration of another important facet of the Armstrong talent—his sense of drama. *Tight Like This* is intelligently built up over sixty-four measures (four choruses) so gradually and smoothly that the listener is scarcely aware of the increase in tension and excitement until the final bars are reached.

In each period of Armstrong's career, there has been a recorded clue to his next venture. With Oliver, his rare solos were hints of the virtuoso performer featured with Henderson; from his New York stint came the Red Onion Jazz Babies sessions with Lil that were the forerunners of later Hot Five recordings; and during the period just discussed, a single Carroll Dickerson record pointed the way Louis was to go within a year's time. Though Dickerson appears to have been a competent leader, his full band was not in demand on recordings, and his only record was not even issued, except in Argentina. It is, however, valuable for the glimpse it affords of the band in which Louis played at the Savoy in 1928. The titles are *Symphonic Raps* and *Savoyager's Stomp*. *Raps* is a forward-looking arrangement studded with unusual harmonies, whole-tone devices, and bustling solos. One can hear, too, the influence of Jean Goldkette and Paul Whiteman scores in this ambitious display piece. It is also related to *Fireworks* (and, indirectly, *Tiger Rag*), which Armstrong's small group recorded only a few days before. The big band seemed to have a salutary effect on Armstrong, whose ear picked up the involved harmonies of *Symphonic Raps* as easily as it had the more elemental changes of old New Orleans numbers. Louis' fleet and authoritative solo on this recording was at least ten years ahead of itself. *Savoyager's Stomp*, a dressed-up version of *Muskat Ramble*, underscored again how ready Louis was to record with a big (ten-piece) band.

By late 1928, Louis had built his reputation to a new peak. He was earning $200 a week with Dickerson and picking up extra money from record dates and casual appearances. Melrose Brothers had added *Louis Armstrong's 125 Jazz Breaks for Cornet* to their catalog some time earlier, and trumpeters in every city of the country were attempting to copy his phrases. The Savoy was making regular broadcasts that were heard for hundreds of miles around Chicago.

Louis was already big time, but he had yet to take on the toughest and most important show business town of all—New York. The prospects had been good when he appeared there with Henderson, but that was four years before. What would it be like now? When the Savoy attendance began to drop a bit and the club professed a shortage of funds for paying the band, Louis and the Dickerson band made a collective decision to strike out for New York. As Armstrong was the drawing card and had some connections in the East, he would front the band. Dickerson would remain as musical director. It sounded like a good arrangement, and they started out for New York in the dead of the winter of 1928–1929.

Over the years, Armstrong's luck has been almost as phenomenal as his trumpet playing. Of course, his position as one of the great figures in jazz and as a gifted entertainer has brought many opportunities his way, but his reception in New York can be considered only sheer plunger's luck. After a few odd jobs such as one at the Audubon Theater, where the group substituted for Duke Ellington, the Armstrong-Dickerson band landed in Connie's Inn, one of the three biggest nightclubs in town. The club's regular band (Leroy Smith's) was hired for an upcoming Broadway stage show called *Connie's Hot Chocolates,* leaving a vacancy that Louis and his friends simply walked into.

Connie's Inn was even larger and more impressive than the Savoy in Chicago. The show began at midnight, drawing an after-theater crowd, and evening clothes were required. A conservative couple would have had trouble spending less than $40 in a single night at Connie's. Despite the Great Depression, customers poured in to hear Louis and his audience-proven routines.

Another stroke of luck came with an offer for Louis to join the *Hot Chocolates* cast on Broadway. Through the spring of 1930, the trumpeter-singer-entertainer stopped each show with his version of the revue's hit number, *Ain't Misbehavin'.* Within a year of arriving in the big city, Armstrong was established as a leading name in show business. Okeh Records responded by giving him more musical latitude and a larger share of the talent budget. Although Louis' recordings from this point on were almost entirely big-band dates, there were a couple of small-group sessions. One was a dismal "Hot Five" affair—the last in the line—with singer Victoria Spivey. The other was a fine casual jam session with Joe Sullivan, Zutty, Eddie Lang, Jack Teagarden, and others, on which Louis played a splendid blues solo. Pianist Sullivan has recalled that Louis tossed off this chorus while "standing against the wall with his eyes closed."

The first New York date produced *Mahogany Hall Stomp,* a big-band New Orleans-style performance of charming simplicity, and, more importantly, *I Can't Give You Anything But Love,* which presented Armstrong for the first time on records as a superior, sensitive ballad singer. The wide-voiced instrumental backing by Luis Russell, created solely for the purpose of supporting Armstrong, invited Louis to reach out for new melodic and harmonic ideas on his horn as well. (He was already familiar with this tune, incidentally, for he had recorded it with singer Lillie Delk Christian in Chicago a few months earlier.)

From the moment he landed in New York, Louis also became an object of adoration for all New York jazzmen. Some admired him primarily for his finesse, others for his power and range, still others for the emotional depth of his work. No one argued any more about his supremacy. The Dorsey brothers arranged for him to play on a couple of their recording dates, with generally good results (an exception is a curious version of *To Be in Love*, on which Louis seems to attempt an imitation of Bix Beiderbecke, without success).

A gifted trumpeter named Jabbo Smith was in and out of New York about this time, and some competition-minded jazzmen began to regard Smith as a possible contender for Armstrong's crown. Cornetist Red Nichols remembers a night when the two met.

"Jabbo had a wide range, but his high notes were more falsetto, not full-blown like Louis'," recalls Nichols. "He played a lot of notes, but some of them were just faking, while Louis maintained a high musical level at all times. When they played together, there just wasn't any comparison."

(Smith did, however, point out the possibilities of an even more advanced style than Armstrong's. With his impish, many-noted flights and his harmonic daring, he foreshadowed the later styles of Red Allen, Charlie Shavers, and Roy Eldridge, although these trumpeters were primarily inspired by Armstrong.)

Between July, 1929 and early 1932, Louis reached the height of his creative and physical powers as a trumpet player. This period is thoroughly documented by a prodigious outpouring of magnificent recordings. Of some sixty titles cut in less than two years, nearly every one has remained *the* classic, definitive version by which jazz trumpeters (including Armstrong) ever since have had to measure their own work. Recording the best popular tunes of the time, Louis was responsible for many of these songs becoming jazz standards. His were the first recorded jazz interpretations of *Ain't Misbehavin'*, *Black and Blue* (both from *Hot Chocolates*), *Rockin' Chair*, *Body and Soul*, *Memories of You*, and dozens of others. The usual format was trumpet solo (muted)-vocal-trumpet solo (open), which allowed plenty of room for Louis to build his ideas. As it turned out, it was also a sound commercial formula; Armstrong records began to be heard on jukeboxes and to move briskly in stores. Louis' good luck was holding up as well as was his celebrated embouchure.

In September, 1929, he recorded *Some of These Days*, a superlative example of the art of logical construction in an extended solo. In this case, the vocal becomes part of Louis' overall melodic blueprint, serving as a natural bridge from the low-key, insinuating opening to the jubilant concluding chorus. A final, inevitable sustained high note finishes off one of the earliest (and still one of the best) extended solos in the annals of recorded jazz. Only a few jazzmen (Lester Young, Jess Stacy, Sidney Bechet, and Sonny Rollins come to mind) have demonstrated a comparable ability to increase the dramatic pitch of a long solo without losing either melodic control or thematic unity in the course of their own creation.

Judging from his records, Louis' tone acquired still more body and strength at this time. Sometimes he played with almost no vibrato, yet his sound was warm and intimate. More and more, he employed a legato manner of phrasing, leaving behind the heavy-tongued "punching" style so characteristic of hornmen in the twenties. On almost straight readings of tunes like *When You're Smiling* and *Song of the Islands*, Louis underscores the quality of majesty in his work with trumpet phrases that seem lifted from the Golden Era of opera singing. Indeed, on a piano-trumpet duet recording of *Dear Old Southland*, Louis gives a veritable trumpet recital, quite unlike the musical cat-and-mouse game he indulged in with Earl Hines less than two years before.

In early 1930, *Connie's Hot Chocolates* wound up its successful season, Leroy Smith returned to Connie's Inn, and the Dickerson band, without immediate prospects for work, broke up. In June, Louis opened at Frank Sebastian's New Cotton Club in Culver City, California, with Les Hite's orchestra. This was a good band (trombonist Lawrence Brown and drummer Lionel Hampton were members), one that could do justice to Armstrong on a series of records that caught him at the summit of his musical life. Together they sailed through great performances like *Ding Dong Daddy*, a beautifully conceived set of improvisations as logical as the earlier *Some of These Days* and as thrilling as *Tight Like This*. By now, Louis was playing fast, compressed figures, held together by inner discipline and outward assurance, that were radically advanced for 1930. The same characteristics turn up in his remarkable ballad performances with Hite—*I'm in the Market for You, Confessin', If I Could Be with You, Memories of You,* and *Body and Soul.* Sometimes embellishing the straight melody, sometimes creating new themes of his own, Louis established with these ballads a lush, unsentimental, "singing trumpet" approach that affected every trumpeter of the thirties and is still widely used today. By selecting the most harmonically sophisticated songs of the period (*Star Dust, Body and Soul, You're Lucky to Me, You're Driving Me Crazy,* etc.), Armstrong also set up new criteria for future jazzmen to apply in their search for challenging raw material.

The culmination of Louis' development as a trumpet player and jazzman can hardly be pinned down to a specific date, but with his October, 1930, recording of *Sweethearts on Parade* Armstrong took his music about as far as it could go. Here all the elements of Louis' extraordinary style seem to come together—technique, taste, tone, advanced harmonic ideas, understatement, rhythmic enlightenment, bravura declarations, drama, melodic sureness, balanced construction, and humor. Historically, *Sweethearts on Parade* ranks with *Ding Dong Daddy* and the later (1931) *Star Dust* as a preview of the style that brought fame to Roy Eldridge and set the stage for further explorations by Dizzy Gillespie. (It should be noted that not all observers share this view. Critic Charles Edward Smith once wrote in *Down Beat* that Louis' *Sweethearts on Parade* is an example of "Low Jive, synonymous with plain kidding.")

Following his run at the New Cotton Club, where the trumpeter had again enjoyed the benefits of regular radio broadcasts, Louis went to Chicago in early 1931 to at last form his own band. He picked up some old friends—trombonist Preston Jackson, drummer Tubby Hall, and New Orleans bassist John Lindsay—and opened at the Showboat Cabaret. From this point on, Louis spent most of his time on the road. He is still traveling in the sixties, and he has toured many countries, beginning with his first European trip in 1932.

Even as his own band took shape, a new emphasis crept into Armstrong's recorded work. With a few gratifying exceptions, the new releases stressed his role as entertainer and singer. Gradually, the quality of his song materials declined, and there were more frequent lapses of taste and musical judgment. There was still much wonderful trumpet playing, but the humor became forced and the band incredibly sloppy. (The band problem was eventually solved by Louis' turning over the entire matter to Luis Russell.)

In 1931, Louis and Lil separated, although their divorce was not final until 1938. At 31, the trumpeter was still a robust young man of infinite good will who attracted more friends than he could handle. The Depression had not harmed him very much, and he was beginning to realize just how important a musician he was—the serious enthusiasm of European fans and critics for his work was soon to make a deep impression on Armstrong. With this solid foundation of contentment, he settled into a relatively predictable groove, where he has remained to this day. Not that Louis was lazy—far from it; he simply could not push beyond his 1930 level. Eventually, he dropped below it, but he has never permitted himself to play less than first-rate trumpet.

Armstrong's influence on other jazzmen has been greater than that of any other single trumpeter in the short history of the music. The roster of Armstrong-inspired performers reads like an all-star poll. Even some of those who had been counted at one time or another as Bix Beiderbecke disciples—Bill Davison, Bobby Hackett, Rex Stewart, and others—cite Armstrong as their main influence. Trumpet men like Buck Clayton, Muggsy Spanier, Lips Page, Joe Thomas, Wingy Mannone, Red Allen, Taft Jordan, Bunny Berigan, Joe Newman, Harry James, Billy Butterfield, Ruby Braff, Cootie Williams, and Roy Eldridge have left no doubts about their deep regard for Louis. So multifaceted was Armstrong's huge talent that most of these trumpeters have created their own musical identities around but one or two characteristics of the master's style. Spanier concentrated on Armstrong's early Oliver-like drive and pure tone; Thomas went after his gift of understatement and melodic symmetry; James struck out for Louis' range and technical powers; Williams, when not saddled with the task of re-creating Bubber Miley solos for Duke Ellington, achieved something like Armstrong's majesty of phrase; Berigan came startlingly close to Louis' emotional warmth and dramatic eloquence; Eldridge and Allen used Armstrong's most complex melodic and rythmic figurations as points of departure; Page came close to Louis' intense blues style, vocally and instrumentally.

Not only trumpet men were deeply affected by Armstrong. There is recorded evidence of his changing the outlooks of countless others—arranger Fletcher Henderson, saxophonists Coleman Hawkins and Bud Freeman, trombonists Jack Teagarden and Lawrence Brown, pianists Earl Hines and Joe Sullivan, and even vibraphonist Lionel Hampton, to name a few.

In a more general way, Louis brought the art of the jazz solo to a new creative peak and to an unprecedented prominence before the listening public. His extended choruses caused jazz musicians everywhere to direct their thinking along similar lines. Ensemble playing skills did not decay with this new emphasis upon solo playing, although collective improvisation by several horns, on its way out anyway, all but disappeared. On the contrary, the soloists led the way to more interesting part writing by arrangers and superior ensemble playing by jazz performers. Armstrong's natural swing and exceptional methods of utilizing syncopation made a deep impression on arrangers of the twenties such as Henderson, Don Redman, Bill Challis, and Tiny Parham.

Louis took the ballad style that found its earliest expression in Bix Beiderbecke, imbued it with oratoriolike dignity, and founded an elegant method of paraphrasing popular songs that has endured. Echoes of Armstrong's finest ballad performances of his 1929–1931 period can be traced in the work of Charlie Parker and Dizzy Gillespie, as well as in that of many of their contemporaries.

After 1929, Louis' voice became a fine musical instrument that affected countless singers, jazz and otherwise. His "jive" vocals led directly to the styles of many minor (though commercially successful) artists, such as Cab Calloway, Louis Prima, the Boswell Sisters, the Mills Brothers, and Wingy Mannone. His ballad singing deeply affected a number of superior singers, such as Bing Crosby, Ethel Waters, Mildred Bailey, Lee Wiley, and Billie Holiday. Without Armstrong, the story of jazz singing, up to and including Ray Charles, might have been quite different.

The substance of Louis' music cannot be explained, in the final analysis, by his remarkable physical equipment, his showmanship, or even his skill with the trumpet. It is the man's *mind* that has produced this vast body of marvelous music. Armstrong has always been utterly serious about his trumpet playing, even in the frivolous years of the twenties, when many jazzmen assumed their music couldn't last and proceeded to blow themselves out at an early age.

"To play it right," Louis stated when he was 50, "you've got to make music a *business*—and I'm not talking just about the money now. A lot of cats get in the money, and then, when you look around, they're not playing *anything*; they can't play. . . . My band doesn't play for any hour before I get on the stand. When that band hits the first note, it's *Sleepytime*, and I'm playing it. And that's the way it's always been. I've watched all that glamorous this-that-and-the-other among the musicians, and I've always said, 'Go ahead, have your ball,' but now it's simmered down, and only the fittest can survive."

Louis Armstrong has entertained royalty, been called his country's most effective ambassador, changed the course of America's music, and become a wealthy man in a wealthy land. For all that, he remains an inner-directed musician of rare humility and sensitivity.

His words, like his magic, are worth pondering: "It's *my* consolation, too, to hit that note the way I like to hear it. I've got to hear my own horn, and it's got to please *me*, don't forget that. That's what a whole lot of youngsters don't seem to pick up on."

Recommended Reading

Armstrong, Louis: *Swing That Music*, Longmans, New York (1936).
Hodeir, André: *Jazz: Its Evolution and Essence*, Grove, New York (1956).
McCarthy, Albert: *Louis Armstrong*, Barnes, New York (1961).
Ramsey, Frederic, and Charles Edward Smith: *Jazzmen*, Harcourt, Brace, New York (1939).
Shapiro, Nat, and Nat Hentoff (eds.): *Hear Me Talkin' to Ya*, Rinehart, New York (1955).

Recommended Listening

Young Louis Armstrong, RIVERSIDE 12-101.
The Perry Bradford Story (one track), CRISPUS-ATTUCKS PB-101.
The Fletcher Henderson Story, COLUMBIA C4L-19.
The Bessie Smith Story, Vol. 1, COLUMBIA CL-855.
The Louis Armstrong Story, Vols. 1, 2, 3, 4, COLUMBIA CL-851, CL-852, CL-853, CL-854.
Jazz Odyssey: The Sound of Chicago, COLUMBIA C3L-32.
Jazz Odyssey: The Sound of New Orleans, COLUMBIA C3L-30.

EARL HINES

No MUSICIAN has exerted more influence over the course of piano jazz history than has Earl Hines. With Hines, the last ties to ragtime fell away and a whole new concept of keyboard improvisation took shape. Earl accomplished all this while operating almost entirely outside New York City, and no major American pianist, jazz or otherwise, had done *that* before, either.

He was born Earl Kenneth Hines in Duquesne, a small town now part of Pittsburgh, Pennsylvania. His father, a crane foreman on the coal docks, maintained a comfortable home, and Earl grew up amid the usual middle-class trappings of the early twentieth century, including a parlor organ that his mother played frequently. The instrument intrigued Earl, and occasionally he pretended to accompany his mother on a newspaper "keyboard" spread out on a chair. The family noted his interest without much surprise, for Earl's father was a fair trumpet player and his uncle, Bill Phillips, played all the brass instruments. Earl experimented briefly with the trumpet, but it didn't take, although he learned to play a few tunes before giving it up. It was about 1914, when Earl was 9, that Mrs. Hines traded in the organ for a piano so that her son could begin serious keyboard studies. His first teacher was Emma D. Young of McKeesport.

Making swift progress, Earl moved on to other teachers and more advanced lesson books. He read from Czerny and acquired a liking for Chopin and Debussy. For six years, Earl was intensively trained in traditional piano techniques, most of which came quickly and easily to him. Dividing his time between sports and music, young Hines was rapidly acquiring the two assets that were to make him one of the most durable and flexible jazzmen of all time—brimming good health and a thoroughgoing command of the keyboard.

Hines has often protested that he went into jazz only because he could make more money faster than in other music. However, he was exposed to all kinds of music during his formative years. There were his father's brass band, the piano rolls of Zez Confrey and James P. Johnson, traveling show bands, and, of course, the classics. Aunt Nellie Phillips, with whom Earl lived in the city, favored light classics and frequently took her nephew to good shows or revues at local theaters, including Lew Leslie's *Black-birds* and the Noble Sissle–Eubie Blake hit *Shuffle Along*. These events were Earl's first contacts with first-rate "rhythm" music, with which he was completely delighted.

While attending Schenley High School in Pittsburgh, the pianist formed a trio with a couple of friends who played drums and banjo. Together they worked out popular songs of the day, probably in the novelty-ragtime style that flourished just after World War I. When music jobs at night began to turn up, Earl accepted them without concern about how the hours might affect his schoolwork. After two years at Schenley, he dropped out for good and turned to music on a full-time basis.

A singer from Springfield, Ohio, named Lois B. Deppe was appearing at the Liederhouse in Pittsburgh about that time and had become dissatisfied with his accompanying pianist, who could not read. Earl took the job, bringing his own drummer with him as part of the contract. Deppe paid his new pianist $15 a week and board. They remained at the Liederhouse for about a year, adding instruments to the orchestra as business improved. By the time Lois B. Deppe and His Serenaders began touring Ohio and Pennsylvania in the early twenties, Earl found himself in a big band, struggling to be heard over a row of horn players. He discovered a time-honored way to make the piano stand out in a large group, simply by playing melody notes as octaves in the upper range of the keyboard. Allowing the natural ring of the octave interval to work for him, Earl was able to hold his own without losing the fast, light touch he had cultivated. This move alone set him apart from many "stomp" pianists, who relied more upon brute strength than finesse in their efforts to penetrate orchestral walls of sound.

The unique Hines style was beginning to take shape now. There were many influences along the way; some came from a pair of impressive local pianists, Johnny Waters of Toledo and a big-band pianist named Jim Fellman.

"Very few pianists were using right-hand tenths then," Hines recalls, "but Johnny Waters could reach twelfths and thirteenths and play melodies with the inside three fingers at the same time! I tried for Johnny with my right and for Jim Fellman, who had a great left, with my other hand."

Pianists like James P. Johnson and Luckey Roberts passed through Pittsburgh with shows, and Earl was quick to hear the New York style and to pick up what he could use from it. In working out his octave style, too, Earl discovered that he could compensate for the inevitable loss of speed by borrowing some ideas from the dramatic syncopated phrasing of good trumpet players. He was particularly fond of trumpeters Joe Smith (who toured with Sissle and Blake) and, a little later, Gus Aiken (who toured with Ethel Waters and James P. Johnson). By 1922, records by singers Ethel Waters and Mamie Smith, along with their jazz accompaniments, were influencing young musicians like Hines all over the country. Playing for singers was one of Earl's specialties.

Deppe made a few records for Gennett at Richmond, Indiana, in the winter of 1923-1924, and Earl, who had joined the musicians' union a few months before, was included on the dates. They are among the rarest items on the collectors' market. Of the four band sides, one—*Congaine*—is a Hines composition. These recordings helped to promote the Deppe orchestra and its piano player as well. The entire group even appeared on radio (KDKA) at that time. Earl sometimes worked casual engagements booked by Deppe and occasionally put groups of his own together. His baritone saxophone player on one such occasion was Benny Carter.

The owner of Pittsburgh's Collins Inn, where Earl had worked frequently, operated another club, called Elite #2, in Chicago near Thirty-fifth and State, the heart of the South Side entertainment belt. He was unhappy with his local Chicago band and sent for violinist Vernie Robinson's quartet, complete with drummer, bassist, and Earl Hines, who happened to be in the group at the time. Earl arrived at the Elite #2 in 1924 and, after playing a month for Robinson, took over leadership of the band and stayed for a year.

There were several good pianists in and around Chicago at that time, including Jelly Roll Morton and Glover Compton, but the best of them—for Earl, at any rate—was Teddy Weatherford, who had a fast, flamboyant style and an adventurous left hand.

Like a well-trained young boxer, Hines studied Weatherford's tricks, drew from them what he wanted, and finally conquered the established pianist in his own territory. Earl's essentially Eastern approach, rooted in a light but firm touch and impressive technical command of his instrument, was too much for the Chicago keyboard men, and the competition melted away. Teddy Weatherford left town in 1926 and never returned (and, his talent spent, died in India about twenty years later).

Earl moved to the larger and more celebrated Entertainer's Café in 1925, playing opposite Carroll Dickerson's excellent big band. Within a short time, he joined Dickerson's group, then began a series of Pantages vaudeville appearances that eventually took Earl and the band to California and back. They were on the road for forty-two straight weeks.

The Dickerson band was a carefully drilled outfit that specialized in flashy ensemble work and clean musicianship, goals wholly consistent with Earl's own. "Hot" solos were featured, of course, by jazzmen like trumpeter Natty Dominique, trombonist Honoré Dutrey, and saxophonist Cecil Irwin.

When the band landed back in Chicago, Louis Armstrong, home again after a stint with Fletcher Henderson, was the man every bandleader wanted. Erskine Tate had him at that moment, but Dickerson and King Oliver, his former mentor, were making offers anyway. Louis was considering rejoining Oliver, but Hines and his friends argued that he should "go with the young guys" and not fall back with the "old" New Orleans men. As it turned out, Hines and Armstrong joined each other's bands and played two jobs for a while, dashing off after an evening with Tate to finish out the night with Dickerson. Tate's specialty was movie theaters, and the work called for a fast, versatile pianist. Teddy Weatherford had achieved much of his local fame in Tate's organization at the Vendome Theater, and Earl, too, became more widely known there. Musicians, though, were more interested in the sound of the Dickerson band at the Sunset Café, for there Armstrong was featured prominently and the sidemen—drummer Tubby Hall, violinist-reedman Darnell Howard, and Hines were a few—seemed more in tune with the brand of jazz Louis was offering.

As the popularity of Armstrong grew throughout 1926, Hines

found his own star rising as well. The Sunset's proprietor, Joe Glaser, decided that Louis was his real drawing card and arranged to edge Dickerson out altogether. In 1927, the band became Louis Armstrong and His Stompers, and Hines was appointed musical director. It was about this time, too, that Earl made his first recordings in Chicago.

In a set of four selections recorded with a group of old-guard New Orleans stylists and Armstrong, Earl seems somewhat ill at ease at the piano. Clarinetist Johnny Dodds, making his initial appearance on records as a leader, establishes such nervously fast tempos that even Armstrong sounds uncomfortable. Earl's solo contributions are brief and perfunctory, revealing a conservative left hand, which was either not completely developed yet or simply inhibited by an attempt to match the mood of the session, and an equally uninspired right hand, concerned largely with dashing off simple on-the-beat melodic fragments in octaves. *Melancholy* has the best Hines of the four Dodds titles; Earl's solo is marked by right-hand tremolos, a Jelly Roll Morton-like glissando or two, and a positive, declarative keyboard touch. But if this was a fair representation of Hines in April, 1927, the pianist must have made some major discoveries in the month that followed; for in May, Earl recorded *Chicago Breakdown*, probably the first good example of his unique artistry to be caught on wax. (Strangely, the recording was not issued until George Avakian discovered it in Columbia's vaults many years later.)

Chicago Breakdown is of considerable interest on several counts. The choice of a Jelly Roll Morton composition hints that Hines and Armstrong might have been more intrigued by the music and arrangements of Morton (whose finest recordings immediately preceded the *Chicago Breakdown* date) than is commonly supposed. The recording is valuable, too, as an only clue to the sound of the Dickerson-Armstrong band of 1927 and to the mutual benefits Earl and Louis derived from playing together regularly. It is unfortunate that Okeh chose to record Armstrong mostly with his old New Orleans friends in 1927, for the decision deprived us of hearing the more modern Sunset Café band and its two star performers during a highly creative period in their professional lives.

Earl's brief solo on *Chicago Breakdown* is a trifle stiff and stodgy, but many of the now familiar trademarks were already there—the sudden break in the regular bass rhythm; the crisp, clean treble-octave voicing; and the short, hornlike melodic phrases. In the ensemble portions, too, Hines cuts through the band sound in characteristic fashion, although he had not asserted himself in this way on the more traditional Dodds session a month before.

Musicians and sophisticated patrons flocked to the Sunset to hear Armstrong and Hines in 1927, but only Louis landed the record dates, which were aimed at a market of displaced Southerners in lower-income brackets. As an entertainer and a highly sophisticated modern musician, Hines had no place in these "down home" recording sessions. Furthermore, the New York pianists had pretty well cornered the solo recording field, so Earl failed to record again until May, 1928, several months after he had left Armstrong as a regular sideman.

The Sunset job finally ran out in the fall of 1927, but Earl and Louis, together with their closest friend, drummer Zutty Singleton, were full of confidence and enthusiasm. The three were regular visitors to after-hours clubs, open jam sessions, and private parties, where they always wound up playing and entertaining as a kind of miniature show. They decided to stick together as long as possible. The trio worked short jobs together in theater bands such as Clarence Jones's and occasionally sponsored dances of their own. In November, Lil Armstrong rented a ballroom called Warwick Hall and turned it over to the three musicians, who tried producing an original revue there. The new Savoy Ballroom opened at the same time just around the corner and wiped them out. It became painfully clear that outstanding musicianship, even combined with showmanship, would not automatically draw customers. Despite a devoted clan of followers (mostly of the non-spending variety), the triumvirate was soon at liberty again.

Earl made an exploratory trip to New York about this time, but nothing came of it. When Hines returned to Chicago in early 1928, Louis and Zutty had grown tired of the uncertain life and joined Carroll Dickerson, who now led the band at the successful Savoy. Earl, somewhat depressed, looked about for a secure job for himself and found a spot, just vacated by Glover Compton, with Jimmy Noone's five-piece band at the Apex Club. He spent most of the year there.

The Apex was a favorite hangout for musicians, and in the course of Earl's stint with Noone, young pianists Joe Sullivan, Jess Stacy, Casino Simpson, and many others were deeply affected by his now mature style. Noone was a New Orleans clarinetist and a bit on the conservative side, but, unlike Johnny Dodds, he was a master craftsman as well as a jazz artist, and Jimmy appreciated the advanced musical ideas put forth by Earl. Happily, Hines's work at this time has been preserved on records, permitting a clear picture of the pianist's progress through early 1928.

In May, the Noone quintet (alto saxophonist Joe Poston, banjoist Bud Scott, and drummer Johnny Wells were the other members) recorded four good performances that effectively combined elements of New Orleans jazz, popular music of the day, honest entertainment, and brilliant musicianship into a highly personal band style. Earl was not yet in the proper setting for his talents, but the small group gave him a good deal of freedom, notwithstanding the jarring clang of Bud Scott's banjo. Indeed, on some selections, one might think it was Hines himself who led the band, for Earl moves right into the foreground alongside the alto and clarinet.

I Know That You Know, a display piece for Noone, suggests that Earl was not entirely comfortable with the breakneck pace established by the leader. The piano solo is neither inspired nor unusual by Hines standards, although Earl never lags behind. *Every Evening* is a stylized stomp played in the New Orleans manner, and heavy-handed stomps were never Earl's forte. However, his solo breaks away enough to show flashes of the arresting scuttling bass lines for which he was soon to become famous and a glimpse of the jagged-right-hand flights which were beginning to fall into place at this time. More satisfying is *Sweet Sue*, in which Earl embellishes the slow, straight melodic lead with a background chorus that is the high point of the recording. The impact of this passage comes largely from Hines's trumpetlike phrasing, complete with "vibrato" at the end of each phrase (achieved by right-hand tremolos) and natural "breath points" inserted just as they might be in a trumpet solo. The use of treble octaves is again important here, for it gives to Earl's short phrases the brassy authority needed to make them completely convincing. *Four or Five Times* has stomp overtones again, but Earl works independently of the idiom most of the way. There is, however, a slight heaviness in the piano bass line despite efforts by Hines to get under and lift the performance with his right hand.

Following an additional pair of Noone sides in June and a date with a dreary new singer named Lillie Delk Christian (Armstrong and Noone also participated in this one), Earl began a historic series of Okeh sessions with Louis and members of the Carroll Dickerson Savoy orchestra. In two hot June days, the old trio— Louis, Earl, and Zutty—reunited and, with trombonist Fred Robinson, clarinetist Jimmy Strong, and guitarist Mancy Cara added, finally recorded the kind of music that had been convulsing other musicians in Chicago for many months. Armstrong's was the overriding voice, but Hines placed such a high second that his name began to be mentioned along with Louis' whenever musicians got together.

Many of the musical devices and tricks on these recordings probably came from the Dickerson band, particularly on pieces like the elaborate *Fireworks,* which concludes with choruses borrowed from the perennial showstopper *Tiger Rag.* The ensemble effect is more that of a small orchestra than of a New Orleans band, reflecting the influence of arrangers Bill Challis, Don Redman, and Fletcher Henderson, among others. For Hines, who never had much use for old-time jazzmen or "back-room musicians" (as he once called Jelly Roll Morton), these were ideal small-band settings in which to stretch out and try some of the ideas he had been developing. One of the best demonstrations of Hines successfully matching wits with Armstrong occurs on *Skip the Gutter,* a relaxed traditional vehicle, where the two musicians trade two-bar and four-bar ideas without interference from the rest of the group. It is really a two-man affair all the way, as each tempts the other to extend himself a little further on successive breaks. Both handle double-time ideas with an easy, sure sense of pulse, and the match finishes a draw.

On *Sugar Foot Strut,* Earl plays with full solo force behind Louis' vocal instead of filling in with an ordinary accompaniment part. As in Noone's band, the pianist constantly pushed himself toward the front line, only reluctantly dropping back into the rhythm section when absolutely required to. This tendency can also be heard on *Squeeze Me* and on Hines's composition *Monday Date*. Now and then, as in Armstrong's monumental *West End Blues,* Earl retires to a more conventional supportive role, boosting the trumpet player with rolling bass tremolos and provocative treble harmonies, but it was not his nature to hang back for long.

Hines was and is a large, aggressive man who enjoyed the musical challenge of working with the gifted Armstrong but, like many Eastern-style pianists who came up in a world of ragtime, elaborate stage shows, and cabaret entertainers, lacked the deep identification with the blues that marked the work of the best New Orleans players. When inspired by Armstrong, the pianist occasionally came close to the idiom, but his later work was almost entirely devoid of the earthy, relaxed spirit so fundamental to successful blues playing. It does not follow, however, that the blues played no part in the Hines style, for he was perceptive enough to realize that good jazz phrasing must borrow something from the blues if it is to avoid academicism.

Now established as a leading pianist, Earl was asked to sit in on a July, 1928, Carroll Dickerson recording. The result is of special interest because it is the only recorded document of the excellent Savoy orchestra of that period. The two selections, *Symphonic Raps* and *Savoyager's Stomp,* are remarkably like big-band extensions of the Hines-Armstrong recordings—full of potential harmonic pitfalls, advanced scoring techniques, and dazzling solos. Although the current of influence must have flowed in both directions, these recordings underline the suggestion that part of Hines's unorthodox bravura style may have stemmed from the arranged music he played with the Dickerson orchestra.

Earl continued to work with Noone throughout the summer months of the year. The group's first batch of records had sold well, and they returned to the studios in August to try six more selections. Again Hines reverted to a more conservative style than he had shown on the Armstrong sessions. His attempts at understatement (*Apex Blues*) seem awkward and unnatural, while his more usual arabesques (*Sweet Lorraine*) are closer in spirit to Jelly Roll Morton than to Armstrong. Another *Monday Date* was recorded, and, unlike the Armstrong version of two months be-

fore, this one has Earl in an almost frenzied mood. Oddly, this
solo suffers from an overabundance of zeal.

A splendid Hines solo in this final Noone series occurs on *King
Joe*. Except for some barely audible timekeeping by the drummer,
the rhythm section drops out for Earl's solo, and this simple device provides the pianist with exactly the kind of freedom he
needs for his extraordinary rhythmic explorations.

In the fall of 1928, Earl began rehearsing with a group of
friends and, apparently with no specific plans for making public
appearances, building a small library of arrangements that all enjoyed playing. It was a natural thing for Earl to do, for his experience with Deppe and Armstrong, which had put him in direct
command of two very different big bands, had left the pianist
without much enthusiasm for serving as a sideman. He finally left
Noone and was replaced by Alex Hill and, later, Zinky Cohen,
two qualified Chicago pianists much affected by the Hines style.

By December, Earl had hit his full musical stride. In this single
remarkable month, the pianist from Pittsburgh recorded fourteen
titles with Louis Armstrong, cut twelve piano solos, and, on his
twenty-third birthday, launched his own ten-piece orchestra at a
leading Chicago ballroom.

Of the Armstrong dates, ten are enduring expositions of Louis
and Earl at their creative peak as a team. There could be no un-
certainty now about the status of Hines; each performance
affirmed and reaffirmed that a spectacular and influential stylist
had been developed in South Side Chicago.

On tunes like *Beau Koo Jack*, Earl approaches his solo as if it
were an extended break, with the rest of the band (again Dickerson men, with altoist Don Redman added) obligingly suspending
all other sounds for that moment. In this happy environment, Earl
demonstrated some new ideas. The octave melody phrases were
now frequently replaced by streaking single-note lines, sometimes
arching gracefully over four or eight bars in a continuous pattern
bearing little or no resemblance to the pianist's famous "trumpet"
style. In the tradition of all good Eastern pianists, Earl's bass figures were masterpieces of eccentric design and spontaneous wit.
It was this feature of his style that made his rhythm men readily
agree to drop out during the piano solos; a bass player, for example, courted disaster if he tried to follow Earl's rhythmic peregri-

nations. Hines, however, never lost the pulse, even when it was completely out of sight, and this remarkable ability had much to do with the success of his music. Broken rhythms were, of course, older than ragtime, but no pianist before Earl Hines—not even James P. Johnson—ever took so many chances in the heat of spontaneous improvisation without experiencing many failures. Hines seemed never to miss.

Fast countermelodies, long lines of sixteenths, thirty-seconds, and sixteenth-note triplets (many suggesting ideas that were to come much later with Lester Young and Charlie Parker), harmonic adventures sometimes actually over Armstrong's head, brilliant use of double-time figures to increase tension, intelligent spacing of pauses for dramatic impact, and a mature sense of musical architectonics were some of the characteristics of Earl's work in late 1928 that amounted to a milestone in the annals of keyboard jazz. Other notable Hines-Armstrong titles are *Save It, Pretty Mama, No, Muggles, Tight Like This, Hear Me Talkin' to Ya,* and *St. James Infirmary.* On *Basin Street Blues,* Earl plays celeste with his usual positive air.

Hines's ambition to be heard as a front-line instrument was given free play in one other Armstrong recording. It is a duet transformation of an old King Oliver tune called *Weatherbird Rag,* and the two jazzmen obviously had a merry time testing each other's strength without the normal restrictions imposed by a conventional jazz band. One need only to contrast this extraordinary collaboration with a rather hidebound Jelly Roll Morton–King Oliver duet recording of some four years earlier to understand how far Hines and Armstrong had helped to bring jazz in that short time.

Earl's solo recordings in 1928 present a curious contradiction: though even more impressive in strictly pianistic terms than his Armstrong work, they occasionally suggest a man to whom music is a kind of advanced game of wits and perhaps little more. "Music is like baseball," Hines has said. "The reason we didn't go for back-room musicians much was that it didn't take anything to figure it out. If it's not a challenge, there's no fun in it."

Many jazzmen would agree, but perhaps not so many would want the kind of compliment that a Hines sideman once offered, quite sincerely: "Earl is just like a machine—but a machine that swings!"

There were moments of tenderness, real or posed, for the "machine that swings," though. His *Blues in Thirds* is a charming mood piece, if not a true blues in its depth of emotional expression. It was recorded first in Chicago as *Caution Blues*, but Earl's QRS version, made in New York a couple of weeks later, is the more sensitive rendition.

When QRS, ordinarily a piano-roll company, asked Hines to make phonograph records in December, he went immediately to New York for the date. Entering the studio without music or even very much idea of what he would do, Earl sat down and played eight tunes: *Blues in Thirds, Panther Rag* (obviously *Tiger Rag*, already recorded in part as *57 Varieties*), *Monday Date*, two other blues, and three originals titled *Chicago High Life, Stowaway*, and *Just Too Soon*. Beneath the elaborate superstructures, these last three compositions are made up largely of stock progressions borrowed from songs like *Sister Kate, Big Butter and Egg Man*, and other good jam-session favorites.

That Earl hoped to make an impression in his New York recording debut may be deduced from these recordings in two ways: his tempos are exhibitionistically fast; and in several instances (*Monday Date* is one), he paraded his command of the Harlem "stride" style, perhaps added for the benefit of critical local pianists like Johnson and Waller.

The QRS solos (and those recorded in Chicago as well) are unique virtuoso performances. Though the Armstrong stamp still appears on some of Earl's ideas, this group of records marks his break with the trumpeter as a co-musician and as a continuing influence. From here on, each man went his own way.

Actually, too much has been made of the impact of Louis on Earl. It is likely that the trumpeter's manner of phrasing encouraged Hines to develop his hornlike treble lines more convincingly, but there is little evidence of wholesale borrowing of musical concepts. Armstrong was a master builder, one who constructed a solo from the ground up; Hines tended, at this time, to think in four-bar or eight-bar fragments, each a unit unto itself. Louis moved with the rhythm section, often relaxing just behind the pulse; Hines pushed the beat, creating the illusion of accelerating while keeping perfect time. Most importantly, Armstrong thought in essentially *vocal* terms; Hines improvised primarily in abstract *instrumental* fashion.

It was while he was in New York that Earl heard from Lucky Millinder, a sort of middleman between the Chicago underworld and the local music business, who was looking for a known musician to head up a band at the Grand Terrace Ballroom. Hines thought of his rehearsal group, assured Millinder that he was ready to go, and took the next train for home.

It was a good choice by Millinder, for Earl's knowledge of showmanship, staging, and musical directing put the fast-moving Grand Terrace show on a par with the revues at the Sunset and the Savoy. The band was a good one, if a little rough at first, and included top men like trumpeters George Mitchell and Shirley Clay, a Miff Mole-inspired trombonist named William Franklin, ex-Dickerson saxophonist Cecil Irwin, and Lester Boone, a good jazz tenor saxophone player. For a couple of months, trumpeter Jabbo Smith also worked with this band. Franklin, Alvis, and Irwin contributed original arrangements to the band's book, which was already expanding rapidly. By early 1929, the Hines band offered a respectable sound of its own that seemed to lie somewhere between the loose swing of Bennie Moten's Kansas City band and the advanced ensemble precision of William McKinney's Cotton Pickers. There were, too, overtones of smaller stomp bands in arrangements like *Beau Koo Jack* and of the strutting Harlem style in numbers like *Everybody Loves My Baby*. These and several other titles were recorded for Victor in February, 1929, barely two months after the band opened at the Grand Terrace.

During these early band years, Earl expanded his harmonic scope, partly through the influence of Cecil Irwin, whose arrangements for the band reflected the saxophonist's formal studies of harmony and increased interest in "modern" voicing. Ninths, elevenths, sixths, and minor sevenths began to appear more frequently in Hines's piano improvisations, adding new dimensions to his already complex style. An intriguing example of this new turn is contained in a February, 1929, solo recording of *Glad Rag Doll*. Two separate versions, takes from the same recording session, have been issued that offer some clues to Earl's transitional position at that time. Take 1 is a straightforward compound of Morton, Johnson, Waller, and Hines, full of strutting Harlem devices, that concludes on a major chord with the sixth added for interest. The second take is slower and more thoughtful, ending with a tense flatted fifth—a modern touch, indeed, for 1929. Throughout, Hines's affection for Waller's frothy stride manner is evident. Earl's bass lines, alternating chromatic tenths with harmonically sophisticated *oom-pah* figures, are a mixture of Waller and his own ideas as originally developed from Jim Fellman in Pittsburgh.

As he continued to work with a large band, Hines began to rely more upon his supporting musicians, causing the full semiorchestral sound of his piano to undergo subtle changes. The rhythm section took over many of the functions of the pianist's left hand, leaving Earl free to experiment further with running-bass countermelodies. Right-hand octaves were still useful in many instances, but more and more single-note improvisations were appearing in the pianist's solos. (By now, the widespread use of electric microphones had encouraged pianists everywhere to play with a faster, lighter touch.) Finally, Earl no longer had to prove his ability to other jazzmen, for he was acclaimed by musicians throughout the country and, as a bandleader, could send his music in any direction he wished without having to force the issue from the keyboard. This, too, had its effect upon his playing, now becoming less frantic and more contemplative—but no less venturesome—with each passing month.

By 1932, Earl had enlarged his band to twelve men. Cecil Irwin, Darnell Howard, and Omer Simeon made up the sax section; trumpeter Walter Fuller, who also arranged for and sang with the band, was a major asset; guitarist Lawrence Dixon, trumpeter-saxophonist George Dixon, bassist Quinn Wilson, trombonist Louis Taylor, and saxophonist Irwin all contributed original tunes and arrangements. British composer and arranger Reginald Foresythe formed a close friendship with Hines at this time and wrote a theme song, *Deep Forest,* for him. Foresythe's advanced harmonic concepts again affected the pianist's personal musical outlook. The Grand Terrace landed a network radio wire about that time, and regular broadcasts of the band from Chicago began to be heard across the nation. It was a happy period for Earl, despite the raging Depression that was crippling most of the American economy at the time. There was security, little travel, musical satisfaction, personal celebrity, and the excitement of planning musical shows around performers such as Ethel Waters and Bill Robinson. Young players like Teddy Wilson were coming around to learn from him, and visiting jazzmen from out of town frequently asked to sit in. For a green bandleader of 27, Earl Hines was doing rather well.

At this time, Earl turned out a pair of recorded solos, *Love Me* *Tonight* and *Down Among the Sheltering Palms.* The second is an especially notable performance, for it reveals a new level of maturity in its orderly progression from simple melodic statement to conservative embellishments to an agitated climax of broken rhythms and fuguelike cross-melodies. The solo, in short, is built to stand as a single spiral of variations on a theme, and it represents an advance from Hines's earlier montage methods.

The band took on a more positive identity in 1933, when arranger-saxophonist Jimmy Mundy joined up. With Mundy arrangements like *Cavernism* and *Madhouse,* the reputation of the band soared, and musicians began comparing the Hines band with Fletcher Henderson's superb organization. In this setting, Earl's playing took on a new warmth that had only occasionally been revealed before.

Hines continued to strengthen his band from 1933 to 1935. Trummy Young, a modern trombonist and an entertaining singer, joined the brass section. Singer Herb Jeffries became a prime attraction with recordings like *Blue.* The best addition of all, however, was tenor saxophonist Budd Johnson, replacing Cecil Irwin, who was killed in a car accident. Johnson was a first-class soloist and a highly skilled, forward-looking arranger. He was also a good organizer and eventually took over many of Earl's personnel problems.

In 1934, the band started recording for Decca, a new company that took over many of the old Brunswick label's established artists, including Hines. Someone at Decca had the singular notion that the band ought to turn out a string of modernized Dixieland tunes, so Earl recorded *Sweet Georgia Brown, That's a Plenty, Angry, Maple Leaf Rag, Copenhagen,* and *Wolverine Blues.* The balance of the Decca output of 1934 and 1935 was made up of new versions of old hits: *Cavernism, Rosetta* (Hines's best-known composition), *Blue, Bubbling Over,* and *Julia.* The material was not really suited to a band as good as this one was, but Earl tossed off a number of impressive solos, particularly those on *Copenhagen* and *Wolverine Blues.*

The best of the Grand Terrace era was over by 1936. From the time the Hines band commenced broadcasting some five years before, more and more months of each year had been devoted to traveling. Now the band was away from home more often than not. In 1936, Benny Goodman lured arranger Jimmy Mundy away from Hines, and Fletcher Henderson became the darling of the Grand Terrace operators. Earl was, in fact, lucky to get even six weeks at the ballroom between Henderson runs. And there was no arguing with the Capone-trained backers of the Terrace—it wouldn't have been good for the "health," as contemporary movie villains were wont to say. The Decca contract lapsed, and no one bothered to record the band at all that year. Hines stayed on the road.

Most of the trouble, of course, came from Earl himself. He was not a good businessman and always seemed to make the right move at the wrong time. He also was, it must be added, neither popular among musicians nor skilled in public relations.

Though its fortunes rose and fell on the waves of mismanagement, the Hines band was still a musically rewarding outfit to hear. In 1937 and 1938, a few more records were released. By now, Earl had updated his playing again, featuring light, airy solos over buoyant swing-band arrangements. The crisp, almost metallic, and very authoritative keyboard touch was still there, as were the broken rhythms and double-time figures, but a fresh, graceful quality that hadn't been noticeable before appeared in some of his work now. The melodic lines were longer and smoother, with fewer stops and starts, and seemed to ride easily *over* the band rather than welling up from *within* it. The Morton-Johnson dicta, which held that a good pianist must imitate a full orchestra, were almost completely put aside. The new piano hero of the period was Teddy Wilson, and it is quite possible that Earl borrowed an idea or two from the fleet and precise Wilson, just as Teddy had once learned much from him. It is likely, too, that Hines's deep regard for the clarinet style of Benny Goodman caused some modification of his old Armstrong-like "trumpet" lines. Much of the pianist's work from this time on was closer to clarinet-saxophone conception than to trumpet ideas. Good examples of this new phase of Earl's development are *Pianology, Rhythm Sundae,* and *Flany Doodle Swing. Honeysuckle Rose,* a concurrent quartet performance featuring clarinetist Simeon and tenor saxophonist Johnson, was a happy affair in which Hines and Johnson explored some outside harmonies while remaining inside the familiar Fats Waller composition.

From 1938 to 1940, Earl's band continued its downward slide. Though still bound by a one-sided contract with Ed Fox of the Grand Terrace, most of Hines's time was spent on tour. Budd Johnson returned to the group after a year or so with Gus Arnheim, but at one point about half the band, including Walter Fuller, quit altogether. Earl switched booking offices, but it didn't seem to help. In an era of successful big bands and unprecedented public enthusiasm for jazz, the Hines unit, though offering good music, might as well not have existed. *Metronome* magazine's 1938 annual readers' poll, in which swing fans voted for the "Best of All Bands," listed Earl Hines and company in seventy-ninth place. There wasn't much cause for rejoicing, either, when the magazine's 1939 poll pulled the band up to the sixty-first spot.

Walter Fuller's departure in 1940 was another blow. (The popular singer-trumpeter took his own band into the Grand Terrace but was pulled out by the union some months later when manager Fox failed to meet the payroll.) Budd Johnson was in and out for a while, but he finally returned to help Earl shape a totally new kind of band. The old contract with Fox had been adjudged worthless by the musicians' union, and Hines decided to give the band business a fresh try. He already had a new record contract with Bluebird, a hit record shaping up in *Boogie Woogie on the St. Louis Blues* (a commercial and uncharacteristic piano specialty), another new booking agency, a fresh band put together by Johnson, and he was soon to have a new singer named Billy Eckstine. When Billy recorded *Jelly Jelly* for Earl in December, 1940, the upward swing had already begun, but it was Eckstine who finally brought Hines the success he had been unable to find alone.

Just as he was beginning his term with Bluebird, Earl recorded two long solos for the very young Blue Note label, *The Father's Getaway* ("Father," often pronounced "fatha," being a nickname Hines had acquired from a radio announcer in the Grand Terrace days) and *Reminiscing at Blue Note*. They were his first recorded unaccompanied solos in seven years. The first is an explosive burst of energy and ideas into which Earl seems to be trying to cram everything he had ever learned. There is a segment of pure James P. Johnson, a sustained tremolo suggesting his *Boogie Woogie on the St. Louis Blues* routine, a series of wild rhythmic gyrations and some melodic broken-field running that seem on the verge of getting out of hand but never do, and an incredible tangle of block chords, suspensions, and breaks within breaks. The result is a kind of amalgam of new and old Hines in a display of virtuosity that no pianist of 1939, save one, could have matched. (The one, of course, would be Art Tatum, who himself began as a Hines-Waller disciple.) *Reminiscing at Blue Note* is a curious hodge-podge, full of references to boogie-woogie, pseudomodern harmonies of the twenties, Harlem piano, and smatterings of Hines favorites like *You Can Depend on Me*.

Three solos for Bluebird recorded in 1939 and early 1940 deserve mention. One is the inevitable *Rosetta*, which begins conservatively enough but eventually winds up as a tightly compressed knot of ideas, concluding, it seems, just before the snapping point. *Body and Soul* reminds the listener that Earl was still, though a more modern musician than before, a little too much the hard-boiled pianist to lose himself completely in a sensitive ballad performance. *Child of a Disordered Brain* is essentially a solo in the style of Fats Waller, upon which is superimposed a dizzying succession of out-of-time breaks and other familiar Hines devices.

The development of the Hines band from 1941 to 1943 is an important early chapter in the story of modern jazz and is better told elsewhere. Suffice it to point out that Budd Johnson gathered the best modern players he could find, helped to build a distinctive library of advanced arrangements, and acted as a valuable liaison between Hines and his men; that during this period the band included outstanding performers like Dizzy Gillespie, Charlie Parker, Sarah Vaughan, Scoops Carry, Freddy Webster, and

Benny Green; and that Eckstine's departure to form his own band
in 1943 sent Earl's rating down to the bottom of the polls again.

During this period of intimate contact with modern jazz, Earl's
own style moved ahead somewhat on his band recordings but appeared to stand still on solo records. *On the Sunny Side of the Street*
and *Melancholy Baby*, for example, are 1941 solos that actually
seem to go back to the stomping and romping of Morton and
Waller, although Hines flourishes are present, too. Yet Earl's short
solo on his 1941 band recording of *You Don't Know What Love Is*
is built on a hard, firm line that was thoroughly modern for its
time. The exploratory urge and the fondness for musical puzzles
that distinguished the musical character of the budding jazzmen
in the early forties were exactly the drives that propelled Hines. It
is unfortunate that the sound of Earl's greatest band (1943) was
never preserved, owing to a recording ban called during that year
by the musicians' union.

Earl's next venture grew out of an anomalous ambition he had
nurtured a long time: to front a huge stage orchestra built along
Paul Whiteman lines, complete with a string section. (Strings
with dance bands were in vogue again by the early forties.) He
added a covey of draftproof female violinists and some French
horns to his new seventeen-piece band and featured concert arrangements of selections from *Showboat* and other old war-
horses. The experiment lasted a few troubled months, after which
the strings and horns suddenly vanished. By mid-1944, Earl was
back to seventeen men, including reedman Scoops Carry, trumpeter Willie Cook, and tenor saxophonist Wardell Gray.

The recording ban was over in 1944, and Earl recorded some
twelve-inch sides for Keynote, featured with groups led by Cozy
Cole and Charlie Shavers. Amazingly, they were the first records
Earl had made since 1928 with a group of jazzmen who were not
only reasonably modern in outlook but also near Hines's own musical level in ability. The Cole releases are especially satisfying, for
Hines was matched with Coleman Hawkins, and both men
seemed to enjoy the experience enormously. Each had passed
through much the same learning processes in the preceding two
decades, and each stood on the threshold of modern jazz in 1944.
Earl was uncommonly relaxed for the date, employing a light but
authoritative touch and even trying his hand at some uncharacter-

istic bits of understatement. The four excellent performances are *Blue Moon, Just One More Chance, Father Cooperates,* and a re-worked *Honeysuckle Rose* called *Through for the Night.* With trumpeter Shavers, Earl recorded another *Rosetta,* an uncommonly slow version of *Star Dust,* and two other on-the-spot compositions. Again one man on the date matched Earl's skill and artistry—drummer Jo Jones. With Jones assisting, Earl's background chording for front-line soloists is decidedly modern, totally unlike his work behind Armstrong in 1928.

A session for Apollo during this period found Earl once more in the company of his peers, in this instance altoist Johnny Hodges, bassist Oscar Pettiford, and drummer Sidney Catlett. Of six titles, *Life with Father* is the best example of Hine's 1944 style.

A set of four 1944 recordings with a trio that again included bassist Pettiford points up even more clearly what was happening to Earl at this time. Many of the arresting left-hand figures had fallen away in favor of light chromatic accents and occasional harmonic punctuations. The advent of bold, modern string-bass lines had made this move by Earl not only possible but musically desirable. In addition, Earl had long been hinting at a more soft and gentle approach, although his own best work never seemed to lean very much in that direction, and the modern rhythm section encouraged him to bring out that side of his musical personality.

"In the twenties," Earl recalls, "much of the music was loud, two-beat gutbucket stuff. It was like shouting all the time. I preferred musicians who played soft and beautiful things—men like cornetist Joe Smith, who used to stop the crowds cold using a coconut shell for a mute. Trombonist Tyree Glenn has some of that quality today."

Earl once selected Tommy Dorsey as his favorite trombonist, because Dorsey had "technique, good taste, experience, and a real knack for organization and selecting song material." These, it seems, were the qualities Hines now tried to stress in his own work. It was a more feasible proposition from 1944 on, when the prerequisites for jazzmen that prevailed in the twenties and early thirties—volume, powerful attack, heavy rhythmic emphasis, and a "down home" blues feeling—had been superseded by a new set of values—harmonic research, long melodic lines, rapid-fire articulation, and rhythmic experimentation. The only drawback was that Hines at 39 was not in a position to build an *entirely* new style on the principles of bop, and his middle-of-the-road approach, while perfectly sound musically, led nowhere commercially. Not wishing to play Dixieland or early forms of swing, but unable to participate fully in the modern movement of the mid-forties, Earl relied instead upon his new, softer, less aggressive mode of expression and entered what might be called his "bland" period. He has never entirely emerged from it since.

In 1945, the Hines band was still a rocking one, with jazzmen like Wardell Gray, Benny Green, and tenor saxophonist Kermit Scott featured, but Earl kept his own solos to a bare minimum. When the piano was spotlighted, the result too often amounted to an undistinguished porridge of pseudo-boogie-woogie and melodic clichés. This strange phase is documented by a handful of recordings—including still another *Rosetta*—on the ARA label.

Earl's last sustained fling at big-band jazz was in 1947. He had just recovered from a serious automobile accident, his second in ten years, that had left him temporarily without sight. The economic picture grew darker, and he finally gave up, after nineteen stormy years as a leader, and accepted Louis Armstrong's offer to join his new All-Star sextet. It was not a good musical solution to Earl's dilemma, but the pay was good and the headaches few. He stayed nearly four years.

Two decades had brought many changes, and the Hines-Armstrong team was no longer the formidable musical *Gestalt* it had been in 1928. Louis had, if anything, retreated from his once-modern position and arrived at a kind of theatrical New Orleans style, while Earl had moved on from his early modern approach to a musical posture consistent with later developments in the forties. Furthermore, Hines had long since grown accustomed to the limelight and could not be content as a sideman—even an All-Star sideman.

Not surprisingly, Earl's best recordings during these Armstrong years were made with others. A number of dates in 1948 and 1949, some with trumpeter Buck Clayton and clarinetist Barney Bigard (also an All-Star), found Earl in good form and occasionally up to his old creative level. One called *Keyboard Kapers* is first-rate Hines from beginning to end. Another mixed batch recorded without Armstrong while on tour in Paris is less impressive, but

Earl repeatedly breaks through the prevailing air of indifference to offer some bracing ideas.

A set of solos for Columbia in 1950 features mainly the bland side of Hines's contradictory musical personality, but there are absorbing moments when Earl reveals what he could still do when the mood struck him. In his new *Rosetta*, for example, he constructs, over simple bass patterns, a long, single-note melodic line that could easily be the work of a modern horn player. Hines was still, when the spirit moved him, a unique and impressive talent.

The inevitable departure from Armstrong in late 1951 triggered some uncharacteristically hostile remarks from the trumpeter (reported in *Down Beat* at the time): "Hines and his ego, ego, ego! If he wanted to go, the hell with him. He's good, sure, but we don't need him. . . . Earl Hines and his big ideas. Well, we can get along without Mr. Hines."

Earl lost no time in putting an excellent semimodern band together, but he soon found himself a victim of his own poor business methods again. Leonard Feather, reviewing the group in *Down Beat,* sensed the problem: "It's not surprising that Fatha Hines has one of the brightest little bands in the country. The only surprise is that he's been working so sporadically and that so few people seem to know about the group. (One possible reason: D'Oro Records keeps his releases top secret.)"

Featuring versatile jazzmen like trumpeter Jonah Jones, former sideman Benny Green, bassist Tommy Potter, drummer Art Blakey (later replaced by Osie Johnson), and reedman Aaron Sachs, this little band represented Earl's last bid for a place in the contemporary music scene. When it failed, the pianist seemed ready to try anything to earn his living. He worked for a while with a small unit featuring Dickie Wells, but that petered out as well. In September, 1955, Earl turned up at the Hangover Club in San Francisco with a pickup Dixieland band that included his old Chicago colleague Darnell Howard and New York trombonist Jimmy Archey. He learned an appropriate list of traditional tunes, discovered how to hold back improper "modern" chords to an even greater extent than had been necessary in Armstrong's All-Stars, and settled down to a long, if musically unrewarding, sojourn at the Western saloon.

For several years, the pianist covered up his Dixieland activities by recording and traveling with more modern trios and quartets, but in 1960 he finally went on the road with his traditional band and immediately found wide acceptance in Eastern nightclubs. Weary of resisting the unavoidable, Earl began rehearsing his little traditional band so that at least some part of each performance would reflect his penchant for organization and showmanship. Hines remained, as he must, very much the leader of his own band.

Shortly after settling in the West, Earl recorded two albums for Fantasy, one devoted to Fats Waller specialties and another containing twelve unaccompanied solos. The second set suggests that Hines's powers were undiminished; he soars effortlessly through a superb version of *Piano Man,* a blues named for the late Art Tatum, some new thoughts on *Monday Date,* and others. However, the records did not sell well, favorable reviews notwithstanding.

Along with a couple of uneventful sessions, including one conducted during a 1957 Paris visit, Earl recorded at least one outstanding performance during the next couple of years. This was *Brussels' Hustle,* a blues put together by Hines and some San Francisco musician friends for a Felsted recording. It is a hearty and imaginative affair, not at all like his playing in a Dixieland context. *Brussels' Hustle* reassured those who cared that Earl was still vitally concerned with music—and rather modern music at that—when he wanted to be.

A 1958 Benny Carter–Hines collaboration, with bassist Leroy Vinnegar and Shelly Manne added, should have provided the ideal showcase for Earl's finest work, and indeed there are many good moments in the twelve performances they recorded, but Carter's unbending alto and Hines's cool piano failed to inspire each other. It was, however, a noble experiment (by Contemporary Records) and a rare instance of intelligent handling of the enormous Hines talent.

Earl's next trip to the studios occurred a year later, when MGM tried once more to sell the natural and timeless Hines style rooted in the music of the mid-forties. An engagingly handsome quartet treatment of *Willow Weep for Me* and a happy *Stealin' Apples* place this date among Earl's best later efforts, but it was followed by a long silence—a silence broken only in 1961 by a new recorded collection of Earl's Dixieland band numbers: from his 1927 recordings with Johnny Dodds, Earl had traveled nearly full circle.

In early 1963, Hines dismissed his traditional group and for a while tried operating his own nightclub in Oakland, California. From time to time, he toyed with a big band, worked with a semi-commercial swing sextet, and even experimented with a trio consisting of piano, organ, and tenor saxophone. Though reluctant to leave his well-appointed middle-class home and family in Oakland, he found his greatest success on trips to the East. A long overdue jazz piano recital at New York's Little Theater in 1964 enthralled critics and led to new record dates, as well as to an engagement at Birdland, a club generally reserved for modern musicians. In strapping health and still a persuasive improviser, Hines appears ready to carry on his search for musical and financial fulfillment for many more years.

Hines's influence over other pianists has been so extensive that it is difficult to assess it clearly. Broken-bass rhythms, treble octaves, frequent use of tenths in both hands, and even trumpet-like melodic ideas were not new or original with Hines; it was *how* he combined them into a refreshing new style that made such a deep impression on other pianists. Unlike most of the barrel-house keyboard men before him, Earl captured the spirit and substance of jazz without sacrificing classical finesse. He used, for example, all the foot pedals for shading, tone control, and heightening the dramatic value of certain passages. His arched fingers, long enough to cover a tenth but seldom more than that, struck the keys in the crisp, forceful manner of a concert pianist. Earl's tremolos were never the sloppy affairs that one heard from blues and boogie-woogie specialists; each note sounded strong, clear, and evenly spaced. And there were no phony diatonic runs or other shortcuts to flashiness; Earl conceived and *played* every note.

Hines's solos differed from those of, say, Jelly Roll Morton in one fundamental way: Morton and other early pianists attempted to emulate the sound of an orchestra; Earl wanted to achieve the sound of a horn soloist over supporting rhythmic and harmonic figures. The older view followed logically from ragtime and New Orleans preferences for ensemble playing. (King Oliver once scolded pianist Lil Hardin for making fancy runs by reminding her that "we *have* a clarinetist in the band.") Earl's attitude made perfect sense in the light of new trends toward solo exposition ushered in largely by Louis Armstrong.

It was the Hines theory that appealed to young pianists in the late twenties and early thirties. Jess Stacy rejected the violent broken-bass figures, but he made extensive use of Earl's hornlike treble phrasing in octaves. Joe Sullivan elaborated on the powerful on-the-beat attack that marked much of Earl's work and borrowed some of his jagged-bass-line concepts as well. Teddy Wilson arrived at his own influential style by way of Hines's octave work in the right hand, his handling of chromatic tenths in the bass, and his advanced harmonic inversions and alterations. Art Tatum picked up and extended some of Earl's most spectacular tricks—overlapping counterrhythms, breathtaking suspensions, fiery double-time figures, and startling changes of pace and direction. Hundreds of others learned from Hines, many of whom tried to copy his style outright.

Though Earl's playing was agitated and "hot" (in the best sense), it was seldom earthy. Stacy and Sullivan avoided this trap by combining the blues message with their Hines-derived styles; Wilson and Tatum, like Hines, evinced little interest in the blues and remained "cool," though highly effective, jazzmen. Through these two channels, Earl affected virtually every jazz pianist who came after him—until the arrival of Bud Powell and Thelonious Monk in the forties.

Because Hines is still an outstanding pianist and a robust, restless man, those who admire his music are hopeful that he will yet achieve rightful recognition for just what he is—an unclassifiable improviser, a primary contributor to the art of jazz piano playing, and a performer still capable of sustaining intensity and excitement as few jazzmen can. Only in Europe, especially in England (where Earl appeared with Jack Teagarden in 1957), has Hines found widespread enthusiasm for his work. It is a pity the country that planted the flower will not permit it to reach full bloom in its own soil.

Recommended Reading

Feather, Leonard: *Inside Be-Bop*, Robbins, New York (1949).

Gleason, Ralph J. (ed.): *Jam Session*, Putnam's, New York (1958).

McCarthy, Albert, and Max Jones (eds.): *Piano Jazz #2*, Jazz Music Books, London (1945).

Ramsey, Frederic, and Charles Edward Smith: *Jazzmen*, Harcourt, Brace, New York (1939).

Shapiro, Nat and Nat Hentoff (eds.): *The Jazz Makers*, Grove, New York (1958).

Recommended Listening

The Louis Armstrong Story, Vol. 2 (one track), COLUMBIA CL-852.

The Louis Armstrong Story, Vol. 3, COLUMBIA CL-853.

Earl Hines: QRS Solos, ATLANTIC LP 120.

The Art of Jazz Piano (three tracks), EPIC 3295.

Guide to Jazz (one track), RCA VICTOR LPM-1393.

Great Jazz Pianists (one track), CAMDEN 328.

Earl Hines: Oh, Father!, EPIC 3223.

Earl Hines, Mercury MG 25018.

Earl Hines: Plays Fats Waller, FANTASY 3217.

Earl Hines: Solos, FANTASY 3238.

Earl Hines: Earl's Pearls, MGM E 3832.

Earl's Back Room, FELSTED 7002.

Earl Hines: A Monday Date, RIVERSIDE 398.

The Grand Terrace Band: Earl Hines, RCA VICTOR LPV-512.

BIX BEIDERBECKE

BIX BEIDERBECKE seemed born to play jazz. Possessed of a spirit of quiet rebellion, endowed with a sharp sense of humor as well as a fantastic musical ear, he was psychologically constituted to seek the handiest medium of self-expression as early in life as possible —and he discovered jazz as naturally as a baby discovers its mother. In his 28 years, Bix burned up most of his energies trying to satisfy his urge to make music and spent much of his adult life attempting to reconcile his musical individualism with the demands of America's entertainment industry in the twenties. He was doing pretty well on both counts until his physical stamina gave out in late 1928.

Apparently, health was no problem during Bix's childhood in Davenport, Iowa, for he is remembered as a solid and active little boy who enjoyed sports almost as much as music. His extraordinary musical ear was something of a local natural wonder, remembered by those who knew him long after he had left Tyler Elementary School. Alice Robinson, Bix's kindergarten teacher around 1908, never forgot the boy with the big brown eyes who could go to the piano after singing with the class and, with one finger, pick out the same tunes on the keyboard.

"Bix loved to stand by the piano," reminisced Miss Robinson in 1953, "and play with the class pianist, imitating on the high notes whatever she was playing. He was a dreamy little fellow and was happy finding his own niche rather than joining the larger group."

Bix's older brother, Charles, recalls hearing the piano almost continuously in the years that followed. When the family had all they could stand, Mrs. Beiderbecke, a pianist herself, sent Bix out to play. He played hard, too, at baseball, ice skating, and especially tennis, but music was always first.

In a sense, Bix was practicing jazz before he knew what it was. Mildred Colby, his sixth-grade teacher at Tyler, observed that young Beiderbecke participated in classroom part singing in a rather special way, adding second or third parts by ear even when no written parts were furnished.

It was his remarkable ear, in fact, that ultimately led to serious problems for Bix. Piano lessons never worked out very well, for he easily memorized the lessons instead of reading them, thereby disrupting the conservative teaching plan of his instructor. Today there might be teachers who would know how to handle such a gifted student. Because music came to him without effort, Bix apparently developed an early indifference to formal studies that eventually harmed him in his professional life. He also revealed a tendency toward laziness and frequently traveled whatever path offered the least resistance. In school, he customarily ignored his studies until exams came around, barely scraping through at the last moment. The pattern did not change appreciably in later years: Bix got by on a vast natural talent for music and a quick, searching mind, adding to these assets as little hard work as possible.

It was while he was in high school that Bix acquired a cornet and, at about the same time, heard the Original Dixieland Jazz Band on records. Both events were major steps toward the creation of a musical personality that was to have far-reaching effects on jazz. Bix never lost his fondness for the tunes associated with the Original Dixieland Jazz Band, and he stayed with the cornet to the end, although most cornetists switched to the sharper-edged sound of the trumpet in the middle and late twenties. Indeed, there was something rather inflexible about this man—a kind of unconscious perverseness that had both positive and negative sides. There was a single-minded dedication to perfecting his own concept of jazz but, working against him, a defiance of authority and accepted behavior that finally prevented Bix from attaining the artistic satisfaction that should have been his. (It has been suggested by some that Bix's strong ties to his mother, combined with the sternness of his father, were revealing clues here, but that is a separate subject.)

Bix's high-school days were full of music, spirited horseplay, and bad grades, and here he set the adolescent way of life he was to follow for the next decade. There were lots of jam sessions, sitting in with bands of every persuasion, and endless hours of listening. Bix was sent to Lake Forest Academy, near Chicago, in an effort to salvage his sagging high-school career. There he was put back a year, given an opportunity to play more often, and, finally, dismissed from the school in 1922 for failing to meet academic requirements before ending his spring term.

During his stay at Lake Forest, Bix and a drummer named Cy Welge formed the Cy-Bix Orchestra, accepting engagements in nearby towns as well as playing for school functions. The young cornetist was already a popular and influential figure among students and a widening circle of musical friends from Milwaukee to Chicago. He made himself known, too, to the New Orleans Rhythm Kings at Chicago's Friar's Inn. Much has been written and many arguments kindled about individual influences on Bix Beiderbecke's style, but the New Orleans Rhythm Kings seem to have had a kind of collective effect on his musical thinking. The group that Bix and some fellow NORK admirers formed in late 1923 borrowed in many ways from the New Orleans unit. Other bands and individuals had left their mark, too, including local Davenport groups (and possibly the fleeting example of an obscure itinerant New Orleans cornetist named Emmet Hardy), assorted bands on the Mississippi boats that visited the Tri-Cities (Rock Island, Moline, and Davenport), King Oliver's band (with Louis Armstrong), maybe Louis Panico, and, of course, the Original Dixieland Jazz Band, particularly its clarinetist, Larry Shields. Most jazzmen learn from many musicians, jazz or otherwise, but a style as distinctive as Beiderbecke's is the creative product of one man's musical mind rather than a montage of borrowed characteristics. In any event, the question of influence, while intriguing, is not of primary interest. What matters most about Bix Beiderbecke is his own music and, secondarily, how his music affected those who came after him.

After Lake Forest, Bix gained experience and confidence in a wide variety of short engagements, including one that took him to New York (where he heard the by now dated Original Dixieland Jazz Band in person), and a lake-boat job working for one Bill Grimm. The most musically satisfying of these seems to have been a series of fraternity jobs with several friends who shared his enthusiasm for the New Orleans Rhythm Kings. Whatever Bix had to offer at that point, the college kids, including a worshipful young Hoagy Carmichael, loved it. This group evolved into the Wolverines in late 1923, by way of a couple of good regular jobs in Cincinnati. Ohio. The men who worked with Bix in the Wolverines were George Johnson (tenor sax), Jimmy Hartwell (clarinet), Dick Voynow (piano), Bob Gillette (banjo), Min Leibrook (tuba), Vic Moore (drums), and, for a while, Al Gandee (trombone).

It wasn't an all-star band, but the Wolverine Orchestra had a total impact as impressive as the New Orleans Rhythm Kings themselves. The group strived for an ensemble blend, and the brilliance of Beiderbecke's lead cornet gave the entire unit a surprising amount of class, as well as rhythmic force and melodic content. Success in the Midwest led to an opportunity to record for a Midwestern record firm, Gennett, in Richmond, Indiana. The first date, in February, 1924, was used up recording four tunes from the Original Dixieland Jazz Band repertory: *Fidgety Feet, Lazy Daddy, Sensation Rag,* and *Jazz Me Blues.* Two were rejected, and the first and last were released on a single record, thereby launching Bix Beiderbecke on six and a half prolific years of recording work that now stands as the only reliable evidence of his enormous talent. The endless anecdotes, the volumes of misinformation (even today, professional jazz writers sometimes refer to Bix as Leon Bismarck Beiderbecke, although he was christened Leon Bix), the fuzzy fantasies dealing with his idiosyncrasies—all these grow rather tiresome with the passing years, cherished mainly by the diminishing body of aging men to whom Bix was a living, breathing man with a magic touch on the cornet and piano. Whatever the "real" Bix was, he lives today, for most listeners, only through his recordings, which begin with *Fidgety Feet* and *Jazz Me Blues* on the 1924 Gennett record.

As near as we can tell from the crudely recorded sounds of *Fidgety Feet,* Bix had already, on his very first record, eclipsed his early hero, Original Dixieland Jazz Band cornetist Nick La Rocca. The Wolverine performance is relaxed, in the manner of the New Orleans Rhythm Kings, and the pulse is in 4/4 time rather than in the jerky 2/4 "cut" time that mars the ODJB recordings. Bix's rhythmic sense is sure, but his tone is undeveloped (he was not quite 21 at the time of this recording), his vibrato tense, and his melodic inventiveness only suggested. *Jazz Me Blues,* however, has Bix in better form, contributing an ordered solo that seems more inspired by clarinetists Larry Shields of the ODJB and Leon Roppolo of the NORK than by other trumpet players. Bix's early interest in harmonic alterations in melodic lines, undoubtedly stemming from his passion for keyboard improvisations, suggests that clarinetists, weaving inner harmonic-melodic parts, may have held more fascination for him than cornetists, many of whom, like La Rocca, were limited to simple rhythmic variations on straight melodies. In any event, *Jazz Me Blues* is the first of many recorded performances in which Bix moves with the fleetness, grace, subtlety, and harmonic sophistication that had previously been heard in some reedmen but seldom in brass players. (New Orleans trumpeter Bunk Johnson had a similar outlook, but there is no evidence of Bix and Bunk coming in contact with each other.)

With recordings, other musicians suddenly became very aware of the gifted cornetist with the Wolverines. Red Nichols, a skilled cornetist with a fair reputation of his own at the time, recorded Bix's *Jazz Me Blues* solo note for note in a commercial dance-band arrangement. The Benson Orchestra of Chicago, recording for the Victor label, picked up material from the Wolverines. Bix was becoming a local sensation and a nationally known "hot" player, at least within the jazz fraternity.

College students, too, were impressed by the band's first records, and, with the help of Hoagy Carmichael, the Wolverines pulled out of Cincinnati and went back to weekend campus work, filling out the balance of each week in an Indianapolis nightclub. Trombonist Gandee stayed in Ohio and was not replaced. During August, 1924, the band played in Gary, Indiana, on a job booked by drummer Vic Berton, who split rhythm-section duties with Vic Moore.

Berton's kid brother Ralph, who spent that August in ecstatic worshiping range of Bix, wrote thirty-four years later (*Harper's,* November, 1958) of the moonshine, marijuana, and music that seem to be part of every Beiderbecke story, but also remembered the celebrated cornet sound, "like shooting bullets at a bell," and Bix's dissatisfaction with his own recordings, which did not do him justice. Other writers have tried to describe Beiderbecke's sound with varying degrees of success. Eddie Condon, an early admirer and colleague of Bix, claimed it was "like a girl saying yes," and Hoagy Carmichael talked of a mallet hitting a chime. Mezz Mezzrow wrote that every note stood out "like a pearl" and was as "sharp as a rifle crack." Berton was probably right; the records suggest a firm attack and a fine round tone, but hardly the sound these musicians talk about.

In May and June, seven more selections were successfully recorded, including Carmichael's *Riverboat Shuffle;* two from the ODJB and NORK books, *Tiger Rag* and *Royal Garden Blues;* a new tune furnished by bandleader Charley Davis, *Copenhagen;* and three ordinary songs called *Oh, Baby, Susie,* and *I Need Some Pettin'.* Throughout, Bix shows sharp improvement in his playing and confidence over the February session and reveals a predilection for blues phrasing that may have been a result of his enthusiasm at that time for King Oliver's band. (According to one observer, Bix was one of the few musicians welcome to sit in with Oliver's band at any time.) *Riverboat Shuffle* and *Copenhagen,* both of which have Gillette playing guitar instead of banjo, are excellent examples of how well Bix could incorporate blues phrases into nonblues material. *I Need Some Pettin'* may be the closest Bix ever came to the spirit of King Oliver and Louis Armstrong. Again the blues is there in his performance, and there are broken-chord figures that tell much of Bix's regard for Armstrong.

Though some of the figures in *Tiger Rag* sound like reworked NORK ideas, the group's rhythmic drive, loose-jointed abandon, and astonishing modernity are best represented by this recording. Bix plays tricks with the lead, darting in and out of strict time, insinuating other compositions as yet unwritten, and prods the entire band from start to finish. His solo is full of brilliant bursts that foreshadow the music he was to produce in later years. While remaining close to a forceful simplicity of style, Bix now begins to utilize short scale passages, unusual neighboring tones (a raised ninth here, a flatted fifth there) as strong melodic rather than passing notes, and intriguing rhythmic accents, causing unsyncopated passages to sound syncopated.

Royal Garden Blues is again a strong blues-based performance (this time the structure matches the mood), and the configuration of Bix's solo bears a striking resemblance to his work on *Tiger Rag,* which was recorded the same day. As before, Bix seemed to be thinking along saxophone-clarinet lines rather than in brass terms. His long, lazy phrases are not unlike Roppolo's.

Some idea of how it felt to play alongside Bix at this point in his career can be had by way of Mezz Mezzrow: "Playing with Bix was one of the great experiences in my life. The minute he started to blow, I jumped . . . into the harmony pattern like I was born to it, and never left the track for a moment. It was like slipping into a suit made to order for you by a fine tailor, silk-lined all through."

The Wolverines were on the periphery of the big time now. Their next engagement, following the happy summer in Gary, was as relief band at the Cinderella Ballroom in the heart of Manhattan. This was, though they could hardly have known it at the time, the beginning of the end of the Wolverines. Bix was the inspiration of the band, but he was becoming too good to stay with them. Within a month of his arrival in New York, he gave his notice and prepared to return to the Midwest, where he probably felt more at home. New York, then as now, could be a highly indifferent city, full of hustle and offering little sympathy to "dreamy little fellows." It must have been clear even to the other Wolverines that Bix was ready to graduate. He did, however, record again with the group in New York, turning out four more titles for Gennett—*Sensation, Lazy Daddy, Tia Juana,* and *Big Boy.*

The first two selections were remakes of the rejects from the band's initial recording session in February. George Brunis, a former New Orleans Rhythm King, enlarged the ensemble and contributed some humorous kazoo work, but the date was not a striking success. The New York studios give us a better representation of the Beiderbecke tone, however, which shows steady improvement but as yet is not the perfectly controlled, finely polished sound that can be heard on later recordings. *Sensation* has provocative moments in which Bix dabbles with thirteenths, ninths, and unusual passing tones and anticipates chord changes (that amazing ear at work again), but the larger part of his contribution here is pedestrian Beiderbecke. *Lazy Daddy,* available in two takes, is full of whimsy and strange passages in which Bix sounds aggressive and bashful at the same time, but it is not a significant Wolverine recording.

Tia Juana does not seem as bad as tenor saxophonist Johnson implied in later years ("the less said the better") and, indeed, reveals Johnson as one of the few early tenor men to produce a good sound on his instrument. Bix again sounds much like Armstrong in places, shows more command and power than before, and ends *Tia Juana* with a characteristic cornet break that implies one of his favorite devices from this time on—the whole-tone scale.

Big Boy is notable for several reasons: it is the final Wolverine recording, a new level of maturity in Bix's cornet playing is reached, and there is a glimpse of the Beiderbecke piano. Tales of Bix's private piano improvisations are frequently superlative-laden written accounts or smug I-heard-the-truth narrations suggestive of religious experiences. This brief solo is hardly of that order. Working within the framework of a popular tune and an ordinary rhythm section, Bix appears to have been a limited pianist (the modulation in *Big Boy*, from E-flat to the easier key of F before the piano solo, was obviously for his benefit) with a clumsy left hand. It is difficult to tell which of Bix's left-hand chord clusters are "advanced" harmonic thinking and which are mistakes, but one can understand the discomfort that some listeners felt while listening to the restless probing of Bix at the piano. Judging from this recording, the substance in Bix's keyboard improvisations would seem to be in his effective use of harmonic dissonances in the right hand.

Ralph Berton is one of several who have attempted to describe the effect of Bix's piano:

> I can say only that it more than once moved this listener to baffled tears, that its subtlety and variety were seemingly infinite, that the way it modulated between Debussy-esque nuance and the dirtiest cathouse stomp had an impact I had never experienced before and never have since.
>
> The reason why none of this was ever captured on records is simple enough. Bix was unhappy even about recording on trumpet [cornet, of course]; on piano, he found it impossible. On trumpet, though he was perpetually dissatisfied, he did at least consider himself a professional justified in accepting wages for work done; on piano he regarded himself as such a wretched fumbler that it was only rarely that he would play at all except in private. As far as I know, the few piano recordings of Bix that exist he was more or less trapped into.

Bix's keyboard work in *Big Boy* is, at least, forceful and rhythmically true, but it is of less melodic interest than his cornet playing on the same recording. And he had now achieved the authoritative Beiderbecke ring that dazzled musicians wherever he went.

There was another Gennett date in New York before Bix headed West. Three of the Wolverines—Beiderbecke, Moore, and Leibrook—joined trombonist Miff Mole, pianist Rube Bloom, and C-melody saxophonist Frank Trumbauer to record *Flock o' Blues* and *I'm Glad*. Both performances are in the rather subdued and precise jazz style that was probably characteristic of several New York bands in 1924. (The three non-Wolverines were from Ray Miller's semi-"hot" orchestra of that time.) The prevailing musical outlook on the date seemed to be away from the blues (despite Bloom's title on the first side) and toward a calculated series of musical tricks within a jazz setting. Bix does not appear to be as involved as he was in the Wolverine recordings.

Bix Beiderbecke has seldom been painted as an intellectual man, but perhaps the portraits are not really accurate. His father, a successful Iowa businessman, and his mother, who had received musical awards in her childhood, were typical of the American middle class that turns out most of the country's college students. Bix, too lazy and too caught up in music to attempt serious higher studies, nevertheless belonged with the college crowd. His relationship with Hoagy Carmichael and, for a brief period, with Hoagy's intellectual friend Bill Moenkhaus may have been as close as Bix came to revealing himself to anyone. ("Nobody could get close to Bix," said pianist Joe Sullivan recently.) Moenkhaus decided to try Bix one day by reading his typical piece of sophomoric surrealism called "The Wheatena Test":

1. Spell Wheatena in four different directions.
2. What horse when it rained.
3. Define freight luner, and amelia.
4. Tell all you know about vetter.
5. Tell all you know about the defeat of New Mexico.
6. Write a short diary about skates. Leave out page three.

According to Carmichael, Bix thought it over and replied simply, "I am not a swan." His friends were delighted. Most of the professional musicians that Bix knew, except the college-trained Wolverines, were either pranksters (Joe Venuti, Wingy Mannone, Don Murray) or confirmed anti-intellectual types who saw music primarily as emotional release (Mezzrow, Art Hodes, Condon). Probably none of them would have understood Moenkhaus, as Bix did instantly. Those who could talk from all sides (drummer Dave Tough was one) were rare, and this may have been part of the reason for Bix's loneliness.

While Moenkhaus and Bix hit it off immediately, some fellow musicians, such as Wingy Mannone, never did penetrate the protective fog that Bix kept around him. "Bix was a genius, and we just didn't understand him, I guess," remembers Mannone. "He was always talking music, telling us, 'Let's play this chord,' or 'Let's figure out some three-way harmony for the trumpets after the job tonight.' It seemed to us he didn't want us to enjoy our life."

Eddie Condon tells of an unexpected conversation with Bix that took place during a time when Condon was brushing up on his schooling: " 'By the way,' I said, 'who is Proust?' He hit a chord, listened to it, and then said, casually, 'A French writer who lived in a cork-lined room. His stuff is no good in translation.' I leaned over the piano. 'How the hell did you find that out?' I demanded. He gave me the seven-veils look. 'I get around,' he said."

Other acquaintances have commented on Bix's ability to communicate verbally when the setting was right. "Bix had a great brain," recalled Trumbauer a few years ago. "He could talk about *any* subject, not just music."

His stay in New York seems to have increased Bix's interest in formal music, too. His fondness for impressionistic composers and orchestrators exerted a large influence on his harmonic concepts in jazz until his death. Joe Sullivan, who had a good deal of classical training himself, remembers Bix introducing him to the work of Eastwood Lane, and others have spoken of his love of Stravinsky, Debussy, and Edward MacDowell. The harmonic devices employed by these composers, although old stuff to classical musicians—and even to advanced ragtimers like Scott Joplin— were strange and new to most jazzmen. Beiderbecke, who could play the blues *and* the "modern" harmonies, was a real phenomenon.

As 1925 came in, Bix must have had mixed feelings about his life. He was too advanced for the Wolverines but not yet a skilled enough reader for bandleaders like Charlie Straight (who fired him after four weeks) and Jean Goldkette. (Bix cut a test record for Goldkette in late 1924 that was not considered acceptable.) Playing jazz had come to him without work or even much formal practice, but composition and orchestration were not that simple. He was both an artist and a speakeasy entertainer, both a middle-class mama's boy and a nomadic bum, both a star performer and a jobless horn player.

Goldkette furnished some work for Bix around Detroit with jazz groups made up of his key "hot" men—Tommy Dorsey, clarinetist Don Murray, banjoist Howdy Quicksell, and others. Some of these men accompanied Bix to Richmond for a January record date, and one of the selections turned out that day, *Toddlin' Blues*, another Original Dixieland Jazz Band number, sounds dated and is of no special interest, save for Bix's flowing clarinet-like style. *Davenport Blues* is another matter. In this, Bix's first known composition, many of the best and most characteristic Beiderbecke flourishes can be heard throughout some one hundred measures of brilliant improvising. There is the ingenious use of accents, in one instance placed on every fourth note in a twelve-note figure made up of four triplets. There is the whole-tone scale ascending from the flatted fifth of the underlying chord. There are the wide interval skips, in which almost any harmonic alteration may occur, such as in the figure where Bix attacks an F diminished chord and comes out with something resembling a G-thirteenth with a flatted ninth. But all these delightful events occur with no disruption in the smooth, orderly flow of melody and with no slackening of rhythmic thrust. With this record, Bix left his formative period as a jazzman, requiring now only a final polishing to reach his creative apex.

In February, 1925, Bix attended the University of Iowa in an effort to bring his formal training in music up to his intuitive grasp of improvisation, but he was unable to cope with college regulations and departed eighteen days after enrolling. Had he lived thirty years later, there would have been schools to accommodate his desire for an all-music curriculum. Stopping briefly in Davenport for piano lessons (again to no avail), Bix returned to Chicago and spent the spring and summer playing odd jobs and short engagements, including a couple of weeks with Ollie Powers at the Paradise Inn, a week with Frank Quartel at the Riviera Theater, and doubtless occasional single nights with Goldkette groups in and around Detroit.

In the fall, Bix joined a major Goldkette unit (there were many, from small ones with Mezz Mezzrow to large and elegant bands like McKinney's Cotton Pickers) stationed in St. Louis under the leadership of Frank Trumbauer. Nourished by his compatible group of players, coddled by Trumbauer's almost paternal interest in his music, and never too far from home should the going get rough, Bix thrived and grew into a much improved musician. Trumbauer, probably learning from Bix at the same time, nudged the cornetist along until he was able to handle a section part with a fair degree of confidence. During this period, too, Bix played a great deal of piano and took a still deeper interest in pieces like Lane's *Adirondack Sketches*. It was a good winter for Bix, playing in a band with men like Pee Wee Russell and Trumbauer, participating in jam sessions, experimenting at the piano, and sitting in with members of Charlie Creath's excellent orchestra. Creath's bassist, Pops Foster, who recalls playing casual jobs as well as jam sessions with Bix in St. Louis, regarded Beiderbecke as a better pianist than cornetist.

Obviously, a kind of workshop atmosphere marked the stay in St. Louis and led to some interesting results, but unfortunately this organization never recorded. The band's pianist, Louis Feldman, has been quoted (in *Bugles for Beiderbecke*) to the effect that Bix and Pee Wee were so far ahead of their time that even some of the musicians in the band didn't appreciate what they were doing.

Russell himself has confirmed this in *Hear Me Talkin' to Ya:* "We used to have little head arrangements, written by some of the men in the band. We would do little things once in a while so drastic, or rather so musically advanced, that when we had a damn nice thing going the manager would come up and say, 'What in God's name are you doing?' I remember on *I Ain't Got Nobody* we had an arrangement with five-part harmony for the three saxes and the two brass. And the writing went down chromatically on a whole-tone-scale basis. It was unheard of in those days. Bix was instrumental in things like that."

In the summer of 1926, Trumbauer took a slightly different Goldkette unit to Hudson Lake, Indiana, and Bix and Pee Wee went along. From all reports, everyone had a marvelous time and the music was good. By fall, Bix and Trumbauer were ready to join and tour with the first-string Goldkette band, which was by now seething with jazzmen ready to blow at the slightest provocation. Ray Ludwig and Fuzzy Farrar (who is supposed to have instructed Bix somewhat) were the other trumpeters; trombonist Bill Rank, reedmen Don Murray and Trumbauer, bassist Steve Brown, and Bix were the principal "hot" men. There was another important member of the troupe, too, named Bill Challis. His arrangements for Jean Goldkette were often as advanced and jazz-oriented as were the contemporary scores of Don Redman, Fletcher Henderson, and Duke Ellington. His and Bix Beiderbecke's talents appeared together on record for the first time in October, 1926, with a tune called *Idolizing*.

After his 1924 recording failure with Goldkette, Bix seemed to be taking a cautious stand in his initial appearance on the Victor label. The band was clearly a superior one, sparked by Steve Brown's booming bass and Eddie Lang's incisive guitar. (Lang and violinst Joe Venuti were frequently added to the orchestra for recording purposes.) Challis contributed a clean, balanced arrangement calling for 4/4 rhythm rather than the jittery 2/4 of so many popular orchestras of the day. The band began to swing.

In all, only a dozen or so Goldkette titles were released that could interest an admirer of Bix Beiderbecke, but among them are some superb examples of the now fully matured cornetist. Happily, these were electrically recorded, permitting us to really hear Bix's exquisite tone for the first time.

That Challis was enchanted by Bix's work was evident from the start. Time and again he wrote out trumpet section parts based on Beiderbecke phrases and assigned Bix to a loose lead, leaving space for a bit of improvisation. Except for the collaboration of Miles Davis and Gil Evans thirty years later and the constant example of Duke Ellington, it is doubtful that any skilled arranger has ever taken more care in writing for a single jazz instrumentalist than Bill Challis displayed in his best work for Goldkette and, later, for Paul Whiteman.

Bix can be heard leading his section and, in fact, lending his character to the entire band on *Sunday, Hoosier Sweetheart,* and *My Pretty Girl.* In other instances, Bix was allowed to improvise in and around the entire arrangement, filling holes, amplifying the brass or the reeds at will, and inventing countermelodies as the band moved toward the final measure. It was a remarkable assignment, one that probably no other cornetist could have handled properly. Examples of this can be heard on *I'm Looking Over a Four Leaf Clover, I'm Gonna Meet My Sweetie Now, Slow River, In My Merry Oldsmobile,* and *Clementine.*

The only Goldkette recording that really offered Bix a solid solo was *Clementine.* On this, his last appearance on record with the band, Bix makes relatively simple but powerful musical statements over rich sustained chords that were presumably worked out between Challis and Beiderbecke.

By far the most valuable legacy left as a result of Bix's two years with Jean Goldkette bands is a set of sparkling performances recorded with Trumbauer in February and May, 1927, representing Bix at the peak of his creative powers. The groundwork for these successful Okeh records was laid in St. Louis during the many hours Bix and Trumbauer spent together working out head arrangements and unusual harmonic progressions.

For his first date, Trumbauer came up with a pair of classic performances. *Singin' the Blues* left an impression on virtually every saxophone and trumpet player and, with the exception of Louis Armstrong's *West End Blues,* has probably been more widely copied than any jazz performance recorded in the twenties. With this record, a legitimate jazz ballad style was announced—a method whereby attractive songs could be played sweetly without losing authentic jazz feeling and without sacrificing virility. Prior to *Singin' the Blues,* "pretty" tunes were either cloyingly sentimental or cranked up to an awkward jogging pace. Jazzmen generally played the blues or blues songs when slow tunes were called for. Bix Beiderbecke, with the help of the electric microphone (which permitted an *intimate* performance by singers and instrumentalists, on the stage or in the recording studio, for the first time), changed the pattern almost single-handedly. Trumbauer, who at best was a bright reflection of Beiderbecke, contributed substantially by proving that the ballad idea wasn't a one-man phenomenon but a workable way for anyone to play certain song material.

It is reasonable to assume that Bix's concept of playing a ballad in moderate 4/4 tempo came, at least in part, from his passion for romantic and impressionistic melodies in formal music. His ear for harmony, too, meant that Bix could hear enough alternate chords within each measure of a popular song to sustain his improvisations at a slow pace. *Singin' the Blues* may not seem very slow by today's ballad standards, but in 1927 it was about as slow as anyone dared to be without strings and "sweet" arrangements.

As usual in his finest work, Bix's solo on *Singin' the Blues* is architectonically sound and as ordered as a written composition. It was, in fact, included in later orchestrations as originally played, and at least two cornetists, Rex Stewart and Bobby Hackett, recorded the Beiderbecke solo in later years. Bennie Moten's 1929 recording of *Rite Tite* is also full of references to Trumbauer's *Singin' the Blues* solo.

Clarinet Marmalade, in an arrangement sketched by Bill Challis, reached back once more to the Original Dixieland Jazz Band library. It is played at a fast clip and is one of Bix's very best recordings. It showed him to be, too, one of the most agile horn players on the scene in 1927. Few men could execute clean, precise, fully formed notes while improvising at this pace, and probably only one or two (Armstrong and Jabbo Smith come to mind) would have been able to conceive original ideas rather than clichés while carrying it off. Bix's *Clarinet Marmalade* is, too, a triumph in terms of logical overall structure, melodic symmetry, and rhythmic drive, a most extraordinary jazz recording.

The performance, which builds in intensity with each phrase, puts to work many of the personal devices that Bix had been toying with for some time. An emphasis on sevenths, ninths, and thirteenths in the melodic line lends color and surprise to the work. There are several examples of Bix's interest in scales as substitutes for arpeggios, a notion that was about three decades ahead of 1927. Using the diatonic scale freely, Bix suggests harmonic extensions reaching into the eleventh and thirteenth intervals of the tonic tone, and this practice, like the use of the whole-tone scale, implies a movement away from tonality and conventional chord playing. Bix's melodic inventions in this work are all the more intriguing because he places each note into his patterns with intuitive care. His use of scales, for example, is not simply an easy way to sound flashy, as with lesser players, but a purposeful musical maneuver.

The roots of Bix's *Clarinet Marmalade*, incidentally, can be discerned quite plainly in two earlier recordings of the tune, one by the Original Dixieland Jazz Band and another by the New Orleans Rythm Kings. For all his advanced concepts, Bix's playing here is a kind of atavistic compendium of the work of cornetists La Rocca and Mares and clarinetists Shields and Roppolo.

The second and third Trumbauer recording dates are of equal interest. On these occasions, *Ostrich Walk* (another nod to the ODJB), *Riverboat Shuffle, I'm Comin' Virginia, Way Down Yonder in New Orleans,* and *For No Reason at All in C* were produced.

Ostrich Walk, like *Clarinet Marmalade*, has Bix in full stride, combining, in his paradoxical way, ten-year-old material with prophetic intimations of music to come after his own lifetime. Bop, or modern jazz, was also built on time-tested popular song patterns. It may be unrealistic to expect a revolution in both jazz instrumental procedure *and* underlying harmonic structures simultaneously. By employing already familiar materials, Bix, for one, was able to become more adventurous in his cornet improvisations. (He did, however, seek new structural forms through his keyboard experiments.)

With the help again of Bill Challis, *Ostrich Walk* moved swiftly and effortlessly through some breathtaking ensemble playing to a brilliant cornet passage in concert A-flat and into a driving final chorus in E-flat. The entire performance sparkles with wit and whimsy and is one of Bix's happiest records. However, there is also a mildly disturbing element in *Ostrich Walk*. Creeping into Bix's work was a slightly stilted manner, a trifle too much emphasis on staccato articulation, suggesting that he might have been in need of a few weeks of playing the blues, at this point, to recover his former balance of expressive techniques. (For historical perspective, we might remember that Louis Armstrong recorded his classic *Potato Head Blues* in the same month that these Trumbauer sessions were held.)

I'm Comin' Virginia displays Bix in his best ballad form and, in this instance, somewhat more in touch with the blues, with a chorus that is perfectly formed and shows no lapses in taste or imagination. On *Way Down Yonder in New Orleans,* Bix contributes a restrained but appealing ballad chorus. There is a hint of awkwardness, though, and one has the feeling that Bix may have been taking the easy way out again—by playing figures already worked out and pretested for effectiveness.

Riverboat Shuffle provides an interesting contrast with the Wolverine version three years earlier. There is no doubt about Bix's growth and increased authority. He easily gallops away from Trumbauer here, working up to a final flare on cornet high C that he probably could not have brought off in earlier times. But amid the excitement and invention, there is a trace of the self-caricaturization that was to damage his work in the months to come.

For No Reason at All in C is a trio performance with Trumbauer, guitarist Eddie Lang, and Bix on piano. The title supports those acquaintances (Jack Teagarden, for one) who remember Beiderbecke as a pianist who was comfortable only when he was playing in C and F. Bix seems less clumsy at the keyboard here than he did on *Big Boy,* if more conventional in his approach. The touch is firm and the sound pleasing, but there is no evidence here of a pianist to be even remotely compared with the outstanding keyboard men of the day—Fats Waller and Earl Hines, for example.

In August, 1927, Bix and Trumbauer turned out a pair of recordings based on *Three Blind Mice* (with a Challis arrangement) and *Blue River.* The former is full of tricks, and the arrangement becomes the focal point rather than the improvised solos. Bix discloses one of his mechanical problems on this one. In his desire to achieve an uninterrupted flow of ideas, he waits too long and is unable to finish his phrase, for lack of breath. This is worth mentioning only because it points up a weakness in Bix's concept of melody as applied to a wind instrument. Bix did not *sing* his choruses, he *composed* them. Armstrong, whose work of the period remains even less dated than Bix's, accomplished both at once, which is an important factor in his greatness.

Blue River tells us the same thing in a different way. Bix plays well behind the vocal but shows no regard for the singer's breath points. (It must be admitted that the singer, Seger Ellis, hardly deserved serious attention.) Instead, he simply "solos" in the background, in marked contrast to the sensitive blues accompaniments played by King Oliver and Louis Armstrong in the mid-twenties.

In a Mist, Bix's best-known composition, was released about this time. It is solo piano, well played, and reveals as much about Bix's aspirations as any single record he made. Having started work on this piece several years earlier, Bix was constantly making changes or adding to it as new ideas came to him. The very act of recording it probably helped to freeze some of its features into place, but the ultimate printed version, put together by Bill Challis, is not the same as the recorded example. One can easily guess another of the paradoxes in Bix's life—the dilemma of wanting to compose pieces that would endure, despite a lack of the technical equipment needed to compose on paper and notwithstanding a natural inclination to improvise something new each time he sat at the piano. *In a Mist* is a charming piece, full of characteristic broken chords, provocative passing tones, whole-tone tidbits, and romantic but not sentimental melodic fragments. As in previous piano solos by Bix, the left hand remains at an elemental level, filling in with parallel fifths and tonic chords while the right hand does most of the work. The four-bar coda sounds derived from the codas that Challis and others wrote for Goldkette and Whiteman.

Challis wrote down three other piano compositions before Bix died: *Candlelights, Flashes,* and *In the Dark.* The first is a kind of extension of *In a Mist; Flashes,* the weakest of the group, is an exercise in broken chords ranging over nearly five octaves of the keyboard; *In the Dark* is a simple melodic piece of considerable charm, featuring long eighth-note lines reminiscent of Bix's cornet improvisations. All four are in C and are quite properly presented by their publisher, Robbins Music, as *Bix Beiderbecke's Modern Piano Suite.*

Bix's final piano recording was *Wringin' and Twistin',* cut in September, 1927, with Trumbauer and Lang. It would be interesting to hear Bix's piano with some other rhythmic support, which might have freed him from the task of keeping time, as he must here; but the way it stands, this record is little more than a pleasant curiosity.

Two other "modern" recordings are worth mentioning. One is

Humpty Dumpty, written by the talented arranger Fud Livingston, which contains an eight-bar gem by Bix in which the cornetist relates to the tonic scale of the composition rather than to the
chord underlying his figures. The implicátions of this tactic are
significant and extraordinary for 1927. The other experimental
number is *Krazy Kat,* utilizing fast and uncommon chord changes
that Bix rides over with confidence and aplomb. His sixteen-bar
solo stresses once more the reliability of that remarkable ear,
which allowed him to anticipate an upcoming chord and, before
reaching the harmonic root that would resolve his phrase, be off
on an anticipation of the next chord. It is this practice that creates
in much of Bix's work a sense of floating and searching, in lines
that almost seem to begin and end in some other song. Fortu-
nately, Bix's unerring good taste brings him back to solid harmonic ground often enough and long enough for the listener to
maintain his bearings and to prepare for the next flight.

The Greystone Ballroom in Detroit was home base for Goldkette. It featured his own bands and groups in his stables, such as
McKinney's Cotton Pickers. It is said that Bix and trumpeter John
Nesbitt of the Cotton Pickers occasionally swapped chairs, and
the two bands probably borrowed a number of musical ideas from
each other. Matching Goldkette's Challis was the Cotton Pickers'
arranger, Don Redman, who also directed and rehearsed the
band. Thus surrounded by top musicians, good arrangers, and
close friends, leading a life of record dates, dances, musical experimentation, and jam sessions, earning both good money and a
wide reputation, Bix was enjoying what must have been the most
rewarding months of his life. True, he was a spoiled child, the pet
of the band, but he was getting better and better at reading his
parts in the section and was earning his keep as a widely known
and most extraordinary jazzman.

By this time, Bix had become, at 24, firmly set in a mode of life
that was decidedly unwholesome. He had a musical protector in
Trumbauer, but no one bothered to steer Bix into desirable social
patterns, and it is not likely that he would have responded had
anyone attempted it. Irregular hours, random diet, and too much
alcohol were beginning to tear him down. Conventional relation-
ships with the opposite sex were, as far as one can tell, not important enough to occupy Bix's thoughts for very long at a time.

There was a special girl named Vera Cox back in Davenport, but she had become tired of waiting and married someone else. He was, like many intelligent men who are preoccupied with their life's work, absentminded and sometimes removed from all that went on about him. Even among jazz musicians, a notoriously individualistic lot, Bix was regarded as a rather odd duck.

Goldkette's band finally collapsed in September, 1927, under the weight of an inflated payroll and poor prospects for the coming year, but Paul Whiteman stepped in to rescue Trumbauer, Challis, Steve Brown, and Bix by offering them permanent positions in his lumbering organization of thirty-odd performers. Actually, there was an interim period of several weeks with Adrian Rollini at the New Yorker Club, but this band (which made a single record for Okeh) was not a success.

Just before joining Whiteman that fall, Bix recorded six selections under his own name (Bix and His Gang) for Okeh. The first three titles, once again connected with the records of the Original Dixieland Jazz Band, were *At the Jazz Band Ball, Royal Garden Blues,* and *Jazz Me Blues.* The second three, more in keeping with Bix's current musical world, were *Goose Pimples, Sorry,* and *Since My Best Gal Turned Me Down.* The men appearing with Bix on these records were selected from Rollini's short-lived band, which in turn was made up largely of Goldkette alumni: trombonist Bill Rank, clarinetist Don Murray, drummer Chauncy Morehouse, pianist Frank Signorelli, and Rollini himself on bass saxophone. The musical results were new testimony to Bix's old paradoxical attitude toward jazz. While other jazzmen of consequence in the twenties were moving away from the Dixieland idea, Bix, whose instincts placed him musically ahead of almost all his contemporaries, chose to play in just that outmoded idiom for his own record dates. By so doing, however, he established the basic principles for playing Dixieland in a new way that have endured to this day. Drawing upon standard ODJB-NORK repertory and popular songs of the day, adding sophisticated harmonies and the 4/4 rhythm of swing, featuring a relaxed, even whimsical, cornet lead, and highlighting each member of the ensemble in solo passages, these Beiderbecke recordings served as prototypes for hundreds of Dixieland bands—some good and some not—to follow in the next thirty years.

Jazz Me Blues and *Royal Garden Blues,* both previously recorded by Bix with the Wolverines, are indices of the extent of the
cornetist's development. Bix was even more his own man. *Jazz Me
Blues* has the same relaxed air as the 1924 performance, but there
are new ideas, new harmonies, and greatly increased authority.
Then, too, there is the constant probing of upper harmonic intervals that marks all of Bix's best work and yet is so unobtrusive
that it is more felt than heard. *Jazz Band Ball,* for example,
sounds like an uninvolved, hard-hitting selection, but the cornet
line is bristling with accented sixths, ninths, thirteenths, ingenious
scalelike figures, and unusual passing tones.

Bix's own recordings have an abandon and freedom that Trumbauer's do not; and for many, these six 1927 selections represent
Bix at his very best. *Sorry* is a superb performance all the way, full
of most of the typical Beiderbecke touches already discussed.
Goose Pimples, a rhythmically disguised blues, offers some of the
most relaxed and forceful (these two qualities *do* go together) Bix
on record. *Since My Best Gal Turned Me Down* is impressive, too,
but the feeling that Bix has typecast himself begins to grow with
this recording, his last before joining Whiteman. The clipped
eighth notes, the triplet runs, the high-note flare—all are effective
enough, but suddenly they begin to resemble a proved formula
rather than spontaneous excitement. The same cloud hangs over
the otherwise excellent Trumbauer-Beiderbecke record cut that
day, *Cryin' All Day* and *A Good Man Is Hard to Find* (both obvious attempts to re-create the success of *Singin' the Blues*).

Rollini deserves special credit for his work throughout these
sessions. His ability to swing on the cumbersome bass saxophone
is in itself noteworthy, but he was also a jazzman of exceptional
ability and taste and probably came closer than any other man
except Pee Wee Russell to understanding, absorbing, and playing
the Beiderbecke way without loss of his own identity.

Whiteman paid high wages to obtain the men he wanted. In
the case of Bix Beiderbecke, he was buying a useful commodity, a
man who could improvise on any given piece of music and lend
an authentically "hot" sound to the band whenever the effect was
called for. The price to Whiteman was $200 a week, plus putting
up with occasional unexplained lapses and tolerating a third chair
man who couldn't read very well. For Bix, it was lots of money, an

opportunity to improve his reading, and intimate contact with light concert music, which had always interested him. It seemed a fair exchange. There would still be recording sessions under his and Trumbauer's names on which to let off steam.

But, as it turned out, Bix stopped growing as a jazzman as of the time he joined Whiteman. It wasn't especially Whiteman's fault; Bix had played in commercial bands before, and this was a good one. A factor may have been Trumbauer's change of direction into more commercial recordings at that same time. Probably the largest reason, though, was Bix himself. He was drinking more (who ever heard of a drinking man consuming *less* with each passing year?), and it was becoming an effort simply to stay at his own high level, let alone worry about further development. Whiteman's music, too, was demanding and required attention to more than merely one's ability to improvise. The job was Bix's severest test as a real professional musician, and he was, as in childhood, earning barely passing grades. Concerts and, later, radio shows, unlike records or fraternity dances, demanded accuracy on the first try. It is a little amazing, in retrospect, that Bix lasted as long as he did—almost two years—with the orchestra.

Bix was still, after joining Whiteman, a superb jazz cornetist. Perhaps his failure to develop further in jazz was simply because he had already reached his highest plateau and, as all jazzmen must sooner or later do, leveled off at or near that point. It is more likely, though, that Bix would have entered a significant new creative phase after 1927 if more time and health had been his.

The first Whiteman release on which Bix could be heard was encouraging, although it had little real jazz to offer. It was a twelve-inch record (Bix always wanted to make longer records), friend Hoagy Carmichael was featured, singing his own Bix-like *Washboard Blues,* the arrangement was by Challis, and there was a brief explosion of Beiderbecke between vocal passages. Best of all, the whole performance had a sense of humor, one of the prerequisites of a jazz band. Other Whiteman items of the period have Bix in varying quantities, from four to sixteen bars at a time. Some have been made available in alternate takes, affording fascinating glimpses into the Beiderbecke musical mind at work. Because the arrangements surrounding Bix's solos remained the same, it is of special interest to observe how the cornetist varied his ideas with each successive take. *Changes*, for example, has a good but relatively conservative sixteen-bar solo on the second master, or take. But on the third master, the one that was chosen for issue in 1927, Bix reaches into the harmonic entrails of *Changes* and develops a splendid short solo that alternates between melodic statements suspended on sixth, ninth, and eleventh intervals and simple but colorful blueslike exclamations.

On *Mary*, Bix again plays reservedly for the first take but works up to a highly expressive eight-bar solo by the time take 4 comes around. His lead work in the section also puts a fine veneer on an otherwise uninteresting Matty Malneck arrangement. *Lonely Melody* has Bix in better form on take 3 than take 1, especially in his manipulation of rhythmic accents and syncopation. Interestingly, the two solos are the same in general structure, differing mainly in terms of internal detail. (Both Whiteman and pianist Irving Riskin have since pointed out—in *Metronome*, November, 1938—that Bix would often develop a solo until he had what he wanted and thereafter play it essentially the same way each time.)

The arrangement of *San* was an attempt to capture the essence of small-band Bix in written form. Challis did an impressive job for his time, but Bix does not solo, and the whole performance has dark implications, reminding one of Mezz Mezzrow's feelings about the effect that formal music was having on Bix:

> "Once, back in Chicago, a bunch of us went over to the Wurlitzer store, and there in the window we saw our whole philosophy on display . . . a kind of animated-doll symphony orchestra set up there, run by some hidden electrical clockwork. 'Wonderful!' Dave Tough said when he caught sight of that window exhibit. 'There it is—that's the answer.' We all laughed like hell. But when we tried to tell Bix about it later, our story only got a feeble grin out of him. There had always been a touch of the militaristic, the highly disciplined and always-under-control, in his horn technique, and it was showing up stronger in his attitude toward music all the time, till he couldn't see what was so funny in that puppet orchestra with its mechanical-doll conductor."

Bix was still very much of and for jazz, however, and his improvisations of this period, unlike Mezzrow's, have endured as some of the best jazz produced in the twenties. Despite pompous scores, all was not mechanical recitation of clichés in Whiteman's orchestra. There are lighthearted recorded moments when Bix, Trumbauer, and Bing Crosby virtually take command of the entire performance, as in *There Ain't No Sweet Man That's Worth the Salt of My Tears*, and transform Whiteman's musical leviathan into a rollicking jazz band for several minutes. At times, it seems almost as if it were Bix's band, as in the long opening solo in *From Monday On*—particularly in the fourth take, which Bix lifts right off the ground by charging in on a sustained, shouting high C.

But these were the occasional high points. Sometimes Bix's aims were blocked by the elephantine stirrings behind him. On *Sugar*, for example, he attempts a kind of shuffle rhythm, in the manner of clarinetist Frank Teschemacher (who had recorded the same tune a couple of months earlier), but there is no response or support from the unwieldy rhythm section, and the solo does not really come off. On some tunes (*Lovable* is one), Bix seems to give up, merely tossing out a smooth and uneventful solo in the pleasing manner of Red Nichols.

Though he may have wished for more opportunities to play jazz, Bix was gaining on his reading problem as the months went by with Whiteman. Jack Teagarden remembers Bix telling him that he enjoyed the big orchestra because it represented valuable experience to him, especially in sight reading. That he managed to survive at all without a thorough grounding in legitimate techniques is further testimony to the efficacy of the remarkable Beiderbecke ear. "Bix would hear something *once*," recalls Teagarden, "and he had it. It beats me how he could pick up intricate modulations and tricky arrangements on just one hearing."

Trumbauer's recordings after the switch to Whiteman are mostly dismal commercial affairs. At first (*There'll Come a Time* and *Mississippi Mud*, cut in January, 1928), Bix was permitted to romp with some freedom, but the jazz content dropped sharply after that, and soon Trumbauer was recording inferior stuff like *Our Bungalow of Dreams* and *Dusky Stevedore*. On these records, as well as Whiteman's of the period, Bix frequently plays a muted horn, despite his long-standing preference for the unmuffled sound of the open cornet. When he played into a metal derby, the resulting timbre was much like a saxophone. This probably pleased Bix, for he had, as we have seen, frequently borrowed from reedmen in putting together his personal style. (A number of reed players, in turn, were deeply affected by Bix, including Pee Wee Russell, Frank Teschemacher, Adrian Rollini, and Benny Goodman. Listen to Goodman's alto on his 1928 recording of *Blue*.) Good examples of Bix's "saxophone" approach with Whiteman's band are *Louisiana* and a pair of 1929 recordings, *Sweet Sue* and *China Boy*.

In mid-1928 Whiteman had two of the best first and second trumpet men around in Charlie Margulis and Harry Goldfield, and Bix must have felt the pressure of playing third to such musicians. Yet when a cornet soloist was called for in the Whiteman recording of George Gershwin's *Concerto in F*, Bix was assigned the part. His moody, muted opening statement, sounding curiously like Miles Davis in the late fifties, comes off without hitch or hesitation.

Bix recorded several more titles on his own, including *Thou Swell, Somebody Stole My Gal, Ol' Man River, Wa-Da-Da, Rhythm King*, and *Louisiana*, but they are not up to the level of his earlier sessions with Adrian Rollini. The leader tries desperately to swing his Whiteman colleagues (Whiteman apparently saw to it that he recorded only with them), but they remain rigid and uninspired. Even Bix plays stiffly and without real enthusiasm on these dates. Ironically, his short solos with the full Whiteman orchestra sound less contrived than his contributions to his own final small-band recordings made at the same time.

When Bix's health faltered in late 1928, Paul Whiteman sent him on leave (with pay) to pull himself together. He came back in better shape in February, 1929, but by now the pace was even faster—regular radio broadcasts had been added to the busy schedule—and Bix was not taking care of himself any better than he ever had.

During this difficult period with Whiteman, though, Bix turned out at least one first-class recorded solo. In May, the band cut *China Boy*, an old favorite of most jazzmen at that time, and in sixteen bars Bix steps in from his private musical world, creates an engaging new melody, makes use of sixths, ninths, and augmented chords that were never there in the first place, changes the mood and quality of the entire arrangement for the better, and quickly vanishes into the musical ferment that follows. It is a cool, modern solo, a little like the way Lester Young played ten years later.

But these flashes were rare now. Bix finally left the band in October and went home to Davenport to spend the winter. And even at home he could not escape the thoughtless friends who wanted to promote and be part of the already forming Beiderbecke legend. "In a sense," said Pee Wee Russell years later (*Hear Me Talkin' to Ya*), "Bix was killed by his friends. Bix couldn't say no to anybody."

It was nearly over now, although Bix kept going well into 1931. By curious coincidence, the American economy collapsed at the same moment in history that Bix did, and the nation was in no mood to spend large amounts of money on music any more. Bix was something of a celebrity in Davenport (characteristically, he sat in with every last local band whenever he visited his hometown, in order to avoid hurting any feelings), but when he got back to New York in 1930, he was just one of the many jobless jazzmen set adrift by a wave of economy moves among top bandleaders. There was no place now, with Whiteman or anyone else, for a Bix Beiderbecke.

A couple of record sessions with Hoagy Carmichael were thrown together, but Bix was no more than a specter of his old self. Although he had returned from Davenport in fairly good physical condition, the long rest probably did temporary damage to his embouchure, which had never been considered very strong anyway, and that may have been part of the trouble at the Carmichael date.

Bix even recorded three titles under his own name for Victor, but that same inability to say no resulted in abortive commercial products, complete to glandless vocal refrains. One suspects, too, that the magic was gone from the Beiderbecke tone, for Bix played almost entirely with mutes on his last recordings, possibly hoping to prevent the decay from showing too much. As if to put an exclamation point at the end of his recording career, though, Bix's final burst on Carmichael's *Bessie Couldn't Help It* is wide open (the tone *is* worse) and, though far below his peak of three years before, is full of enthusiasm and hope for the future. He was, after all, still a young man of 27.

Once again, Bix went home to Davenport and struggled

through another winter of odd jobs, heavy drinking, and poor health. He returned to New York in 1931 and found some radio work, but he was unable to stay in good enough condition to perform well after a few months. He tried to join the Casa Loma band, but that didn't work out either. Now he was reduced to casual work, a night here with the Dorsey Brothers (sometimes sitting next to young Bunny Berigan), a night there with Benny Goodman or someone else.

Even in his last confused days, Bix stuck to his music. He played piano, worked with Challis to get his compositions printed and published, and talked music with friends at Plunkett's speakeasy. (Bassist Joe Tarto preserved an unusual six-measure coda, concluding on an unresolved major seventh, that Bix composed at the bar one day.) He had dreams of taking a jazz band to Europe, recording jazz with a concert orchestra, and perhaps even of going on the wagon someday.

The end came in August, when Bix developed "lobar pneumonia" (according to his New York death certificate) and had no strength left to fight it off.

Beiderbecke's contributions to jazz were major in four distinct ways. For one, he was the first real modernist in jazz, both in his attitude toward music and in the way he went about playing. Introducing the use of flatted fifths, sixths, ninths, elevenths, thirteenths, whole-tone scales, and augmented chord harmonies in improvised single-note melodic lines, Bix opened the way for all innovators who came after him. An entire body of music, largely inspired by his improvisations, sprang up around men like Red Nichols, Miff Mole, Eddie Lang, Vic Berton, and Fud Livingston, and this music in turn had considerable effect on players like Teddy Wilson (who recalls the Nichols records as his favorites in the late twenties), baritone saxophonist Harry Carney (strongly influenced by Adrian Rollini's bass saxophone work), Benny Goodman, Jack Teagarden, and countless others. Through Frank Trumbauer and Pee Wee Russell, Bix's music reached jazzmen of the thirties such as Lester Young and Bobby Hackett. According to the pioneer modern trumpeter Benny Harris, Teddy Wilson was an important early influence on modern jazzmen because of his tasteful and precise use of unusual extended harmonies, and cornetist Hackett was also much admired by Dizzy Gillespie and by Harris himself for his easy command of ninths, elevenths, thirteenths, and so on, in his solo lines. Tenor saxophonist Young, who cited Trumbauer as an early influence, is, of course, generally acknowledged as a key figure in the early development of modern jazz.

Bix's imaginative use of rhythmic accents on weak beats, while not original with him, was also influential. Finally, the Beiderbecke piano pieces, which still sound fresh today, have been rediscovered by jazzmen every decade or so for the past thirty years.

The second major contribution Bix made was his method of playing in what is best described as a "ballad" style. The whimsical, probing ballad playing of Pee Wee Russell, Bobby Hackett, Bud Freeman, Bunny Berigan, probably Lester Young, and many others (Gerry Mulligan, Paul Desmond, and Miles Davis are contemporary extensions of this tradition) grows directly out of the easy, contemplative approach of Bix and Trumbauer. The melodic and harmonic flavor found in a number of Hoagy Carmichael compositions, too, undoubtedly stems from the songwriter's long association with Bix.

Bix helped to revitalize the dying art of Dixieland playing, which had, by the mid-twenties, reached an impasse in sterile groups like the Memphis Five, the Indiana Five, and so on. The young Chicagoans of the period turned to Louis Armstrong and Bix and evolved a virile Dixieland-swing style that continued to be vigorous and exciting for more than fifteen years. Some of these players were Eddie Condon, Joe Sullivan, Frank Teschemacher, Bud Freeman, Rod Cless, Dave Tough, Jess Stacy, George Wettling, Jimmy McPartland, and Pee Wee Russell. Following Bix's example, they carried on material from the Original Dixieland Jazz Band library (*Jazz Band Ball, Jazz Me Blues, Sensation, Tiger Rag, Clarinet Marmalade, Fidgety Feet,* etc.) as well as many tunes associated with Bix (*Riverboat Shuffle, Copenhagen, You Took Advantage of Me, Singin' the Blues, I'm Comin' Virginia,* etc.). The New Orleans Rhythm Kings and King Oliver's band were other sources of inspiration for this group, but Bix was a kind of personal hero to most of the Chicagoans. The early Commodore recordings of the late thirties, directed by Condon and featuring many of the men mentioned above, are full of Bix's music.

Finally, there is the less important matter of direct stylistic influence. It has been said that in the late twenties, most trumpet players sounded like either Bix or Armstrong. Many, like Bill Davison, went through a Beiderbecke *and* an Armstrong phase before arriving at their own styles. Some tried to combine both from the start. The obvious examples of direct Bix leanings are Red Nichols, Jimmy McPartland, Andy Secrest (who replaced Bix in Whiteman's band), Doc Evans, and Bobby Hackett (with much Armstrong added). Less obvious are the styles of jazzmen Pee Wee Russell, Brad Gowans, Joe Rushton, Rex Stewart, Yank Lawson, and Bud Freeman.

The saga of Bix Beiderbecke is not any more tragic, in personal terms, than the stories of dozens of jazzmen who lived through the twenties. Romance aside, Bix died mostly from pneumonia. Of course, pneumonia caught him when it did partly because Bix's consuming passion for music blinded him to the essentials of a healthful life. And there we see the basic ingredients for real tragedy.

Recommended Reading

Carmichael, Hoagland Howard: *The Stardust Road,* Rinehart, New York (1946).

Condon, Albert Edwin, and Thomas Sugrue: *We Called It Music,* Holt, New York (1947).

Condon, Albert Edwin, and Richard Gehman: *Eddie Condon's Treasury of Jazz,* Dial, New York (1956).

De Toledano, Ralph (ed.): *Frontiers of Jazz,* Durrell, New York (1947).

Evans, Phil, and William Myatt: *A Bio-Discography of Bix Beiderbecke,* scheduled for future publication.

Green, Benny: *The Reluctant Art,* Horizon (1963).

James, Burnett: *Kings of Jazz: Bix Beiderbecke,* Barnes, New York (1961).

Mannone, Wingy, and Paul Vandervoort: *Trumpet on the Wing,* Doubleday, New York (1948).

Mezzrow, Milton, and Bernard Wolfe: *Really the Blues,* Random House, New York (1946).

Ramsey, Frederic, and Charles Edward Smith: *Jazzmen,* Harcourt, Brace, New York (1939).

Shapiro, Nat, and Nat Hentoff (eds.): *Hear Me Talkin' to Ya,* Rinehart, New York (1955).

Shapiro, Nat, and Nat Hentoff (eds.): *The Jazz Makers,* Grove, New York (1958).

Venables, R. G. V., and Clifford Jones: *Bix,* Clifford Jones, Willesden, England (1945).

Wareing, Charles H., and George Garlick: *Bugles for Beiderbecke,* Sidgwick & Jackson, London (1958).

Recommended Listening

Bix Beiderbecke and the Wolverines, RIVERSIDE RLP 12-123.

On the Road Jazz, RIVERSIDE RLP 12-127.

Jean Goldkette and His Orchestra, "X" LVA-3017 (deleted).

The Bix Beiderbecke Story, Vols. 1, 2, 3, COLUMBIA CL-844, CL-845, CL-846.

Thesaurus of Classic Jazz (four records), COLUMBIA C4L-18.

Paul Whiteman's Orchestra, "X" LVA-3040 (deleted).

The Bix Beiderbecke Legend, RCA VICTOR LPM-2323.

Hoagy Carmichael: Old Rockin' Chair, RCA VICTOR LPT-3072 (deleted).

Ralph Sutton: Bix Beiderbecke Suite, COMMODORE FL 30,001.

Bud Freeman: Wolverine Jazz, DECCA DL-5213 (deleted).

THE CHICAGOANS

THE CHICAGO STORY is, if one wants it to be, part of the nation's romantic image of the Roaring Twenties, complete with hip flasks, illicit gin mills, Midwestern provincialism, dynamic migration patterns, organized crime, and some new rumblings of social protest. Though these aspects of the decade may lurk in the background, the history of the Chicagoans has to do with their *music* and how it grew, and that's quite a story by itself.

There were many Chicagoans in jazz, but they are usually discussed as a group, for most of Chicago's young jazzmen of the twenties who became important were part of a loosely knit single gang, the core of which was an almost fanatic, exclusive inner clique. These men listened, practiced, worked, recorded, drank, and finally found fame together. They regarded themselves as a kind of musical family devoted to the task of nurturing in each member a valid form of personal expression, a family bound together by an overwhelming mutual desire to make music just as exciting, but not the same as, that which the men from New Orleans played. Some were highly successful, a few gave up the quest, and others were simply not endowed with enough talent; but their average level of achievement was high and had an influence on later jazz developments.

Any man with a horn who stopped in Chicago for a while was eligible to be a "Chicagoan" if he listened to the right bands and really believed in jazz as a way of life. There was a nomadic, one-handed trumpeter from New Orleans called Wingy Mannone and there was a well-trained clarinetist from Arkansas named Volly de Faut. A good clarinet player from Iowa whose name was Rod Cless became accepted as a "Chicagoan," as did a first-rate pianist from Missouri named Jess Stacy. Even after the hard-core Chicagoans had moved to New York in the late twenties, they went on recruiting new members for the club, some of whom had seldom been west of New Jersey.

The first wave of well-known Chicago jazzmen included drummer Earl Wiley, who worked the Mississippi riverboats and traveled to New Orleans prior to 1920, and Ben Pollack, a highly skilled drummer who landed a job with a direct-from-the-source band, the New Orleans Rhythm Kings, and in turn became an important influence on Chicagoans only slightly younger than Pollack himself. Mezz Mezzrow, a kind of combination jazz preacher, clarinetist, and, later, marijuana dealer, was another enthusiast-musician who discovered New Orleans jazz in Chicago through performers like Tony Jackson, Freddie Keppard, and Sidney Bechet during and just after World War I.

By 1920, a 14-year-old boy named Muggsy Spanier was permitted to sit in the shadows of the Dreamland Café's balcony to listen to cornetist King Oliver's New Orleans band. When Spanier began to play creditable cornet a little later, it was Oliver's forceful, bluesy style he went after and came close to capturing. About that time, cornetist Paul Mares came up from New Orleans and put together the New Orleans Rhythm Kings, who played the same sort of music—with perhaps less drive than the Oliver band —and the new group became another model for the Chicagoans.

Other kids were finding out about the South Side dance halls and coming to listen. Those who couldn't arrange to get in free usually sat outside, catching whatever sounds drifted out the windows and doors. By 1923, when Louis Armstrong was appearing with Oliver at the Lincoln Gardens, there would be fifty or more young musicians down front trying to remember every note the two cornetists played. Among the most avid listeners were young apprentice jazzmen like drummers Dave Tough and George Wettling, who were there mostly to learn about Baby Dodds. Every college musician in the area knew about and visited the places where the New Orleans Rhythm Kings and King Oliver played, and commercial band leaders frequently dropped in looking for musical novelties to add to their books.

Some students at Chicago's Austin High School, most of whom had had some musical training, heard a few recordings by the New Orleans Rhythm Kings in 1922 and decided to form a band around that style. They had listened to the latest records by popular musicians like Isham Jones, Paul Whiteman, Paul Biese, Ted Lewis, and even the Original Dixieland Jazz Band, but it was the Rhythm Kings who finally struck the right chord. Their activities centered about the home of Jimmy and Dick McPartland, who wound up taking over the cornet and banjo functions in the new band. Frank Teschemacher had played a little violin, so he eventually became the clarinetist. Bud Freeman, who had attended Austin briefly and quit to take a job at Sears Roebuck, obtained a tenor saxophone after an early bout with the C-melody saxophone (an instrument now passé). Other friends filled out the initial unit. Drummer Tough, from the well-heeled Oak Park district, joined the gang and eventually brought a trombonist, Floyd O'Brien, into the fold.

Other teen-age players were popping up around Chicago. Pianist Joe Sullivan, who at 17 had had twelve years of classical keyboard training, began to play popular music in a nonunion gangster hangout in the bohemian sector. It turned out that the club had also hired an authentic jug band from the South, and the group was for Sullivan—whose listening experience had been confined to theater pianists and records by Art Hickman or Paul Whiteman—a first contact with something resembling honest jazz.

In 1922, a precocious West Side boy of 13 named Benny Goodman was playing clarinet remarkably well after only three years of instruction. His sources of inspiration were shifting and improving rapidly, from Ted Lewis and Bailey's Lucky Seven (a New York recording band) to Leon Roppolo (clarinetist with the New Orleans Rhythm Kings) and Jimmy Noone. Goodman studied alongside Buster Bailey (an experienced Memphis jazzman seven years Benny's senior) under Franz Schoepp, an outstanding teacher and symphony man who at one time counted Jimmy Noone among his pupils.

The inner circle at Austin High, including bassist Jim Lannigan (then courting the McPartland boys' sister, Ethel) and pianist Dave North, were rehearsing tirelessly to achieve the sound of the New Orleans Rhythm Kings. The McPartlands, as sons of a music teacher, had a slight advantage and led the way. Teschemacher was also learning fast, but Freeman, without earlier musical training, lagged behind. The Austinites, whose ages in 1923 ranged from 16 (Jimmy McPartland) to 21 (Lannigan), were something less than men of the world at this point. "We were too young to get into Friar's Inn, so the only way we could hear the Rhythm Kings was to go down and stand in the doorway and listen," Mc-

Partland has recalled. "It was great when someone opened the door and we could hear it louder." Dave Tough knew his way around Chicago, however, and had come in contact with other young musicians who were finding their way into the New Orleans style—clarinetist Don Murray, cornetist Bix Beiderbecke, pianist Dick Voynow, and drummer Bob Conselman were a few. More resourceful than his Austin pals, Dave imposed upon slightly older musicians like Volly de Faut to accompany him to South Side clubs where he could hear Baby Dodds, King Oliver, and Louis Armstrong. Through Tough, the Austin crowd began to open its ears to more than just the sounds of the New Orleans Rhythm Kings.

1923 and 1924 were eventful years for the Chicagoans. A new band grew out of a series of Northwestern University fraternity jobs involving clarinetist Jimmy Hartwell, drummer Vic Moore, and saxophonist George Johnson. Pianist Voynow and cornetist Beiderbecke brought a touch of class to the group, and they called themselves the Wolverines. They decided to stick together, made some records, and the sound of Beiderbecke's cornet became a new major influence on the kids back in Chicago. At the same time, King Oliver's band began turning out recordings on which Louis Armstrong and clarinetist Johnny Dodds could be heard. The McPartland-Freeman-Teschemacher-Tough axis was making fine progress as the Blue Friars (named for the Friar's Inn, of course) and began to be talked about by musicians on the South Side. Professionals called them the "wild West Side mob," but alert listeners could tell they were coming into a worthwhile style of their own. Teschemacher was still playing violin a lot of the time, especially when talented guests like Benny Goodman sat in.

Goodman played off and on with the "wild West Side mob" at high-school gym dances or in sessions at public park recreation areas and worked an amusement park job in the summer of 1923 with Jimmy McPartland, but he found that he could make better money with real professional bands. He joined the union the same day that Dave Tough did.

"I got along better than they [the Austin gang] did because I could read right from the start and played correct clarinet," Benny remembered some years later. That word "correct" is the key to a philosophical dichotomy that set Goodman and some others on a course quite different from that traveled by the West Side mob, although their final musical goals were not entirely dissimilar. Goodman, like his fellow music student Buster Bailey, was primarily a *clarinetist*, and jazz was his favorite mode of expression. For Teschemacher and Freeman, and to a lesser extent their comrades, becoming a *jazzman* was the important point, and the instrument was simply whatever chance had dropped into their hands. It was a distinction that became more subtle as the performers improved, but it was still there. Curiously enough, Goodman's attitude toward his instrument was much closer to the outlook of the New Orleans clarinetists and several older Chicagoans who came under their direct influence than it was to the West Side gang's musical position. Chicagoans Darnell Howard and Omer Simeon, for example, picked up the clear-toned, flowing New Orleans style, without leaving home, from Lorenzo Tio, Jr. (Simeon was born in New Orleans but began playing in Chicago.) The Tios (junior and senior) had already taught New Orleans reedmen Jimmy Noone, Albert Nicholas, and Barney Bigard. Most of these Tio-trained musicians later regarded Goodman as, at the very least, their equal. It was a judgment not so readily bestowed upon Teschemacher and others in the young Chicago gang.

Chicagoans like Teschemacher, Freeman, Tough, Mezzrow, and Sullivan were probably the first self-conscious *students* of jazz to appear. For them, the music was not merely a functional aspect of the entertainment world but a challenging art that required deep thought and study. They tried to weed out what they regarded as trivial or tasteless (the side of King Oliver that involved imitations of a baby crying or Clifford King's barnyard squeals on the clarinet) and to listen instead to the musicians who were totally involved with the art of jazz (Beiderbecke, Earl Hines, Armstrong).

About this time Tough was also participating in poetry and jazz sessions at a Chicago bohemian hangout called the Green Mask. Among his intellectual friends there were poets Kenneth Rexroth, Langston Hughes, and Maxwell Bodenheim, as well as an odd assortment of musicians, entertainers (comic Joe Frisco was one), and artists. A few other Chicago jazzmen may have shared

Tough's enthusiasm for such gathering places, but most of the Austin High gang was not concerned with much of anything outside music in those early days of discovery.

It was about 1924 when 20-year-old pianist Jess Stacy hit town, after a long apprenticeship on Mississippi riverboats with Tony Catalano's band. Stacy had come under the New Orleans jazz spell in much the same way the Chicagoans had, except that Jess worked more from first hand experience than from recordings. He had spent the winter months in ballrooms along the river, such as the Coliseum in Davenport, where he was charmed by the playing of Bix Beiderbecke. He had heard Louis Armstrong and Baby Dodds on the boats when they put in at Cape Girardeau, Missouri, where Jess was born. Like Bud Freeman, he had started out wanting to play drums; and like Joe Sullivan, he had put in long years of formal study and classical training. Like Muggsy Spanier, but unlike the West Side mob, Stacy was in 1924 a thoroughgoing professional. As soon as he arrived in Chicago, he belonged.

Chicago was a vital music center in the mid-twenties, and almost any musician who could carry a tune and go through the motions of "getting hot" found work of some kind. For the young players, nearby summer resorts were a favorite outlet. Youthful patrons, informal surroundings, and an impudent spirit that came from constant defiance of Prohibition laws added up to a good setting for a troupe of iconoclastic kid musicians. The Blue Friars found work at Lost Lake. Benny Goodman picked up odds and ends, including a lake-boat job with Bix Beiderbecke, an engagement at Waverly Beach in Neenah, Wisconsin, and other casuals in and out of Chicago. Joe Sullivan worked the lakes in Wisconsin or Indiana, sometimes with drummer George Wettling, and was beginning to move away from popular novelty tunes (*Get Out and Get Under, San, Abba Dabba Honeymoon*, etc.) toward jazz-based material (*Panama, Farewell Blues*, etc.).

By 1924, most of the Chicagoans had left school (the law then allowed one to quit at 14) and had begun playing music in earnest. Goodman, whom Tough had talked into attending Lewis Institute because classes began at 11:30 A.M., dropped out to take a steady job at Guyon's Paradise with Jules Herbeveaux. Joe Sullivan had played a few dances at Lewis Institute with some of the boys, but continued at Lakeview High School, finally leaving after his second year there. The Blue Friars couldn't have cared less about school, for they were beginning to attract attention as an organized unit.

There were several important people to know in Chicago at that time. They were the men who operated booking offices and found work for individual musicians or entire bands. Charlie "Murphy" Podolsky was a prominent figure in this field, through whom the Chicagoans obtained many of their jobs and thereby met men of similar musical interests from other quarters of the area.

In late 1924, Jimmy McPartland was called to replace Bix Beiderbecke with the Wolverines in New York, leaving the Blue Friars leaderless and somewhat adrift for about a year. They spent much of that time listening, theorizing, discussing, and arguing about jazz. Tough, the youngest, was the intellectual in the gang and was constantly turning over, questioning, and evaluating everything he heard. Teschemacher had improved so rapidly that the others often looked to him as their musical leader and guide. Freeman was still attempting to catch up to the rest, hampered by a lack of fundamental training and the inherent problems of trying to produce an acceptable tone on a saxophone and mouthpiece manufactured before instrument companies learned how to make them very well. Eddie Condon, a one-eared banjo player and promoter who ran into the gang about this time, remembers that Freeman's horn appeared green with corrosion and sounded the way it looked.

A South Side youngster of about 15 heard the gang in a movie theater job about this time. He was Gene Krupa, an intense fellow who had taken up saxophone briefly but had finally settled on drums, and he admired Dave Tough's Dodds-inspired playing. Krupa had worked summer jobs, too, including one at Wisconsin Beach with a group called the Frivolians. In 1924, he was preparing for priesthood, but it never worked out. Like most of the Chicagoans, he became utterly and hopelessly fascinated with playing jazz and with the endless struggle to master his chosen instrument.

Discounting records by the New Orleans Rhythm Kings (a hybrid group of Chicagoans and New Orleanians), the first Chicagoan jazz recordings of any consequence were turned out by the Bucktown Five in early 1924. Muggsy Spanier sparked this session with a jumping, biting cornet lead that was right out of Oliver; Volly de Faut, who followed Roppolo on clarinet with the Rhythm Kings and later recorded with Jelly Roll Morton, demonstrated why his graceful, flowing style was highly respected in the Midwest. Spanier went beyond Paul Mares (also an Oliver man) to demonstrate that the lead voice, as he felt it, should be neither behind nor in front of the beat but right on *top* of it. The result was electric, something like running downhill and trying to keep up with yourself. The Spanier thrust, although seldom enhanced by a flow of original ideas, was a significant factor in the formation of an independent Chicago style.

The Bucktown Five records were, however, all but eclipsed within a couple of months by a brace of Wolverine recordings, featuring the brilliant ensemble and solo work of Bix Beiderbecke. The Wolverines were, of course, a going band rather than a studio pickup group, and their records showed it. Everywhere musicians began copying Bix's solos and the original riffs of the group. It was, in fact, McPartland's note-for-note knowlege of these records that landed him the job as Beiderbecke's replacement later in 1924. Cornetist Bill Davison, who recorded with the Chubb-Steinberg orchestra in the same year, also borrowed much from Bix.

As the Wolverines struggled along after Beiderbecke's departure, McPartland gradually replaced each member with one of his old Austin friends. Now reunited, the gang found work through booking agent Husk O'Hare, who even put them on radio station WHT as O'Hare's Red Dragons.

A couple of new reed players appeared on the scene in this 1925–1926 period. One was Rod Cless, whom the gang met on a job in Des Moines, Iowa. The other was Pee Wee Russell, an experienced clarinetist-saxophonist whose musical views have caused many to regard him a front-rank Chicagoan, although he was not noticed much in jazz circles in the city before 1925 and never did put in a lot of time there.

Russell was brought up in Oklahoma, heard and liked clarinetist Larry Shields on Original Dixieland Jazz Band records, and was attracted to in-person performances by New Orleans clarinetist "Yellow" Nunez. He studied violin, piano, and drums before getting to the clarinet. Russell played on an Arkansas River pleasure boat and with the band at Western Military Academy in 1920 and 1921 at Alton, Illinois, not far from the St. Louis area where he was born. For a while, Pee Wee attended the University of Missouri, but he spent most of his time listening to jazz on the Mississippi boats, admiring the band of Charlie Creath (a good cornetist with a haunting, aged-in-wood tone), and hanging out with the small but eager jazz gang around St. Louis. There he met New Orleans players like Armstrong, Baby Dodds, bassist Pops Foster, and drummer Zutty Singleton. Saxophonist Frank Trumbauer, playing with Ted Jansen's band, was already a local hero, and youngsters like trombonists Vernon Brown and Sonny Lee, bassist Bob Casey, and clarinetist Artie Gruner were to St. Louis what the Austin gang and their friends were to Chicago. From time to time, wandering jazzmen like Wingy Mannone and Fud Livingston turned up in St. Louis, too.

Russell, unlike the Chicagoans, was a loner. By 1922, he was knocking about the Southwestern states, playing jobs in Phoenix, Arizona, El Paso, Texas, across the line in Mexico, and in Houston, where there was a stint with the celebrated band of pianist Peck Kelley, which, in 1924, included clarinetist Leon Roppolo and trombonist Jack Teagarden. Russell returned to St. Louis and Herb Berger's band. Later, in 1926, the clarinetist played in another celebrated but unrecorded group, a Jean Goldkette unit fronted by Trumbauer at the Arcadia Ballroom in St. Louis. It is said that Pee Wee was so enthused about working alongside Bix Beiderbecke in this band that he refused to be fired and continued to play without pay after receiving his notice. He also tried, without success, to get Peck Kelley into the St. Louis orchestra. Russell absorbed all he heard and played as he pleased, working out the details of style by himself rather than through the group-therapy approach favored by the Austin boys. Happily, both methods worked out rather well for the men involved.

Back in Chicago, the well-schooled players were finding good jobs in 1924 and 1925, and the seat-of-the-pants improvisers were taking what was left. Benny Goodman played the Midway Gardens with pianist Elmer Schoebel (another former New Orleans Rhythm King who had never been to New Orleans). Then Art Kassel took over the band, which included, in addition to Goodman and Schoebel, former Rhythm King Steve Brown (who *was* from New Orleans) on bass, Danny Polo on reeds, and a Mares-Oliver cornet disciple (who sounded something like Spanier) named Murphy Steinberg.

Spanier and de Faut, the Bucktown Fivers, were at the White City Ballroom with Sig Meyers, and Joe Sullivan was grinding out vaudeville assignments with Elmo Mack and his Purple Derby Orchestra. Trumpeter Al Turk and saxophonist Wayne King were working steadily. Jess Stacy was playing with Joe Kayser at the Arcadia Ballroom. The Teschemacher-Freeman-Tough entente had become, in 1925, Husk O'Hare's Wolverines. In 1926, they had a couple of good jobs at the White City Ballroom, about a block from the Midway Gardens, and drew admiration from Beiderbecke, Armstrong, and drummer Zutty Singleton (who had recently arrived from St. Louis). This kind of praise was, of course, highly valued.

The Chicagoans were, by and large, a cocky and self-impressed group. Teschemacher was moody and serious, McPartland brash and outgoing, Tough cynical and questioning, Freeman impulsive and ingenuous, but all were convinced that they had something no one else had, and each member of the gang bristled with enthusiasm. It was, however, inevitable that the band would break up. Each man needed a wider exposure to varying musical climates and a chance to develop his own identity. Whether it was the result of a conscious recognition of this need or not, the first move was made by Teschemacher, who joined Floyd Towne's band, first at the Triangle Café and then at the Midway Gardens in 1926. This group was an outgrowth of Sig Meyers' band and included trombonist Floyd O'Brien, George Wettling, Danny Altier on alto, Towne on tenor, Muggsy Spanier, and eventually Jess Stacy on piano. It wasn't too far from musical home for Teschemacher, after all.

Benny Goodman found a promising spot in August, 1925, when he answered Ben Pollack's call to join his new band in California. Pollack had hopes of building a first-class jazz band that could also present modern, cleanly executed arrangements instead of mere jamming on a select list of "jazz" tunes all night. He hired Glenn Miller, a skilled trombonist and arranger, and Joseph "Fud" Livingston, an imaginative arranger, composer, and reedman.

Fud had been around Detroit and Chicago for about a year, working with Jean Goldkette units and broadening his knowledge of jazz. Although he was born in South Carolina, Livingston fit the Chicago pattern—a deep love for jazz, an aggressive and optimistic instrumental style, an interest in widening the expressive scope of jazz through unusual harmonies (his interest in whole-tone scales may have come in part from Beiderbecke, who was jobbing with Goldkette about the same time Fud was), and, one might add, a colossal thirst for alcohol.

Pollack's idea was a kind of sophisticated extension of the King Oliver band approach: over a steady, swinging rhythmic foundation, make the music *sound* impromptu, but base the improvisations on a real structure, with interesting scored passages worked out in advance. The Pollack unit would not be as free as the unique Oliver band, but it might go beyond it in other respects because its members were good readers as well as skilled improvisers. It would also borrow a little from the outlook of the best Goldkette bands. The idea looked good and sounded good, but Pollack had to make concessions to commercial demands and finally watered the band down with a couple of violins in order to keep working. And then, too, Glenn Miller, as arranger, was less aware of New Orleans music than Pollack and leaned toward the more salable Roger Wolfe Kahn sound.

Goodman's first released record was a Pollack date in December, 1926, when Benny was 17. His solo on an ordinary popular tune, *He's the Last Word,* bubbles with vitality and confidence and contains an explosive staccato burst that may be the first such Chicagoan musical device on record. Livingston's tenor also reveals a feeling for the tense "shuffle" style (sharply accented dotted eighth notes followed by weak sixteenth notes) that has often been identified with Chicago musicians and probably came from the New Orleans Rhythm Kings, Bix, Jimmy Noone, and Johnny Dodds.

The Austinites didn't approve of the Pollack compromise and said so. They held out for the all-improvised sound of the smaller band, although most of them had been working off and on with bands just as commercial and usually not as good as Pollack's.

The Wolverines, under McPartland, secured one more good engagement before breaking up. Art Kassel took them, with Bud

Jacobson in Teschemacher's place, to the Greystone Ballroom in Detroit (another lively jazz center in the twenties), where they were delighted to find themselves playing opposite Fletcher Henderson's excellent 1926 band. Freeman was the one most affected by this circumstance, for it was his first encounter with Coleman Hawkins, who had already lapped all competition on the tenor saxophone. It can be assumed that a different Bud Freeman came away from Detroit after the Greystone job. Even a decade or so later, Bud remembered the stomping, on-the-beat approach of the Henderson saxophonist in 1926–1927 as his favorite of several phases of the Hawkins style that had evolved over the years.

Dave Tough left the group next, then McPartland and Lannigan joined Bill Paley's band, and the others were left to dig up whatever they could find. Mezz Mezzrow had been sitting in with the gang now and then and occasionally had enlarged the sax section to three men for special jobs. He cut quite a father figure among the Austin gang, for Mezzrow was seven or eight years older and seemed very worldly, indeed. He was acquainted with most of the South Side musicians, with several gangsters, with a connection for obtaining quality marijuana, with booking agents, and with the insides of several jails. Teschemacher, Freeman, Sullivan, and Gene Krupa were impressed, but Tough, though friendly, could see through the bluster. Mezzrow favored all-out emulation of the New Orleans players, and gradually the gang lined up against him, stressing instead the development of their own group style. When Eddie Condon moved into the inner circle, he, too, was unconvinced by Mezzrow's arguments, and the Chicagoans ventured further away from New Orleans jazz.

As a matter of fact, the New Orleans men themselves were breaking up their bands and the old improvised marching style. Armstrong had left Oliver, the Dodds brothers (clarinetist Johnny and drummer Baby) were playing a more intimate kind of jazz at Kelly's Stables, Jimmy Noone had a two-reeds-plus-rhythm-section group, and Oliver himself had hired a saxophone section. Only Jelly Roll Morton continued to cling to the earlier forms. Mezzrow's attempts to convince Sullivan of the virtues of playing the Morton style were again unsuccessful, for Sullivan had heard the young and very modern Earl Hines, who was clearly the man of the hour among Chicago pianists in 1926–1927. Tough and

Krupa still regarded Baby Dodds with enormous respect and affection, but now Zutty Singleton seemed more in step with their musical thinking.

Bix was at nearby Hudson Lake with Pee Wee Russell in 1926, and most of the Chicagoans made pilgrimages to the resort to hear the band, play records, discuss music, and drink. Mezzrow went, too, but he had begun to feel left out when the gang discussed nonjazz works by composers like Stravinsky and Eastwood Lane. Even purist Muggsy Spanier had become interested in formal music, and, of course, Sullivan had had plenty of it in his background to begin with. Mezz just wanted to play the blues and was unhappy about this new digression.

Teschemacher was especially fond of Beiderbecke and began to show it in his playing. Like Russell, who had been deeply affected by Bix's melodic and harmonic concepts, Tesch introduced a hard, rasping quality into his tone that brought it closer to the brassy bite of the cornet and carried it away from the more liquid sound of the conventionally played clarinet. Benny Goodman and Fud Livingston had also found this an effective means of adding punch and excitement to their solos. Beyond this characteristic (which Goodman eventually dropped), these four clarinetists also shared an admiration for Jimmy Noone, who had changed during the twenties from a delicate contrapuntal ensemble style to a powerful cornet-like lead with graceful embellishments. Thus was created what many call "Chicago style" clarinet.

Rhythm came first for the Chicagoans. They leaned heavily upon the skills of Tough, Krupa, and Wettling in establishing the fundamental pulse. Stacy and Sullivan picked up pointers from various Chicago blues pianists, as well as from Hines, and pushed the band either by hammering out steady four-beat chords or by adding an eight-to-the-bar pattern borrowed from the popular boogie-woogie specialists on Chicago's South Side. The banjo player was encouraged to maintain a steady four beats to the measure and refrain from the fancy flourishes common in earlier jazz bands. The drummer was allowed to fill in empty spaces, and it required taste and understanding to carry this responsibility. Tough was the ideal man for the job, but Krupa and Wettling were quite acceptable.

As for the bass, it was pretty much up to the individual player, but no one argued with the Steve Brown approach that Lannigan used, which alternated from a two-to-the-bar pattern to contrapuntal triplets and clever off-the-beat accents.

All horns played on the beat or even slightly in front of it. Melodic ideas were important, but they usually came in rhythmic bursts and clusters. How the player pounced on a note was as important to the Chicagoans as the pitch of the note itself. Emotional impact was everything. No group of jazzmen had ever *attacked* music with more vigor and bravado than did this eager fraternity.

Russell and Stacy, who had formed their musical habits independently of the Chicagoans, were not quite so ferociously inclined. They had each investigated the subtle art of understatement in their solo work and had come up with excellent results. Pee Wee's unusual sensitivity at a time when the entire country, including its jazz musicians, seemed caught up in a "get hot" complex, can be heard on a mid-1927 Red Nichols recording of *Ida*. Here Russell explores the harmonic pockets of the song's structure in a restrained, almost recalcitrant manner, borrowing from Bix's ballad approach and adding the unique Russell sense of whimsy that marks all his best work. His solo created a bit of a stir among some musicians at the time, but most of the Chicagoans were not ready for "pretty" jazz yet. They didn't care for cornetist Nichols either, whom they regarded as a mere Bix imitator and not a very convincing "hot" player.

Early Stacy on record is rare, but a glimpse of his 1928 style can be had on a recording by Danny Altier's orchestra, which included Spanier, Wettling, clarinetist Maurie Bercov (who played much like Teschemacher), and guitarist Ray Biondi. Jess, at 24, had already formed the mature style for which he became widely known years later with Benny Goodman's orchestra. His right-hand figures were more linear than those of Hines or Sullivan, but the Chicago rolling bass line was there and so were the hornlike melodic statements so characteristic of the best Chicago pianists of the period. There was, though, no hammering on the keyboard; Stacy displays superb control and an advanced sense of dynamics throughout his solo on *My Gal Sal* and behind the dismal vocal on *I'm Sorry Sally*.

While most of the Chicago gang wrestled with all these problems, Benny Goodman, now back home, was continuing to play with Pollack whenever there was work or to accept casual engagements whenever the band's luck ran out, which was often. In 1927, he recorded a couple of trio performances with Chicagoans Bob Conselman on drums and Mel Stitzel on piano (*That's a Plenty* and *Clarinetitis*) that reveal him as a gifted young clarinetist at that time, with an already recognizable style, but a style yet rooted in the same Dodds-Noone-Beiderbecke idiom within which Teschemacher worked. The vibrato, phrasing, attack, and general ebullience were quite similar to Teschemacher's later work, but the tone was cleaner and clearly Goodman's own.

A favorite hangout for Chicagoans in 1927 was the Three Deuces, where Sullivan, Freeman, Tough, Krupa, Teschemacher, Condon, Wettling, and Mezzrow were regulars at frequent jam sessions held in the dank basement.

Goodman, Beiderbecke, and others dropped in whenever possible and helped to establish the saloon as a kind of recreation center and clubhouse for local and visiting jazzmen. The sessions held there, some still remembered by the participants, marked the arrival of the Chicagoans as jazzmen with their own following of musicians, tyros who were now attracted to them just as they had been attracted to New Orleans jazz groups in the first place.

About this time, Dave Tough picked up his drums and went to France with clarinetist Danny Polo. Dave was a restless man, unhappy with his environment. (Mezzrow recalled in later years how Tough read the *American Mercury* from cover to cover, "especially the section called 'Americana,' where all the bluenoses, bigots, and two-faced killjoys in this land of the free got a going over they never forgot.") It seemed logical to Tough to go where other creative Americans were gathering.

Gene Krupa had met most of the Chicagoans through the Benson booking office, and Mezzrow was already preaching Baby Dodds to the 18-year-old drummer and helping him to fit into the spot vacated by Tough. Gene's enthusiasm was boundless, and by late 1927 he was, after Wettling, the Chicagoans' favorite available drummer. That fall, practically everyone in the gang got a chance to make records, partly as a result of a selling job by singer–promoter–comb player Red McKenzie, who had now settled in Chicago and usurped Mezzrow's big brother role among the Austinites.

The first date was for Charles Pierce, a local butcher and sometime alto saxophonist who admired the Chicago jazz gang and often hired them for his band. Spanier and Teschemacher were the bright lights of the session, which produced *China Boy*, the familiar Chicago war-horse, and a real blues called *Bull Frog Blues*. *China Boy* was arranged for two cornets and three reeds and is of interest chiefly for Teschemacher's agitated, explosive solo, which overcomes a series of clinkers (usually a result of Tesche's pinching and straining in the upper register, causing a higher note than intended to come out) and ignites an otherwise rather stodgy band performance. Spanier blows a disappointing stock chorus on *Bull Frog Blues*, but Tesche grasps the blues idea quite well and is close to the Jimmy Noone sound throughout. The arrangement was probably based on Jelly Roll Morton's *Jungle Blues*, recorded three or four months before *Bull Frog*.

The next record, made the following month, is more satisfactory. Again a straightforward blues was included, called *Friar's Point Shuffle*, as well as a popular song, then about a decade old, *Darktown Strutters' Ball*. The personnel was mostly first-string Chicagoans: Spanier, Teschemacher, Mezzrow (tenor sax), Sullivan, Condon, Lannigan (tuba), Wettling, and Red McKenzie (vocals). Spanier seems happier on this one, plays a good enough blues solo, and Tesch sounds even deeper into Noone, except for a wider vibrato and a nervous, almost frenzied, quality that the more assured Noone never displayed. Sullivan solos with characteristic vitality, featuring a rolling left-hand bass line and closely grouped, powerful chord clusters in the right. Lannigan manages to establish an oscillating rhythm with his tuba by playing a stream of dotted-eighth- and sixteenth-note patterns. The record is, in all, a good representation of what was going on among the more talented Chicagoans in 1927.

Benny Goodman defected from the struggling Pollack band for a while to play with Isham Jones in 1927, but he soon returned, and at approximately the same time, Jimmy McPartland joined the Pollack crew. They got out another record in late 1927, *Waitin' for Katie* and *Memphis Blues*. Oddly enough, the blues side was poor and *Katie* was, in the final passages, an excellent band performance, with almost fully mature Goodman (he was 18) and advanced saxophone section work. On this number, Pollack comes close to the best of Jean Goldkette, a very high level for 1927, indeed. His ace soloist was Goodman, whose ears and fingers were ahead of most of his contempories, including the slightly older Austin gang. "The boys that hung out at the Three Deuces were terrifically talented guys," Benny wrote in his autobiography, "but most of them didn't read, and we thought their playing was rough. We didn't pay them much mind, although we liked to jam with them."

McPartland, who has never shed the Beiderbecke mantle he acquired so early, quite naturally showed great improvement in 1927 over his 1924 Wolverine level (which can be heard on a single record cut at that time), though he was never to be more than a pleasant utility cornetist. He participated in another Wolverine recording session in 1927 with a group that included Maurie Bercov and Dick Voynow, but nothing much came of it.

Prior to his first record date in late 1927, Krupa worked all over the Chicago area with bandleaders like Joe Kayser, Leo Shukin, and Thelma Terry. He studied, at one time or another, with Al Silverman, Ed Straight (from whom Tough learned his rudiments), and Roy Knapp, striving to become a thoroughly trained and highly flexible drummer. At the same time, Freeman played with Herb Carlin's band, followed up casuals through the booking offices, and worked a movie theater job with Tough and Condon in a band fronted by Jack Gardner, a good Chicago pianist. Freeman and Tough were close friends, and when Dave left for France, Bud let Mezzrow talk him into striking out for Hollywood, presumably to make a fortune as an actor. They got as far as Colorado, then turned around and ran for home.

Joe Sullivan was busy with dance bands like Sig Meyers' or Louis Panico's and did occasional radio work. And Teschemacher, according to Condon, was dropping into the Apex Club to hear Jimmy Noone at least five times a week. He also continued to work in Floyd Towne's band at the Midway Gardens with Spanier, Stacy, Wettling, and trombonist Floyd O'Brien.

More than twenty years later, Artie Shaw, who visited Chicago with Irving Aaronson's orchestra about 1928, described (in his book *The Trouble with Cinderella*) his reactions to O'Brien and Teschemacher:

I remember one night—or morning, rather, for it started around four A.M.—when a bunch of us, who had decided to have ourselves a little session, wound up in some dance hall where they were holding one of the Marathon Dance contests that were always taking place in those days. Different musicians floated in and out, sat in for a while, played a few choruses, and then got up to let some other guy blow. There was a piano player named Jess Stacy, and another named Joe Sullivan. There was one trombone player, Floyd O'Brien, who had one of the most peculiar, lazy, deliberately mistaken-sounding styles I've ever heard. He would almost, but not quite, crack a note into little pieces, and each time you thought he was about to fall apart he'd recover and make something out of what started out to sound like a fluff—till after a while you began to get the idea that this guy not only wasn't making any mistakes at all, but had complete control over his horn. He would come so damn close to mistakes that you couldn't see how he was going to get away with it; but he always recovered somehow—and this trick of almost, but never quite, making the mistake, and each time recovering so that the things he played went off in altogether unexpected and sometimes quite humorous directions, was what made his style so peculiar to start with—although it's impossible to give the flavor of it in language. . . . I sat next to him [Teschemacher] and watched him while he played. We were all slightly drunk on bad bootleg gin, but it didn't seem to affect his playing any. He too had this odd style of playing, but in an altogether different way from O'Brien's. Even while he'd be reaching out for something in his deliberately fumbling way, some phrase you couldn't quite see the beginning or end of (or, for that matter, the reason for it in the first place), there was an assurance about everything he did that made you see that he himself *knew* where he was going all the time; and by the time he got there you began to see it yourself, for in its own grotesque way it made a kind of musical sense, but something extremely personal and intimate to himself, something so subtle that it could never possibly have had great communicative meaning to anyone but another musician and even then only to a jazz musician who happened to be pretty damn hep to what was going on.

A recording session for the Okeh company in December, 1927, was arranged by Red McKenzie, whose valuable contacts with that firm were left over from his earlier commercial successes with the group he called the Mound City Blue Blowers. As McKenzie and Condon's Chicagoans, McPartland, Freeman, Teschemacher, Krupa, Sullivan, Lannigan, and Condon cut four sides that obtained wide distribution throughout the country and made a favorable impression on Eastern jazzmen, most of whom had not realized how much the Chicagoans had improved. The biggest surprise was Krupa, an unknown, whose well-recorded drum work on these sessions rocked the New York jazz cliques, and ultimately unseated Vic Berton as their chief percussionist. Krupa's intense study of Dodds, Singleton, and Tough, along with his vast natural energy and superb sense of time, placed him, as of the last days of 1927, in the front rank of jazz drummers.

The tunes recorded were *Sugar, China Boy, Nobody's Sweetheart,* and *Liza* (not Gershwin's), all in F, which must have been the gang's favorite key signature. Tesch wrote out a few connecting passages to give the ensemble fabric more strength, but most of the music was freely improvised in a small-band style that stemmed from the New Orleans Rhythm Kings, various Beiderbecke recording groups, the Dodds brothers' combination, Jimmy Noone, and, inevitably, a number of semicommercial units around Chicago in which the gang had played over the years. Teschemacher's scored interludes were borrowed in part from such standard dance-band sources, and the clarinetist frequently sought similar straight parallel-harmony parts in the improvised ensemble passages rather than a weaving New Orleans contrapuntal line, as advocated by Mezzrow. He also devised an unusual introduction to *Liza,* in 6/4 time.

Freeman, nervous on his first recording, demonstrated that, while his tone was still rough, he had ideas and a rapidly developing command of his horn. Sullivan, after Krupa, emerged as the steadiest and most arresting performer in the group. His powerful left hand and Hines-like right tied the rhythm section together and provided much of the lift for which these records are famous.

Teschemacher was in better form for this date than he had been on earlier recordings, but he was still an uneven player. His solos ranged from breathtakingly inventive melodic paroxysms, with notes flying off in unexpected directions like so many fireballs (*China Boy*), to stilted, groping phrases that amounted to little more than rough caricatures of Jimmy Noone (*Sugar*). For all his faults, though, Tesch had achieved a personal, identifiable, and highly stimulating mode of expression that soon rubbed off on dozens of other clarinetists around the country.

Two Chicagoan ensemble devices that intrigued Eastern jazz-men can be heard on these records. Mezzrow described them some years later (in his autobiography *Really the Blues*) as the "explosion," a sudden flare preceding each repetition of the initial melodic statement in a conventional song structure, and the al-ready mentioned "shuffle rhythm," a staccato, heavily accented eighth-note pattern usually applied to the bridge, or release, of a song. These and other simple but effective methods of increasing and releasing tensions came largely from the mind of Dave Tough, who, more than any other single musician, translated New Orleans musical ideas into the jazz language of the Chicagoans. Had he been in town for the occasion, Tough would doubtless have been the hero of the McKenzie-Condon recordings.

The Chicagoans knew they had left their mark when Red Nich-ols recorded *Nobody's Sweetheart* a couple of months later, com-plete with shuffle rhythms, explosions, and a Chicago-like clarinet solo by Fud Livingston.

For a few months after the Okeh sessions, there was little change in the Chicagoans' job situations. Krupa played for Ben-son orchestras, in Eddie Neibauer's Seattle Harmony Kings, and, for three months or so, with Mezzrow (Milton Mesirow and His Purple Grackle Orchestra); Tesch and Jess Stacy were still with Floyd Towne; Sullivan continued with Louis Panico; Tough was still seeking culture in France. Benny Goodman, encouraged by the success of the McKenzie-Condon recordings that featured his old friend and fellow Pollack sideman McPartland, secured a one-session Vocalion date using the same instrumentation. Bob Conselman played drums, but the others were drawn from the Pollack fold. The titles were *A Jazz Holiday* and *Wolverine Blues*, and the performances were more directly derived from Bix Bei-derbecke's small-band records of the preceding year than from either the New Orleans bands or the Austin gang. The session pointed up a split among the Chicagoans that had been widening for some time and could now be heard in their music. McPart-land, Goodman, Freeman, Wettling, and Teschemacher were drifting away from New Orleans patterns toward a more sophisticated, lighter music that emphasized clean execution, advanced harmonies, and melodic wit. Their guiding light was the modern work of Beiderbecke. Sullivan, Mezzrow, and Spanier were primarily Armstrong-blues men. As Sullivan once expressed it, "I love Bix like I love my right arm, but I go by way of Louis."

Not that Freeman *et al.* didn't have a deep admiration for Louis ("Too much Armstrong," Teschemacher once admonished Bud after one of his tenor solos); nor did Spanier and the others fail to appreciate Bix. Each side still indulged in a good deal of hero worship in both directions, but the split was there.

McKenzie and Condon, figuring they had a winning combination, landed two more record dates. One record, under the heading of McKenzie and Condon's Boys, was not issued, but the other, by the Chicago Rhythm Kings, was successfully released in April, 1928. Three sides, *There'll Be Some Changes Made, I've Found a New Baby,* and *Baby, Won't You Please Come Home?* (the last not issued at the time), feature Teschemacher, Spanier, Mezzrow, Sullivan, Condon, Lannigan, and Krupa. Mezzrow was included because Freeman had gone to New York to join Pollack, who had been impressed by Bud's first records.

The reproduction quality and studio balance of these recordings are superior to the December sessions for Okeh, and Spanier furnishes a solid Armstrong-inspired lead. Krupa, who can be heard clearly this time, is again the lion of the date. Although Gene was not the first to use the then difficult-to-record bass drum on records (Baby Dodds, for one, preceded him), he makes daringly prominent use of it here, filling out the rhythm section in a way that had never before been caught on wax. His tom-tom accents and explosions were, too, unusual and very exciting in 1928, when electrical recording methods, permitting a more extensive use of deep-tone drums, were only about two years old. Also to Krupa's credit was his ability to hold a firm tempo behind Spanier's pushing lead, which caused many weaker drummers to accelerate in a misguided attempt to catch up with the cornetist. Spanier has trouble with drummers on this point to this day.

Teschemacher seems more contemplative here than on previous recordings and is even closer to trumpet phrasing. The effect of the tenor-clarinet-cornet Chicago front line is, in fact, that of three tightly knit parallel melody voices and a distinct departure from the old New Orleans Dixieland format, which calls for a trombone bass line, a simple cornet lead, and contrapuntal clarinet figures. Tesch explored this new idea even further at this time by working out a fourth tune, *Jazz Me Blues*, for three reeds and rhythm. It is, interestingly, the best side of the date, and Tesch seems more comfortable playing lead over the saxophones of Mezzrow and Rod Cless than he had before in his wandering ensemble lines above Spanier's horn. Tesch's *Jazz Me Blues* is rather close, too, to the ensemble approach of the trumpetless band Jimmy Noone fronted at that time.

I've Found a New Baby and *There'll Be Some Changes Made* settled any question that might have remained about the emergence of a new crop of talent from Chicago. These men had created a fine, workable method of small-band collective improvisation that accommodated the newer trends in jazz (solo virtuosity, a steady four-to-the-bar swing, harmonic explorations beyond simple triads with added sevenths, an enlarged set of responsibilities for the drummer) while retaining some of the good things in New Orleans jazz (the blues, a "vocal" approach to personal expression, unified collective spirit, a driving on-the-beat momentum, intelligent use of understatement). For some Chicagoans, this formula for small-band swing, with the addition of a relaxed ballad style, served well for a lifetime; others continued to search elsewhere for musical fulfillment.

The summer of 1928 found many of the Chicagoans in New York. McKenzie, a natural salesman (he had also arranged for Jimmy Noone to record his Apex band in Chicago the previous month), now went to work lining up New York dates for his brood. There was supposed to be an attractive job with Bee Palmer, but for various reasons it fell through. The gang spent a hard summer in a strange city. They found a brief moment of glory backing a dance team at the Palace, but it vanished when a *Variety* reviewer described the gang as the "poorest 7-piece orchestra on earth," even though a writer for *The Billboard* suggested that the band was "commendable."

Teschemacher found a temporary job substituting for Gil Rodin in Ben Pollack's sax section for about three weeks. Then the Pollack band itself was laid off, leaving McPartland with the curious distinction of being out of work with two bands at the same time. Goodman had no trouble picking up dates with commercial bands like those of Sam Lanin, Meyer Davis, and Nat Shilkret, but the other Chicagoans had to share a single hotel room and tighten their belts. A quartet recording date with Teschemacher, Condon, Sullivan, and Krupa helped pay the hotel bill. The titles were *Indiana* and *Oh, Baby*, again in the key of F. Tesch is heard on alto and clarinet, flailing his way through the two sides without accomplishing very much. His stiff reeds and raucous, forced tone prove unsuitable in this case. Krupa's drumming is overbearing and overrecorded, for he whacks energetically on his tom-toms, crash cymbal, and bass drum as though a full band were present. Sullivan, however, reveals steady improvement and a sensitive touch that could not be heard on previous records.

Freeman, who had turned out a couple of commercial records with Pollack in April, became disillusioned and sailed away to join Dave Tough in France. By September, Bud was back in Chicago again. Tough, too, had not profited very much by his stay in Europe. Most of the work there was decidedly nonjazz in character, and by 1928 Dave was working in ships' bands on the Atlantic. He left one disciple in Paris, though, in Maurice Chaillon, who replaced Tough in Danny Polo's band. Another French musician who had heard and been influenced by the McKenzie-Condon recordings was trumpeter Philippe Brun. It was, nevertheless, a poor environment for a young drummer of Tough's ability; despite the flow of good legal liquor and the "cultured" environment, he headed for home in early 1929. (Mezzrow, on his way to see Tough in Paris at that time, passed the drummer going the other way in mid-ocean.)

New Yorkers Red Nichols and Miff Mole were interested in the Chicagoans, especially Krupa and Sullivan, and a recording session was set up that would combine their talents. McKenzie had been talking up Jimmy Noone and Chicago music to Nichols, who seemed ready to give it a try, as long as the date was in Mole's name anyway. The initial attempt was *Shim-Me-Sha-Wabble* and *One Step to Heaven*, and the result was one of Nichols' best records. With no bassist, Sullivan and Krupa set the pace. Tesch, as usual, plays flimsy ensemble parts, challenging rather than complementing the cornet lead, but there can be little doubt that he

LOUIS ARMSTRONG

A GATHERING FOR THE PHOTOGRAPHER. LEFT TO RIGHT, FRONT ROW: TOMMY DORSEY, LOUIS ARMSTRONG, GEORGE WETTLING; BACK ROW: BUD FREEMAN, "POPS" FOSTER, EDDIE CONDON, HENRY "RED" ALLEN

BESSIE SMITH

BENNY GOODMAN AND GENE KRUPA

EARL HINES

BIX BEIDERBECKE

FLETCHER HENDERSON

JACK TEAGARDEN

MA RAINEY

DON REDMAN

JAMES P. JOHNSON IN THE LATE FORTIES

FATS WALLER AND FRIENDS

and the other Chicagoans lit a fire under Nichols and Mole. Nichols was a top jazzman in New York, and this recording amounted to a musical test for the newcomers. They outdid themselves and qualified with room to spare.

Krupa, Sullivan, and Goodman, along with a new friend, Jack Teagarden, spent much time in Harlem listening to pianists and big bands. Earl Hines had suggested they look up Fats Waller, who was but one of several outstanding pianists in New York. The music they heard in Harlem deeply affected the Chicagoans, particularly Sullivan, who absorbed the buoyant, strutting Harlem piano approach (the eighth-note left-hand "stride" technique fit nicely into the Chicagoan "shuffle" idea) and combined it with his blues-*cum*-Hines style. The smooth, even swing and the sophisticated arrangements of the New Yorkers were a logical next step for the still rough Chicago gang, and they began the learning process all over again. Most of them were, after all, in their early twenties and still quite flexible.

Goodman, who was finally finding some security with Pollack at the Park Central Hotel, was especially impressed by Duke Ellington's band and in the summer of 1928 recorded a "Harlem" arrangement, complete with Bubber Miley effects by McPartland, of Jelly Roll Morton's *Jungles Blues*. At the same session, Benny made a rare appearance on alto saxophone, playing a charming Beiderbecke-like solo on *Blue*, and turned out a thoroughly Chicago-style performance with *Room 1411*, the last enhanced by Pollack's skillful drumming. Pollack was one of the first drummers to play four beats to the measure on the bass drum and was actually in a class with Tough and Krupa at this time, but he was too busy as a bandleader to participate in many all-jazz recordings.

The Chicago style had been all but swallowed up in the mainstream of jazz developments by late 1928, and Bud Freeman, back in the hometown, demonstrated some of the new things he had learned in New York on a single interesting Okeh record. Krupa, who had also returned to Chicago because his mother was ill, joined Freeman, Floyd O'Brien, clarinetist Bud Jacobson, and several other friends, mostly from the band working at the Golden Pumpkin with Thelma Terry, to make *Craze-ology* and *Can't Help Lovin' That Man* in December. Freeman's tone was by now lighter and more graceful, his fingers fast and sure, and his conception quite mature for a saxophonist of 22. *Craze-ology* reflects his New York impressions, for there are "jungle" effects, a kind of big-band arrangement (even to a saxophone lead) scaled down to three horns and rhythm, and evidence of an interest on Free-man's part in the kind of tour de force saxophone playing that Jimmy Dorsey, Coleman Hawkins, and Frankie Trumbauer had popularized in the East.

Krupa, too, had changed while in New York. He now played crisp rim shots in place of Dodds-like tom-tom thumps, used sudden explosions more sparingly, and concentrated on achieving a more even flow of 4/4 rhythm. About this time, too, he became interested in the work of a Cuba Austin, drummer with Mc-Kinney's Cotton Pickers.

Can't Help Lovin' That Man is a ballad performance, high-lighted by a good straight vocal by Red McKenzie (who later be-came a direct influence on a number of singers, including Woody Herman) and a Freeman solo that is almost pure Beiderbecke–Pee Wee Russell and represents Bud's first of many recorded solos in that vein. It is interesting to note, incidentally, that the final ensemble flare, which formerly would have been Krupa's signal to open fire with tom-toms, found him accenting with afterbeat cymbals but otherwise maintaining a regular pulse.

By 1929, most of the gang was in New York to stay, except for Teschemacher, Stacy, and Wettling, who continued to play for bands like Louis Panico's and Gene Fosdick's in Chicago. Spanier went with Ray Miller and Ted Lewis, and Goodman was still with Pollack, but New York had become home base. Max Kaminsky, a Boston trumpeter who had worked both Beiderbecke and Arm-strong into his style, settled in Manhattan, as did Pee Wee Russell, who kept alive playing for bandleaders like Paul Specht and Cass Hagen. Condon, Sullivan, Mezzrow, and Teagarden spent much time listening to bands and forming new friendships in Harlem. In the fall of 1928, they had recorded *Makin' Friends,* a fine blues performance featuring Teagarden that again drama-tized the new spirit of the Chicagoans. Most of them were be-coming firmly committed to the even rhythm of Ellington, Henderson, and other good New York bands. The effect this rhythmic change—four uncluttered, evenly accented pulses to each measure—had on the soloists was of considerable importance. The men had grown up when two-to-the-bar was in general use but was interpreted as *four* by horn players. It amounted to laying out *eight* beats in a measure by this new system. Creative use of syncopation and daring double-time phrases were now easier to bring about, and more involved harmonies came naturally as rhythm men broke the monotony of hitting the same chord four times in succession by thinking of new inversions, alterations, and passing chords. The 4/4 revolution—or rather evolution, for the Chicagoans and many others had been leading up to it for a long time—was the first giant step toward the higher creative level at which average jazzmen of the thirties performed.

Dave Tough was back in New York in 1929, but his slight frame and intemperate outlook had led him to illness and irresponsibility. He recorded some fair sides with Red Nichols and even toured in an all-Chicago band fronted by the popular cornetist, but he was not his old self. He eventually returned to Chicago and worked on and off there for the next several years, sometimes substituting for Wettling in Joe Kayser's band and even, at one point, playing for the Capitol Dancing School. Freeman, who was in and out of Chicago during the severest Depression years, remained close to Tough and worked with him whenever possible in places like Carlin's Ballroom.

One group of 1929 Nichols recordings deserves attention, for they include Sullivan, Freeman, Tough, Russell, and Teagarden (a kind of honorary member of the Chicago gang, because he, like Russell, fit comfortably into their musical philosophy). The tunes selected were *That Da Da Strain, Basin Street Blues,* and a blues called *Last Cent.* It was a top-heavy session with four horns and two rhythm, the more so because Teagarden, Russell, and Freeman behaved in typical Chicago fashion, ignoring the traditional functions of their instruments in a Dixieland setting, to improvise around the melody. The recordings do show the participants to be close to musical maturity, however, and, for better or worse, typecast in the roles each had to live down over the years —Russell the poignant clown, Teagarden the blues expert, Freeman the bumptious buffoon, Sullivan the muscular stomper, and Tough the forgotten drummer. It was a raw, undisciplined session, perhaps partly in open defiance of the meticulous Nichols, who always remained an opportunistic outsider to the Chicagoans.

Sullivan had by this time adopted the Harlem left-hand "stride" device and was developing into one of the best pianists in New York. With Teagarden, Mezzrow, Condon, and a couple of men from Charlie Johnson's big band, he had made a pair of excellent recordings in early 1929, and there was one very special date at about the same time that featured Joe, Teagarden, Eddie Lang, and Louis Armstrong—no doubt a satisfying experience for a young man like Sullivan, who had looked to Armstrong for inspiration from an early age.

Goodman, too, was in demand for recordings, jazz and otherwise. Leaving Pollack in the fall of 1929, Benny quickly became part of the New York jazz–studio-recording–free-lance gang that included the Dorseys, Eddie Lang, Miff Mole, and Glenn Miller. These men, who usually gathered at a speakeasy on West Fifty-third Street called Plunketts', fared unusually well during the Depression years of 1930 to 1932 because they could read well and perform according to instruction without delay or fuss. Goodman appeared on countless recordings during this period, but his best jazz solos were those he played on several Red Nichols dates. One of these, *China Boy*, recorded in 1930, is of special interest because it also features Sullivan and Krupa, and it is the same tune that helped bring them into prominence. Goodman, at 21, was now fully formed as a leading jazzman and was becoming a major influence on other clarinetists. His rhythmic figurations, impressive technical equipment, and unfailing ear earned for him respect from all quarters—studio men, dance-band musicians, the jazz clique, and "legitimate" players alike.

Sullivan and Krupa were boiling with enthusiasm for this Nichols date, and they demonstrated that their McKenzie-Condon phase nearly three years earlier was but a rough draft of what they were to become. Krupa, who had made his first recordings with Goodman for Nichols more than a year before (*Indiana* and *Dinah*), seemed to stimulate Benny. It was these and later Nichols sessions that led to the profitable association of Krupa and Goodman in the mid-thirties.

For all the brilliance of Goodman, Sullivan, and Krupa, it was

Teagarden who stole the show on *China Boy* and its companion selections, *Peg o' My Heart*, and *The Sheik of Araby*. Curiously, on *Shim-Me-Sha-Wabble*, an old Chicago favorite, Krupa's memories of Mezzrow's sermons seemed to be revived, as he plays in a "busy" style somewhat in the manner of Baby Dodds.

For Teschemacher and Stacy, there was fairly steady work in Chicago, but the exciting days of discovery in that city were pretty much over. Most of Tesch's remaining recordings, made in a fourteen-month period from late 1928 to early 1930, found him in the company of second-rate jazzmen, except for his final date with Bud Freeman and George Wettling. (The clarinetist's last New York recording in 1928 was with the Dorsey brothers and Don Redman, on which Teschemacher played a brief, awkward tenor saxophone solo.) In December, 1928, Tesch recorded *Trying to Stop My Crying* with Wingy Mannone and Art Hodes (a talented blues-oriented Chicago pianist), but the chief point of interest is a tag lifted from Stravinsky's *Petrouchka* that Spanier and Teschemacher had used from time to time.

An Elmer Schoebel recording of October, 1929, reveals Tesch and a group of Chicago friends completely caught up in Beiderbecke, even to selecting tunes from the old Wolverine book— *Copenhagen* and *Prince of Wails*. By this time, Tesch had cleaned up his tone, improved his intonation and control, and settled into a very attractive style that held to a middle road somewhere between Goodman and Russell. Considering this and the notable improvement Teschemacher displayed a few weeks later in a recording session with a Chicago group called the Cellar Boys, particularly on the stirring *Wailin' Blues*, it might be reasonable to assume that the clarinetist could have developed into a major jazzman of the thirties, alongside Goodman and Russell. As it turned out, this was his last appearance in a recording studio. Teschemacher's final two years, during which he even took up violin again, were spent mostly in commercial bands like those of Jan Garber and Benny Meroff, although there was a brief job with Jess Stacy in a group named Stacy's Aces. The 26-year-old ex-Austinite was killed in an automobile accident in 1932.

Stacy kept playing around Chicago during the lean years, along with those Chicagoans who had decided not to try New York yet. Freeman and Sullivan turned up on Chicago jobs occasionally, but the hometown boys were now mostly second stringers or younger men like Bob Zurke and the Marsala brothers (trumpeter Marty and clarinetist Joe). Jess worked with Paul Mares's jazz band at the Century of Progress Exposition in 1934 and at a club called the Subway in 1935, at which point Goodman sent for him to join his big band.

Dave Tough was around, too, sitting in and picking up occasional work in places like the Liberty Inn, but his drinking problem had become quite serious. Finally, he made an all-out effort to redeem himself and, after a fling in Ray Noble's American band, secured a steady job with Tommy Dorsey in late 1935.

Krupa spent the antijazz years of the Depression in a Red Nichols theater band with Goodman and Sullivan as well as in the orchestras of Irving Aaronson, Russ Columbo (again with Goodman and Sullivan, for Benny put the band together), Mal Hallett, and Buddy Rogers. It was no surprise when Goodman asked Krupa to join his new big band in early 1935.

Sullivan passed the years of the early thirties with a succession of odd jobs, from an engagement at New York's Stork Club with Red McKenzie's revised Mound City Blue Blowers to a road trip with Roger Wolfe Kahn. In 1933, he opened as a single on New York's Fifty-second Street at the Onyx Club, a kind of pioneer establishment that led to a mushrooming of many more jazz saloons along the same strip after the repeal of Prohibition. It was at this time that Sullivan first recorded two of his most famous solos, *Gin Mill Blues* and *Little Rock Getaway* (a theme going back to a piece from King Oliver's book called *Buddy's Habit*). After working with Bing Crosby and serving on staff at KHJ in Los Angeles, Sullivan joined Bob Crosby's big band in 1936.

Bud Freeman ended the on-again, off-again years of the early thirties (the Dorsey Brothers, Zez Confrey, Joe Venuti, Roger Wolfe Kahn) by joining Ray Noble's American band in 1935. Dave Tough was there, too, and, indeed, the two Chicagoans seemed virtually inseparable throughout the decade. Shortly after Tough joined Tommy Dorsey, Freeman became a member of the band's sax section. When Tough went with Benny Goodman in 1938, Freeman followed. One month after Goodman fired Tough for missing a Waldorf Astoria opening, Freeman left, too.

Tough's recordings with Dorsey's band indicate the powerful

influence this little man held over his fellow musicians. His drumming, now a kind of mixture of advanced Baby Dodds and contemporary Chick Webb, determined the whole character of the band and lent a dignity to performances that didn't always deserve it. His sensitivity, subtlety, and humor formed the perfect foil for Freeman's whimsical solo work, but he could also provide a properly stirring backdrop for the majestic trumpeting of Bunny Berigan, Dorsey's best soloist. Excepting Sid Catlett and Count Basie's Jo Jones, Tough was without equal on the crash and high-hat cymbals.

Krupa took a different path. A drummer of drive and proficiency, he began to be carried away with his role as a featured member of the Goodman orchestra and to play to the crowds rather than to the music. Never bashful, Krupa carried the showy Chick Webb approach to its extreme and sometimes turned Goodman's simple swing style into a montage of frenzied drum solos with orchestral accompaniment.

With Count Basie's Jo Jones setting the big-band pace in 1937–1938, it became painfully clear that Krupa was damaging the Goodman ensemble sound. The matter came to a head at Benny's Carnegie Hall concert in January, 1938. Krupa and Stacy were featured on *Sing, Sing, Sing*, a piece almost guaranteed to bring the audience to the edge of hysteria. Stacy turned in one of the best solos of his career—characteristically subtle, perfectly balanced, reflective, and carefully shaded for maximum aesthetic impact. Krupa, on the other hand, was all clamor and gongs. After the concert, members of the band went to the Savoy Ballroom to hear Count Basie's band triumph in a battle with Chick Webb, the first time Webb had been cut down at the Savoy. It was a fitting way to mark the new direction in which jazz was turning.

Within two months, Krupa left Goodman, and Tough (with Bud Freeman in tow) took over the job of putting the rhythm section back into proper perspective. Dave had by now dropped most of the New Orleans tricks that could still be heard behind the Dorsey band and was concentrating on a personal variation of the Jo Jones approach, which suited Goodman just fine.

The day after Goodman's January concert, the Commodore Music Shop made its first records with Stacy (continuing and probing some of the ideas set forth in *Sing, Sing, Sing* the night before), Freeman, Wettling, Pee Wee Russell, Bobby Hackett (who had re-created a Beiderbecke cornet solo for Goodman's concert), George Brunis (original trombonist with the New Orleans Rhythm Kings), Condon, and bassist Artie Shapiro. It was Chicago all over again, but with a difference. The Chicagoans were now established musicians of 1938, no longer dependent upon Bix, Noone, and Armstrong for ideas. They still used the collective-improvisation ensemble system, but it came out valid contemporary music, not a recreation of early forms.

The Commodore recordings brought wider recognition to the old gang, and they went back to make more. Stacy cut several solos, Freeman tried some trio pieces, Jack Teagarden sat in on a few, and a number of friends got into the act—Max Kaminsky, valve trombonist Brad Gowans, Marty and Joe Marsala, Fats Waller, Miff Mole, and Muggsy Spanier. The joy they felt in playing jazz together again after the long dry spell could be heard on each release, and the records began to sell quite well.

The Chicagoans made many small-band records together after that. Freeman, hopeful with this turn of events, launched an excellent eight-man band of his own called the Summa Cum Laude Orchestra. Tough was traveling with Jack Teagarden's big band in 1939, but he joined the Freeman band shortly before it broke up in 1940. Russell and Gowans brought some of the flavor and ideas of the slightly more commercial band Bobby Hackett had fronted a few months earlier. Freeman's unit developed into one of the most cohesive small bands of its time.

Spanier, too, put an outstanding small band together during this period. More tradition-bound than Freeman's, Muggsy's band combined a contemporary rhythm section with ideas borrowed from Oliver, Armstrong, the New Orleans Rhythm Kings, and the Midway Gardens band. Trombonist Brunis, clarinetist Cless, and pianist Joe Bushkin were Spanier's principal soloists.

The two groups stood as final friendly arguments for each side of the Beiderbecke-Armstrong division that had occurred some ten years before. Spanier played *Dippermouth Blues* and *Big Butter and Egg Man* along Armstrong lines; Freeman worked up a library of Wolverine tunes.

After 1940, most of the Chicagoans played in small bands, usually built on a Dixieland pattern, for no one had yet invented a better method of collective improvisation for seven or eight jazz musicians than this basic system of modified counterpoint. Usually, though, the solo passages were of more interest than the ensemble performances, and on the many recordings made by this group of musicians after 1938 can be heard some of each individual's very best work. Russell's melodic and harmonic extensions of Beiderbecke are especially noteworthy and appear on a large share of the Commodore releases. Freeman's explorations along similar lines have been preserved on many recordings, including his provocative trio dates of 1938 and a superb set of 1940 performances featuring Teagarden and Tough. Stacy, too, appears on some of these as well as on many non-Chicagoan dates. His engaging melodic inventions were featured often with the Goodman band and in recording sessions with Lionel Hampton, Ziggy Elman, and Harry James.

Sullivan formed an outstanding swing band about the same time that Spanier and Freeman were fronting their own units. His combination, though it included Chicagoan Danny Polo and New Orleans clarinetist Ed Hall, was a nearly complete break with Chicago. It was a versatile band, one that could do a proper job on the blues (Sullivan worked with blues singer Joe Turner) or slip effortlessly into the contemporary idiom represented by Billie Holiday, Lester Young, Coleman Hawkins, and Benny Carter, all of whom Sullivan recorded with at this time.

Krupa formed his own big band after leaving Goodman and found a fair measure of success, except for a couple of war years, until 1951. He has seldom appeared with the old Chicago gang, preferring to work with players whose styles are rooted in the music of the early and mid-forties. Krupa has returned to a less flamboyant style in recent years. He continues to influence young drummers through his teaching as well.

Goodman, the most gifted of the Chicagoans, ceased to be a creative force in jazz in the early forties and a few years later seemed to be all but burned out as a jazzman. The story of his contribution to the music from 1931 (when his recording of *Basin Street Blues* and *Beale Street Blues* stood as a first definition of the big-band style Benny was seeking) to 1941 is a separate study beyond the scope of this chapter.

Dave Tough worked with a variety of groups during World

War II, including Artie Shaw's Navy crew, but he began a whole new musical life upon joining Woody Herman's remarkable big band in 1944. At this point, Tough began listening to a modern young drummer named Max Roach and altered his musical outlook once more (some recordings with Flip Phillips document this change). But his old problem returned, and by 1946 he was back with the Chicagoans, playing in Eddie Condon's New York nightclub. Sullivan had returned to the gang, too, and sometimes Freeman dropped by to sit in with his old friends. Bud, like Tough, had served in the armed forces and had come out of the war with a few contemporary touches added to his old style.

The Tough-Freeman alliance produced a few more records about that time, but ended abruptly in 1948, when Dave slipped in the snow, hit his head, and died. He was 41.

Tough, who always wanted to be a writer, unwittingly composed his own epitaph in this lighthearted passage from one of his 1937 *Metronome* drum columns:

> Oh, the joy of the wine when it is red! Those lovely summer nights in the Bois with the swift, inner up-take of the Pernod. It turning milky in your glass and the taste of the wine, hard, clean, and tannic, in your mouth, volatile all through you—and you would go to the Birch Tops in the Rue Pigalle and hear her sing *The Boy in the Boat,* and hope you don't meet Ernest. Those dear, dead days! With us almost dead too!

A New York steak house called Nick's was home for many of the Chicagoans and their Eastern friends in the forties. They settled in and, with varying combinations, remained for a decade. (At one point, the band at Nick's used a rotation system in order to be assured of a trumpet player. Of several leading hornmen, he who was sober enough to get through all seven sets had the job that night.)

As the years went by, the Dixieland form had started to wear thin, and Freeman, for one, looked for other possibilities. He studied with Lennie Tristano and began working with more modern rhythm sections. Russell, whose health disintegrated in the early fifties, experienced a musical renaissance after his physical comeback and in recent years has been experimenting with some modern jazz ideas. Sullivan and Stacy work sporadically on the West

Coast, struggling to maintain their former high standards. Goodman is in a semiretirement, occasionally emerging to offer a few thin echoes of his old robust style. Of the other Chicagoans, some are still playing regularly (Hodes, McPartland, Mezzrow, Wettling, Spanier), but age and too many years of corrosive speakeasy gin are making it difficult for others to carry on. Many are already gone.

Every few years, some eager recording executive attempts to revive the Chicago style by gathering some of its surviving founders together again. In 1961, an NBC television show was built around such a reunion, and a recording session was organized by the Verve label that included Freeman, McPartland, Condon, Krupa, Sullivan, Russell, and Jack Teagarden. Once more, the old friends ran down *China Boy, Sugar,* and others, but most of the collective magic had long since vanished. It was just an assemblage of soloists, each with better things on his mind than turning back time. Russell and Freeman had already grown so weary of Condon's brand of Dixieland that both regarded this date as something of a personal affront. The musicians merely plodded through the accepted routines, signed for their money, and fled.

The influence of the Chicagoans on the course of jazz has been strong and direct in some ways, incidental and roundabout in others. No jazz clarinetist of the thirties and forties could escape the Goodman influence, but Benny offered something more than a new level of technical achievement on his instrument. He was one of the first jazzmen to improvise on fairly complex song structures at rapid tempos without falling into a series of clichés or resorting to unmusical tricks. Because Goodman was a superb craftsman almost from the beginning, he was able to develop clean musical ideas and long phrases even at a blistering pace, and his example helped to open the way for other jazzmen. For players like Teddy Wilson, Roy Eldridge, Art Tatum, Lionel Hampton, Chu Berry, Charlie Christian, and, ultimately, Charlie Parker, Goodman was not so much a direct influence as perhaps a breaker of new ground that they were nearly ready to sow.

It is an often overlooked fact that Bud Freeman was a major tenor saxophone stylist who once represented the "other" way for those who would not or could not follow the example of Coleman Hawkins. Freeman's dry tone, often resembling a C-

melody more than a tenor saxophone, was antirhapsodic and unsentimental, and it appealed to budding jazzmen, such as Lester
Young, who could not identify with the heavier, darker sound of
Hawkins. However, with the emergence of Young himself as a
primary jazz voice, beginning around 1937, Freeman's influence
faded rapidly.

Krupa's eminence was not entirely undeserved, although his
boyish good looks and stage manner were large factors in the public acclaim for him. Like Goodman, he caused his contemporaries
to pause and consider their own technical equipment. Krupa was
fast, accurate, and, when he wished to be, a master of dynamics
and tonal shading. He also brought to his instrument an unprecedented celebrity. For better or worse, the extended drum solo in
jazz grew out of Krupa's display pieces in the Goodman band.
The number of drummers, good and bad, Krupa has influenced
probably runs into the thousands.

Dave Tough, despite an erratic sense of responsibility and a determination to avoid grandstand tactics of the Krupa variety, was
a popular figure and rated high among the best drummers of the
thirties. His was an unspectacular influence, for he simply played
in the most supportive and tasteful way possible at all times.
Tough was a model of restraint combined with positive drive, of
steadiness coupled with spontaneous wit. Only Sid Catlett, Jo
Jones, and Chick Webb could surpass him in all these qualities. A
number of thoughtful modern drummers—Mel Lewis, Shelly
Manne, and Ed Shaughnessy are three—learned much from
Tough.

Jess Stacy was perhaps the most underrated Chicagoan of all.
An unassuming and gentle man, Jess looked on from the wings as
Teddy Wilson gathered most of the honors—quite justifiably—
through all the most productive Goodman years. But many pianists were listening carefully to both men. Stacy brought a new
kind of warmth to jazz piano, quite different from the "hot," iron-
fisted fury of Sullivan, the cool precision of Wilson, or the awesome improvisations of Earl Hines. Like Beiderbecke, Russell,
and trombonist O'Brien, Stacy's gift nestled in the realm of the
artfully understated melodic phrase and the painstakingly measured tincture of inevitability and surprise.

One of the most knowing appraisals of Stacy to appear in print was contributed to *The New Republic* by Otis Ferguson in 1937. Ferguson first discusses the pianist as a bandsman:

"What I try to do—" Jess says. "Look, I try to *melt* with the band." It is a simple word, but all the meanings are there in it: nuance, mood, touch, attack, phrasing, harmonic direction, what not. Because it is still in the unspoiled charm of its youth, this jazz music has never troubled to build a complicated breastwork of definitions. Jess and the rest have an *active* knowledge of how a tune may run, of how the value of a chord may be shifted—by its place in the general pattern (where it rises from and leads to), by its attack, duration, the color of its key and measure of its contrast, the sonority dependent on which of its notes are uppermost.

Ferguson goes on to discuss Jess as a soloist on a 1936 Gene Krupa–Benny Goodman recording:

From the deep background of the blues and from his own feeling, mind and hand, Jess made twelve bars of piano on a record that John Hammond supervised for English Parlophone, *The Blues of Israel.* That one is a sport all through, but after a few playings the piano stands out as much as anything. It has so completely that old-time pensive mood in the treble, the slurred second and the close three-finger chord hanging a mood of nostalgia around such a simple progression as sol, fa, mi, re: it is given so thorough a support in the constant working bass, whose left hand mingles intimately with what the right is doing. The song hangs on a trill, doubles the time for a swinging phrase, and slows to an ending of sustained chords, beautifully voiced. The analysis is simple, but the effect runs over into those complexities of the musical spirit that cannot be rightly described.

Pee Wee Russell, who replaced Teschemacher in the affections of many Chicagoans after Tesch's death, has always remained something of a musical entity unto himself. The impact of Beiderbecke can be traced in his work, but beyond that Pee Wee is unlike any musician who ever lived. His spidery, almost fragile, melodic inventions are full of unexpected turns and starts that sometimes leave the listener spent from prolonged anticipation of disaster. As Russell once explained his adventurous style to jazz writer Charles Edward Smith, "If you miss, you miss. If you get lucky, you get lucky—but you take a chance. You've got to get lost once in a while."

Because Russell plays to the music rather than to the house, some of his staunchest fans are other musicians. His presence in a jazz band can often be determined by what the men around him play. If boisterous trombonist George Brunis suddenly becomes reflective and introspective or if Max Kaminsky launches a solo that sounds like whimsical Beiderbecke, Russell is probably there. Even on earlier recordings, such as the 1929 *One Hour* by the Mound City Blue Blowers or Condon's 1933 *Tennessee Twilight*, it was often Pee Wee who established the mood and the musical tone of the moment. Bud Freeman, for one, has often played solos that are undiluted Russell (Condon's 1933 *Home Cooking* is an example), and when it has happened, Pee Wee has usually been present.

A number of modern jazzmen have expressed an interest in Russell, but with the possible exceptions of trombonist Bob Brookmeyer and soprano saxophonist Steve Lacy, there has been no notable Russell influence on younger players in modern jazz. Pee Wee made a deep impression on Bobby Hackett, however, whose influential ballad style, distinguished by explorations into the upper harmonic reaches of each chord, is admired by musicians of all persuasions.

There can never be another group like the Chicagoans, for they represent the coming together of two provincial forces—the New Orleans musical fraternity and the Chicago jazz gang—and the sturdy music that resulted from this meeting. While ingrown cliques will always be with us, it is no longer possible for one self-contained group of jazzmen to find direct inspiration in the work of another self-contained group imported nearly intact from a different part of the country. Today the patterns of change and influence are national and international in scope, a situation that was only forecast before the twenties with the first traveling jazzmen and the first commercial jazz recording. It is a loss, in a way, because the Chicagoans accomplished what they did by playing and listening *together*. The weak members were not rejected but encouraged, prodded, and helped along until they could stand alone. On the other hand, this very feature of the Chicago attitude may be a clue to the vein of melancholy that runs beneath the blithe music of these men. They were a kind of adolescent gang, and some of them never grew up. There is, after all, something fundamentally sad about an adolescent who is pushing 60. As the swing era, during which each of the Chicagoans reached the apex of his creative powers, came to a close, members of the old gang either withdrew from the competitive arena or huddled together for protection again—this time against the shift to modern jazz. Goodman, Krupa, and Freeman explored the new music but failed to become part of it. Only Tough could have done that, and he drank himself into the grave without finishing the job.

So the music of the Chicagoans came and went. Their records tell us how good it was—while it lasted.

Recommended Reading

Anderson, Ernest (ed.): *Esquire's 1947 Jazz Book,* Smith & Durrell, New York (1947).

Condon, Albert Edwin, and Thomas Sugrue: *We Called It Music,* Holt, New York (1947).

Condon, Albert Edwin, and Richard Gehman: *Eddie Condon's Treasury of Jazz,* Dial, New York (1956).

De Toledano, Ralph (ed.): *Frontiers of Jazz,* Durrell, New York (1947).

Feather, Leonard: *The Encyclopedia of Jazz,* Horizon, New York (1960).

Goodman, Benny, and Irving Kolodin: *The Kingdom of Swing,* Stackpole, Harrisburg, Pa. (1939).

Mannone, Wingy, and Paul Vandervoort: *Trumpet on the Wing,* Doubleday, New York (1948).

Mezzrow, Milton, and Bernard Wolfe: *Really the Blues,* Random House, New York (1946).

Miller, Paul Eduard (ed.): *Esquire's 1946 Jazz Book,* Barnes, New York (1946).

Ramsey, Frederic, and Charles Edward Smith: *Jazzmen,* Harcourt, Brace, New York (1939).

Shapiro, Nat, and Nat Hentoff (eds.): *Hear Me Talkin' to Ya,* Rinehart, New York (1955).

Shapiro, Nat, and Nat Hentoff (eds.): *The Jazz Makers,* Grove, New York (1958).

Recommended Listening

Chicago Style Jazz, COLUMBIA CL 632
Chicago Jazz Album, DECCA 8029.
Chicago Jazz, RIVERSIDE 12-107.
Jam Sessions at Commodore, COMMODORE FL 30,006.
Gems of Jazz, Vol. 5, DECCA 8043.
Jazz, Vol. 6, FOLKWAYS FP 65.
Jazz, Vol. 7, FOLKWAYS FP 67.
Jazz, Vol. 9, FOLKWAYS FP 71.
Great Jazz Reeds, CAMDEN 339.
A String of Swingin' Pearls, RCA VICTOR LPM 1373.
The Art of Jazz Piano, EPIC 3295.
Jess Stacy and Others: Chairmen of the Board, MAINSTREAM 56008.
Jess Stacy: Piano Solos, BRUNSWICK 54017.
Joe Sullivan: New Solos by an Old Master, RIVERSIDE 158.
Benny Goodman, 1927–1934, BRUNSWICK 54010.
The Vintage Goodman, COLUMBIA CL 821.
Benny Goodman: Carnegie Hall Concert, COLUMBIA OSL 160.
Portrait of Pee Wee, COUNTERPOINT CPST 562 (stereo).
Pee Wee Russell Plays, DOT DLP 3253.
Swingin' with Pee Wee, PRESTIGE-SWINGVILLE 2008.
Pee Wee Russell and Coleman Hawkins, CANDID 8020.
Pee Wee Russell: A Legend, MAINSTREAM 56026.
Pee Wee Russell: New Groove, COLUMBIA CL-1985.
Bud Freeman: Wolverine Jazz, DECCA DL 5213.
Bud Freeman and His All-Star Jazz, HARMONY HL 7046.
Bud Freeman and His Summa Cum Laude Trio, DOT DLP 3166.
The Bud Freeman All-Stars, PRESTIGE-SWINGVILLE 2012.
Bud Freeman: Something Tender, UNITED ARTISTS 14033.
Swingin' with Krupa, CAMDEN 340.
Eddie Condon: Ivy League Jazz, DECCA 8282.
Eddie Condon: A Legend, MAINSTREAM 56024.
Max Kaminsky and His Jazz Band, COMMODORE FL 30,013.
Wild Bill Davison: Mild and Wild, COMMODORE FL 30,009.
The Hackett Horn, EPIC 3106.
Muggsy Spanier: The Great 16!, RCA VICTOR LPM 1295.
Dixieland–New Orleans, MAINSTREAM 56003.
Chicago and All That Jazz, VERVE V-8441.
The Sound of Chicago, COLUMBIA C3L-32.

FATS WALLER AND
JAMES P. JOHNSON

WHILE THE REST of the country was just beginning to develop its regional attitudes toward and approaches to jazz during and after World War I, New York pianists were putting the finishing touches on a complex and valid jazz language all their own. Keyboard artists like Luckey Roberts, Richard "Abba Labba" McLean, and Bob Hawkins had already built a buoyant "shout" style by adding blues melodies and country dance rhythms to an urbane ragtime bass. New York was the final proving ground for the best pianists, and top players from other music centers—Eubie Blake of Baltimore was one—sooner or later settled there. Most of these men were also composers, and New York, the hub of America's music-publishing industry, attracted them for that reason as well. It was a hotly competitive arena that made no room for musical weaklings.

To understand how Thomas "Fats" Waller fit into this picture, it is necessary to turn first to the man who had much to do with the formation of Waller's approach to playing jazz piano—James P. Johnson. Johnson had arrived in New York in 1908 as a fledgling pianist of 14 with a wide variety of musical tastes. In New Jersey, he had heard country set or square dances, church hymns, marches, stomps, blues, popular tunes, folk songs, and barrelhouse ballads. Once in the big city, James also absorbed the sounds of classic rags performed by front-rank players and the individual creations of New York's best party pianists. He also listened attentively to symphonic concert music, superior cabaret show music, and grand opera. He heard, too, New Orleans pianist Jelly Roll Morton, who played at Barron Wilkins' in Harlem about 1911. All these sounds went into Johnson's music.

By 1912, when he was 18, James was good enough to play professionally in bars and movie houses as well as for parties, where the fees were usually paid in food and drink. He played popular songs, showpieces like *The Dream* (alternately credited to New

York pianists Jack "The Bear" and Jess Pickett and later recorded
by Waller as *The Digah's Stomp*), Scott Joplin's *Maple Leaf Rag*,
hits from current musicals, and some numbers of his own. Johnson
aimed at becoming a first-class "tickler," and he was rapidly
acquiring impressive credentials, even by New York standards.
However, unlike some classical-minded ragtimers of the period,
James did not turn away from folk blues material and dance
music. In a series of remarkable interviews with writer Tom
Davin many years later (published by *The Jazz Review* in 1959),
Johnson described one of his regular jobs around 1913:

> The people who came to The Jungles Casino were mostly from
> around Charleston, South Carolina, and other places in the South.
> Most of them worked for the Ward Line as longshoremen or on
> ships that called at southern coast ports. There were even some
> Gullahs among them.
>
> They picked their partners with care to show off their best steps
> and put sets, cotillions and cakewalks that would give them a
> chance to get off.
>
> The Charleston, which became a popular dance step on its own,
> was just a regulation cotillion step without a name. It had many
> variations—all danced to the rhythm that everybody knows now.
> One regular at the Casino, named Dan White, was the best dancer
> in the crowd and he introduced the Charleston step as we know it.
> But there were dozens of other steps used, too.
>
> It was while playing for these southern dancers that I composed
> a number of Charlestons—eight in all—all with the same rhythm.
> One of these later became my famous *Charleston* when it hit Broad-
> way.
>
> My *Carolina Shout* was another type of ragtime arrangement of
> a set dance of this period. In fact, a lot of famous jazz compositions
> grew out of cotillion music—such as *The Wildcat Blues*. Jelly Roll
> Morton told me that his *King Porter Stomp* and *High Society* were
> taken from cotillion music.
>
> The dances they did at The Jungles Casino were wild and
> comical—the more pose and the more breaks, the better. These
> Charleston people and the other southerners had just come to New
> York. They were country people and they felt homesick. When they
> got tired of two-steps and schottisches (which they danced with a
> lot of spieling), they'd yell: "Let's go back home!" . . . "Let's do
> a set!" . . . or "Now, put us in the alley!" I did my *Mule Walk* or
> *Gut Stomp* for these country dances.

Breakdown music was the best for such sets, the more solid and groovy the better. They'd dance, hollering and screaming until they were cooked. The dances ran from fifteen to thirty minutes, but they kept up all night long or until their shoes wore out—most of them after a heavy day's work on the docks.

By 1916, Johnson had taken his place alongside the most accomplished jazz and ragtime pianists in the city. His own later account of his playing at about that time reveals many of the elements that went into young Tom Waller's style shortly after:

I was starting to develop a good technique. I was born with absolute pitch and could catch a key that a player was using and copy it, even Luckey's. I played rags very accurately and brilliantly—running chromatic octaves and glissandos up and down with both hands. It made a terrific effect.

I did double glissandos straight and backhand, glissandos in sixths and double tremolos. These would run other ticklers out of the place at cutting sessions. They wouldn't play after me. I would put these tricks in on the breaks and I could think of a trick a minute. I was playing a lot of piano then, traveling around and listening to every good player I could. I'd steal their breaks and style and practice them until I had them perfect.

From listening to classical piano records and concerts, from friends of Ernest Green such as Mme. Garret, who was a fine classical pianist, I would learn concert effects and build them into blues and rags.

Sometimes I would play basses a little lighter than the melody and change harmonies. When playing a heavy stomp, I'd soften it right down—then, I'd make an abrupt change like I heard Beethoven do in a sonata.

Some people thought it was cheap, but it was effective and dramatic. With a solid bass like a metronome, I'd use chords with half and quarter changes. Once I used Liszt's *Rigoletto Concert Paraphrase* as an introduction to a stomp. Another time, I'd use pianissimo effects in the groove and let the dancers' feet be heard scraping on the floor.

During this period, James learned and borrowed from every pianist he admired—Eubie Blake, Willie "The Lion" Smith, Sam Gordon ("a great technician who played an arabesque style that Art Tatum made famous later"), Fred Bryant (". . . he invented the backward tenth. I used it and passed it on to Fats Waller

later. It was the keynote of our style"), Fats Harris ("who looked
like Waller did later"), and many others.

By 1917, the 23-year-old pianist was something of a local celebrity. He married and settled into a reasonably prosperous life of
café jobs, songwriting, making piano rolls, Broadway stage work,
vaudeville tours on the TOBA (Theater Owners' Booking
Agency) circuit, and, eventually, coaching promising youngsters
like Thomas Wright Waller.

Waller was only 13 in 1917, but he already had seven or eight
years of keyboard training and experience behind him. His father,
who was working his way up to becoming pastor of Harlem's
Abyssinian Baptist Church, approved of Tom's interest in organ
literature and the classics but took a dim view of ragtime. He tried
the boy at the church organ and even at a folding organ in street
sermons but was unable to stop him from "ragging" his hymns,
although Tom had written a hymn of his own called *Everything
That's Not of Jesus Shall Go Down*. Waller's mother, however, a
pianist and organist herself, encouraged her son's interest in
music, ragtime or no ragtime. In 1915, his father took him to hear
pianist Ignace Paderewski at Carnegie Hall. The boy was deeply
impressed and renewed his efforts to improve his own piano playing. He studied technique and composition while continuing to
play and perform (he was a natural entertainer) at school or anyplace that had a keyboard instrument. By 1918, when he was 14,
Waller quit school and worked at odd jobs outside of music while
waiting for something to turn up.

Tom was lucky. He had been spending much of his time at the
Lincoln Theater, where an organist and a small group led by a
pianist were hired to play during film showings. Because he was
allowed to sit in regularly and to become familiar with the requirements of movie work, the young musician was prepared to
step into either keyboard job as soon as a vacancy occurred. At 15,
Waller became the official organist for the Lincoln Theater. From
that time on, the best New York ticklers, including James P. Johnson, began to notice him.

Harlem was growing fast as a center of musical activities just
after the war. Pianists found work in dozens of small cellars and
clubs from 125th Street to 140th Street. James P. Johnson has told
of pianists gathering at a place called The Rock for cheerful cut-

ting sessions. Willie "The Lion" Smith and others engaged in piano battles at Leroy's. From 1920 on, Waller was a member of the inner circle of pianists who gathered and worked in these places. His experience at the organ had, however, left him with a weak left hand. As Johnson was the reigning tickler at the time, Fats (who had by now eaten his way into the nickname) went to him for help.

"Fats would bang on our piano till all hours of the night," Johnson's wife has recalled. "Sometimes to two, three, four o'clock in the morning. I would say to him, 'Now, go on home,' or 'Haven't you got a home?' But he'd come every day, and my husband would teach."

Many pianists had learned indirectly from Johnson by way of his piano rolls, but Waller, a native New Yorker, had the advantage of private tutelage and the prerogative of playing alongside James in public places and private sessions. He carried the Johnson imprint on his music for the rest of his life.

In 1920, Tom's mother died, leaving her devoted son disconsolate for many months. He plunged into an unwise marriage that broke up after a short time and eventually caused him endless trouble over alimony payments. His second marriage, to Anita Rutherford, turned out well and lasted until Waller's death in 1943. Though still in his teens, Fats had become a favorite entertainer and performer around Harlem by the early twenties. His natural broad humor and easy disposition delighted even those observers who couldn't appreciate the quality of his music. Fats's ability to amuse people finally became his most valuable commercial asset; without it, he might have ended a "musician's musician" (usually a synonym for an unrecognized musician), as did his friend and teacher James P. Johnson.

Fats worked at Leroy's for a while and then went on the road with vaudeville shows for a couple of seasons. On one rainy night in Boston (clarinetist Garvin Bushell, who was with Waller at the time, believes it was New Year's night in 1923), the pianist tried out some variations on an old song called *Boy in the Boat* and named the results *Squeeze Me*. With words added by Spencer Williams, it became the first of many successful songs for Fats. His gift for turning out tunes by the dozen was Waller's second most valuable commercial asset, although he often sold compositions outright for only a few dollars. His take from songs like *Ain't Misbehavin', Honeysuckle Rose, Keepin' Out of Mischief Now, Blue Turning Gray Over You,* and *I'm Crazy 'Bout My Baby* helped cover the alimony payments. They also obscured the image of Waller the organist and pianist. Not that Fats objected to his songwriting role; indeed, he frequently expressed the desire to spend more time composing. In jazz terms, however, it is Waller as a keyboard improviser who commands attention.

Because he had a special affection for the organ, Fats returned to his Lincoln Theater job as often as possible. He learned how to play the blues on the giant instrument, for the Lincoln crowd wanted the old familiar material rather than the modern Tin Pan Alley songs. Sophisticated musicians called the theater the "Temple of Ignorance," but its emphasis on earthiness was probably good for Waller, who lacked James P. Johnson's early contacts with folk blues. One of his staunchest admirers at the theater was Bill Basie, a young pianist just Fats's age who yearned to learn more about the pipe organ. (Basie remains fond of the organ today and plays one whenever the opportunity arises.) After coming off the road with Liza and Her Shufflin' Six ("Liza" was Katie Crippen) one season, Waller sent his friend Basie out as a replacement. It was Count's first tour.

The Lincoln was sold about 1923, and Fats moved to the Lafayette, again in charge of the organ. His rhythmic digressions, sometimes far from the spirit of what was showing on the screen, were generally enjoyed by Harlem audiences, and no one seemed to mind his including his own compositions, such as *Squeeze Me* and *Wild Cat Blues*. It was in 1923, too, that Fats made his first radio broadcast, from the Fox Terminal Theater in Newark, New Jersey.

James P. Johnson, who had been cutting piano rolls for some six years by 1922, recommended Fats to the QRS company. Johnson's good word resulted in new prestige and more than $2,000 for Waller, who made eighteen or nineteen rolls at $100 each and lent his name to still others performed by J. Laurence Cook. Some of these rolls have been transferred to records in recent years, allowing historians to better evaluate Waller's development in the early twenties. To give further perspective, there was also a series of record dates in late 1922, when Fats was 18.

Of the recorded solos, one, *Muscle Shoals Blues,* is of special interest on several counts. It was Fats's first record, and the form is a blues (Waller recorded relatively few blues); also, a piano roll of the same selection by James P. Johnson, cut earlier that year, provides an interesting point of contrast to the recorded version. The song itself is not unusual (apparently patterned after Handy's *Memphis Blues*), but there is ample evidence in Fats's performance that he was a skilled young pianist, if still well below Johnson's level. A striking deficiency in the solo is its lack of rhythmic thrust or even jazzlike syncopation. It is a rather formal performance, not at all in the warm blues idiom that characterized the work of Southern jazz instrumentalists at the time. Johnson's piano-roll rendition of the tune is no closer to a true blues feeling, but this may be due in part to the absence of nuance usually encountered in mechanical rolls. Despite the similarity of styles and faults, Waller's recording and Johnson's roll differ in a fundamental way. Fats had already begun to use single-note treble lines against his conventional bass figures; Johnson was still tied to the use-all-ten-fingers philosophy of the ragtimers. Of the two approaches, Johnson's was the more impressive pianistically, but Waller's held more promise of new ideas to come.

There were more recorded performances in 1922—*Birmingham Blues, 'Tain't Nobody's Bizness If I Do,* and several others with blues singer Sara Martin. Although they show Waller to be a confident pianist with an awareness of the blues, most of these records did not provide opportunities for him to demonstrate the entire range of his skills at that time.

The piano rolls were something else again. Though limited by the mechanical medium, Fats was allowed more latitude to advance pianistic ideas for their own sake. The pyrotechnical outburst in *Your Time Now,* the complex set of variations in triplets in *'Tain't Nobody's Bizness* (a much better version than the recording, by the way), the smooth trills and clean double-time devices in *Mama's Got the Blues,* the harmonically full sound of *Last Man Blues,* the intimations of a perfectly smooth 4/4 rhythmic foundation in *Snake Hips*—all these things that had begun to make up the Waller-out-of-Johnson style can be heard on Fats's 1923 piano rolls. One roll, Johnson's tune *If I Could Be with You One Hour Tonight,* features both Fats and James in a duet performance. Johnson was still the better player, but Fats was beginning to exhibit the more cheerful rhythmic outlook later identified with him and, indeed, seemed slightly more of the jazz world than his teacher—or, to put it another way, Waller seemed less the ragtimer of the two.

With records and piano rolls spreading his name, Fats became a key figure in the Harlem jazz scene. Other musicians began to record his compositions, especially Clarence Williams, who had a publisher's interest in such material. Arranger Don Redman became a close friend, as did Fletcher Henderson, whose band was beginning to gain national recognition. Despite the intensity of Harlem's keyboard cutting contests, New York pianists helped each other along. Williams, Johnson, Waller, Eubie Blake, Henderson, Duke Ellington (who arrived in New York in the twenties partly as a result of Fats's urgings), Stephen "The Beetle" Henderson, Willie "The Lion" Smith, and even George Gershwin, though all of them were busy with composing, publishing, recording, touring, writing for shows, or just playing better piano than the next man, helped promote one another's songs and spoke up for those who tended to be overlooked. Johnson and Blake not only were top pianists, but also scored songs for successful shows like *Dudley's Smart Set, Shuffle Along, Runnin' Wild,* and *Plantation Days* (which toured Europe with James as musical director), and their accomplishments served as goals for younger pianist-composers, particularly Fats Waller.

Fats wrote more songs than ever in 1924. He collaborated with publisher Clarence Williams on a number of ordinary ditties designed to make a quick dollar. This partnership is documented on an obscure recording by the Jamaican Jazzers, for which Williams performed outrageously on a kazoo and Waller contributed a pleasant mixture of rippling swing and lukewarm blues.

In 1925, when Fats was 21, there were still more record dates (mostly with mediocre singers), piano rolls, and new songs (even a waltz, called *The Heart That Once Belonged to Me*). Waller's studies with Carl Bohm at Julliard and his other contacts with modern formal composition may have affected his playing as well as his writing by this time. His lessons with Leopold Godowsky, too, left their mark. It was while working a Chicago theater job (probably on organ) in 1925 that Fats concentrated on Bach

under Godowsky. They went through the toccatas and the two-
and three-part inventions together. Fats referred to this period in
an interview for *Metronome* magazine ten years later, when he
was asked about modern (1935) pianists: "Formerly the right
hand was given all the work and the other left to shift for itself,
thumping out a plain octave or common chord foundation. There
was no attempt at figuration. But that is all in the past. Now it's
more evenly divided and the left has to know its stuff, its chords
and its figuration, just as well as the right. I consider the thorough
bass foundation I got in the study of Bach the best part of my
training."

Apparently, when Fats used the word "training," he meant
training for playing jazz. For all his interest in classical literature,
he regarded himself quite seriously as a jazz musician, and that
by itself sets Waller apart from the many jazzmen who scorned
their own music in the twenties. And Waller *used* European
music in jazz terms rather than dressing up his improvisations
with superficial classical effects. "Whenever you get stuck for a
two-bar harmonic device," Fats explained, "you can always go
back to Liszt or Chopin. Even so, it's all in knowing what to put
on the right beat."

Even in Waller's 1925 accompaniment records, the use of full
tenths in the left hand lent a distinctly "modern" sound to the
piano parts. Tenths were not a new idea, but Johnson himself
could not handle them with Waller's aplomb. Fats had enormous
hands (blind pianist George Shearing once described the experience of shaking hands with Waller as "like grabbing a bunch of
bananas"), and tenths were for him what octaves were to the ordinary piano player. He frequently exercised his left hand, in fact,
by running up and down the keyboard in tenths.

Fats wrote some numbers for Fletcher Henderson in 1926, and
the by now celebrated leader asked Waller to sit in on a couple of
recording sessions. One of these dates included *The Chant* (a Mel
Stitzel tune), Fats's first pipe-organ recording. More impressive,
however, are the piano solos and ensemble parts in *The Henderson Stomp* and *Whiteman Stomp*, both Waller compositions with
Redman arrangements. Fats seems to stimulate the entire band
with his enthusiasm and rhythmic propulsion; his solo ideas here
are more absorbing and individualistically mature than before.

Whiteman Stomp must have been a particularly challenging piece for pianist and orchestra alike, but Waller sails through it easily. Most important of all, rhythmically Fats was now really swinging. Waller's exposure to Louis Armstrong in 1925, both in New York and in Chicago, may have accounted for some of the improvement in this area over his 1922 recordings, but much of it was undoubtedly due to the musical maturation of Waller and of jazz generally during the early twenties.

Beginning in late 1926, Victor launched a series of recordings of Fats at the pipe organ, his favorite instrument. It was a remarkable undertaking for the conservative Victor company, for no one had ever recorded real jazz on the great instrument before. As it turned out, these are some of the finest recordings of Waller's career. His ability to swing on several keyboards and a set of foot pedals while creatively manipulating the various stops and controls has never been surpassed. At jazz organ, Fats Waller was supreme. Moreover, he was deeply serious (but not without humor!) whenever seated at the organ, and his 1926–1927 solos are refreshingly free of the entertaining but superficial distractions that mar many of Waller's later recordings.

After an initial fling at *St. Louis Blues,* Fats (he was still billed as Thomas on record labels) settled into a series of superb originals. *Lenox Avenue Blues* is a fine light piece in which Waller demonstrates his remarkable control of dynamics; *Soothin' Syrup Stomp, Stompin' the Bug,* and *Hog Maw Stomp* are extraordinary sets of variations in the Harlem piano tradition; *The Rusty Pail* is a superior jazz performance by any measure and a definitive essay on the jazz potential of the pipe organ. In short, Waller created a new body of instrumental music within the jazz language that has stood untarnished for more than three decades. Fats's organ work was, as anyone who follows the witless fancies of the listening public might expect, both the least commercial and the most profound of his many musical assets.

What made these organ solos so special was Waller's intimate knowledge of the capabilities of the instrument as a unique mode of jazz expression rather than merely as a piano with extra attachments. The musical style was identifiably Waller's, but his techniques were not the same as those he used at the piano. Fats never succumbed, either, to the temptation to overdramatize his music with trite organ voicings or unnecessary flamboyance. He was especially skilled at drawing the lightest, daintiest sounds from the awesome instrument, always avoiding the obvious and rejecting the sentimental.

The next batch of organ records seems to have been an experiment by Victor. Each of three selections (*Sugar, Beale Street Blues,* and *I'm Goin' to See My Ma*) was recorded twice, first as an instrumental solo, then as a vocal (Alberta Hunter) with organ accompaniment. The solos are excellent, but the vocals probably sold more records, for Victor chose to issue very few pipe-organ solos by Waller after that. Among those pieces recorded by Fats but never issued are two Bach fugues and some light classical material, which the organist played first in a straightforward manner and then as jazz.

The Harlem piano sessions continued throughout the twenties, sometimes at so-called parlor socials (rent parties), other times at favorite clubs and meeting places, such as the Clef Club or the Rhythm Club. The old ticklers, though still highly respected, were gradually being replaced now by young jazzmen like Waller and, out in Chicago, Earl Hines. Johnson and Willie Smith were able to keep up with the shift in rhythm and phrasing, but many of the older men remained rooted in ragtime. Of the new crop of pianists in New York, Waller was the most impressive. His wide-ranging left hand had become, by 1927, a model of metrical accuracy and buoyant swing combined with harmonic daring and tremendous rhythmic power. His right usually delineated delicate but authoritative melodic variations built on rhythmic patterns similar to those used by horn players of the day. Many jazzmen preferred Waller's piano to, say, Willie Smith's because Fats worked better as a member of a jazz band, while Smith seemed to be playing bravura exercises for his own amazement.

Fats stopped touring for a while in 1926 and 1927 to concentrate on developing his contacts in New York more fully. He took on a manager, made downtown appearances in places like the Kentucky Club, and set to work on the music for a new show, to be called *Keep Shufflin'*. He turned out tunes faster than his friends could use them, but Clarence Williams published many, such as *Long, Deep, and Wide, Midnight Stomp,* and *Old Folks Shuffle.* With Thomas Morris, he recorded *Please Take Me Out of*

Jail (a title said to refer to further alimony difficulties in Waller's life) and *Fats Waller Stomp* in a pseudo-New Orleans style. Fletcher Henderson recorded *St. Louis Shuffle* and *Variety Stomp*, which Fats sold to him for $10 apiece.

Waller worked with lyricist Andy Razaf on *Keep Shufflin'*. Fats and James P. Johnson were both hired to play in the pit as well as to compose music for the show. Although the most popular songs from the show were *How Jazz Was Born* and *My Little Chocolate Bar*, the only Razaf-Waller tune of that score to survive the years since is *Willow Tree*. The show opened in 1927 and went on the road in 1928, taking Waller, Johnson, and orchestra with it.

In early 1928, Fats, James, and two more members of the *Keep Shufflin'* orchestra, reedman Garvin Bushell and trumpeter Jabbo Smith, traveled to Camden, New Jersey, to record one of the strangest sessions of all time. The four men went to the huge old church that Victor had taken over for a studio. At one end was Waller at the pipe organ, and at the other were Johnson, Smith, and Bushell, who remembers the distance from himself to Fats as "about a city block." Despite these precautions, the pipe organ all but drowned out Johnson's piano. They recorded four tunes, including James's *'Sippi* and Fats's *Willow Tree*. Aside from Smith's beguiling trumpet and Bushell's unusual effects on bassoon, the center of interest here is the combined sound of Waller and Johnson. James plays cleanly and engagingly but does not show the drive and exuberance that Waller had by this time already demonstrated on both piano and organ. The teacher was losing ground to his star pupil.

The success of *Keep Shufflin'* encouraged Connie and George Immerman, owners of Harlem's Connie's Inn, to underwrite a show of their own for the 1928–1929 season. Fats, Razaf, and Harry Brooks were to handle the scores. Brooks, who helped on both music and lyrics and is a good pianist himself, remembers how he and his partners put together their hit song for *Connie's Hot Chocolates*—*Ain't Misbehavin'*. "It was an attempt to copy the successful formula Gershwin used for *The Man I Love*," declared Brooks. "We imitated the opening phrase that began just after the first beat and the minor part of the bridge, too."

Ain't Misbehavin' became so popular that it swept its composers—and Louis Armstrong, one of the stars of the show—

into the top echelon of American show business personalities. Less noticed perhaps, but equally attractive was *Black and Blue*, the revue's second hit. (Razaf helped Eubie Blake steal phrases from *Black and Blue* for *Memories of You* a year later, which must be some kind of private system of poetic justice.) Fats now had his hands full—writing songs for nightclub floor shows, tossing off originals for friends like Fletcher Henderson or Don Redman, and preparing for another show, to be called *Load of Coal*. He also recorded some superb piano solos in 1929.

Handful of Keys and *Numb Fumblin'* represented a new level of attainment for Waller the pianist, at least on records. Both were waxed casually by Fats, along with a pair of loose band performances, after a long night of serious drinking and a morning of hasty mental sketching of material for the date. From all reports, it was a typical Fats Waller recording session, complete with bottles, last-minute decisions, and gratifying musical results. *Numb Fumblin'* is a splendid blues piece, full of crisp trills, thick harmonies resembling the sound of an entire orchestra, long thirty-second-note runs in the best tradition of Harlem bravura playing, and flawless articulation. *Handful of Keys* is a scintillating "shout" in the James P. Johnson manner, far from profound but a rhythmic delight. The band sides, *The Minor Drag* and *Harlem Fuss,* are marked by Waller's characteristic disregard for ensemble precision but are rescued by a rhythmic ebullience generated almost entirely by Fats himself. (The only other rhythm man, banjoist Eddie Condon, didn't bother anyone.) Other piano solos followed a few months later. *Ain't Misbehavin'* and *Sweet Savannah Sue,* from *Hot Chocolates,* are, oddly, rather uneventful performances. *I've Got a Feeling I'm Falling,* one of Waller's finest songs, seems more an exposition of the tune than a true piano solo. *Love Me or Leave Me, Gladyse,* and *Valentine Stomp* are more interesting, with Fats transfiguring ragtime ideas by the use of current Har-lem "stride" effects and lots of full-bodied chords.

Several solos recorded a few weeks later, in late August, 1929, seemed to wipe out the last vestiges of the old, stilted Eastern phrasing, which Fats had been gradually eliminating over the years. (The jagged staccato phrase, New York style, can still be heard in some older Eastern jazzmen today: Jimmy Archey, Henry Goodwin, the deParis brothers, Hank Duncan, and Garvin

Bushell are examples.) *Goin' About* and *My Feelin's Are Hurt* brought out Waller's own musical personality, by now quite obviously different from James P. Johnson's, more than any of his previous piano recordings.

1929 was a good year for Fats, notwithstanding the Wall Street disaster that fall. His songs were bringing him fame, if less than an equitable share of the publisher's profits, for Waller still had the unfortunate habit of taking the short-term view and selling many of his compositions outright for absurdly small sums. *Load of Coal* became another *Hot Chocolates* revue, and the new Waller-Razaf pieces included *Honeysuckle Rose, Zonky,* and *My Fate Is in Your Hands.* At one point, Fats was featured at Connie's playing a huge white organ. The effect must have been similar to that described by the late Tom Fletcher in *100 Years of the Negro in Show Business:* "One of the greatest performances he [Waller] ever gave was the night in the latter part of the 1920's at Carnegie Hall when he was on a late spot on the bill. When he was introduced some of the audience had started to leave, but when he began playing that immense organ everybody who had started out rushed back to seats and the applause was so tremendous that he was compelled to give many encores." Fletcher probably was referring to one of the Clef Club Carnegie concerts that had been given since at least as early as 1919.

From 1929 to 1932, Fats was one of the most sought-after pianists for recordings and private jam sessions in New York. The Chicagoans (Joe Sullivan, Eddie Condon, Bud Freeman *et al.*) had found him to be just their kind of musician—always swinging right on the beat, iconoclastic, talented, hard-drinking, whimsical, and basically dead serious about jazz. Jack Teagarden, Coleman Hawkins, and others also spent as much time with Waller as possible, for his good nature and musical creativity always seemed to rub off on those around him. Joe Sullivan, who was deeply influenced by Waller's musical outlook at this time, smilingly recalls the gregarious pianist:

> "When Fats had just sold a tune, he would call me and shout, 'Mother! Come on down, I just made a strike!' and this meant the drinks were on him. Still, he was completely serious when it came to playing—particularly when in a cutting contest with someone like The Lion.

"There were several sides of Fats that most people didn't know about. I heard him play background music for a stag movie once, and he did some things that even Hines and Tatum couldn't cut—at least on *that* night! Some nights he and I would go to a Harlem theater after hours—the cleaning ladies all knew him—and Fats would play the organ until six or seven in the morning. He liked to play original compositions and serious classical things. It was beautiful music."

Mezz Mezzrow, who was usually on hand because he supplied Fats and other jazzmen with marijuana, tells in *Really the Blues* of one of the piano contests he attended about the same time:

Fats was a wonderful guy, one of the most jovial persons I have ever met, always bubbling with jokes so it was impossible to feel brought down in his company. He stood about six foot tall and weighed well over two hundred pounds and his feet, that were a stylish size fifteen, he referred to as his "pedal extremities." . . . He'd sit at the piano all night long, and sometimes part of the next day, without even getting up to see that man about that canine. We'd set up quart after quart of bathtub gin for him—one on top of the piano, so when he was playing treble he could reach up with his left hand, and another at his foot, so while he beat out the bass he could reach down and grab the jug with his right hand. . . . Well, this morning out came several quarts of liquor, and it was on.

Corky [Williams] sat down and started to play *Tea for Two*, a number that Willie The Lion could give a fit. All of a sudden Willie jumped up and said to Corky, "Git up from there you no-piano-playin' son of a bitch, I got it," and with that he sat down next to Corky. As Corky slid over, Willie started to play just the treble, while Corky still kept up the bass, and then he picked up with his left hand too, the tempo not even wavering and without missing a beat. Willie played for a while and then Fats took over, sliding into the seat the same way Willie had done. He played for a while, looking up at Willie and signifying every time he made a new or tricky passage. It went on like that, the music more and more frantic, that piano not resting for even a fraction of a second, until finally Fats said "I'm goin' to settle this argument good." He went into a huddle with his chauffeur, who left and returned about an hour later, but not alone. Fats had telephoned to Jamaica, Long Island, and woke up James P. Johnson out of his bed. When the chauffeur brought Jimmy in he was still rubbing his eyes, but as soon as he sat down at the piano that was all. He played so much piano you didn't have to yell, "Put out all the lights and call the law," because the law came up by request of the neighbors. "We been sittin' downstairs enjoying this music," the cops told us, "when we got a call from the station house to see who was disturbing the peace around here. Some people ain't got no appreciation for music at all. Fats, just close them windows and pour us a drink, and take up where you left off." So for the rest of the morning the contest went on, with these two coppers lolling around drinking our liquor and listening to our fine music. It was great.

During this period, Fats recorded with members of Fletcher Henderson's band (called the Little Chocolate Dandies), McKinney's Cotton Pickers, popular singer Gene Austin, James P. Johnson (King Oliver was on the same date), Jack Teagarden, Ted Lewis, and Billy Banks. In each case, his all-pervading *élan* and authoritative sense of time seemed to lift the other performers' spirits and playing levels. It was virtually impossible to avoid swinging with Waller in the band.

There were also some band recordings featuring Fats and some of his friends ("Fats Waller and His Buddies" is the way Victor billed them). These are rather commercial affairs, but jazzmen like Red Allen, J. C. Higginbotham, Jack Teagarden, Gene Krupa, Albert Nicholas, and Pops Foster can be heard on them. Waller, as usual, buoys up the whole band and drives the soloists.

Waller cut his first recorded vocals in 1931 with, enigmatically, Ted Lewis. His facetious, whining shout is prominently featured on *Dallas Blues, Royal Garden Blues,* and his own *I'm Crazy 'Bout My Baby,* setting the pattern for hundreds of vocal performances—from mock tender to coarsely inane—in the succeeding twelve years. A few days after the Ted Lewis affair, Fats made his own Columbia vocal record (Victor apparently lost interest in Waller around 1930, a nasty year for the record industry), *I'm Crazy 'Bout My Baby* and *Draggin' My Heart Around.* With these recordings, the die was cast; Thomas Waller, organist and pianist extraordinary, was destined to play a subordinate role to Fats Waller, entertainer and buffoon. Yet by way of his easy humor, Fats brought jazz to many people who might otherwise have turned away from it. At least one critic, Hugues Panassié of France, has suggested that Waller's extramusical antics were simply part of his total musical personality and to be accepted in the spirit of fun that pervaded much of his playing. "Here was one of those rare people whom one could not misunderstand without misunderstanding the music of jazz itself," declares Panassié in *Douze Années de Jazz.*

Joe Sullivan takes a different view: "Many musicians didn't understand Fats's artistry. They thought he was just a good-time Charlie, but he was much more. Fats was such a sweet guy, he tried never to let anybody down—his publishers, his friends, and his public—although he was often dragged by all of them. The piano meant as much to him as it does to me."

Waller, like many jazzmen, found radio one of the few prosperous media left for entertainers during the Depression. His boisterous singing and lilting playing were perfect for radio, and he worked several shows between 1930 and 1934, including his popular "Fats Waller's Rhythm Club." In 1932, he and songwriter Spencer Williams spent a short time in Paris, where Fats enjoyed the wine as well as the affection of French musicians and fans. It is said that Williams and Waller ground out dozens of songs in a few days to make enough money for their steamship fare to Europe. Williams, who had been in Europe before, stayed on, but Fats quickly returned to New York and to his radio work. There was a successful network stint at WLW in Cincinnati, and later, through a discussion with CBS Radio's William Paley at a George Gershwin party, Fats took his "Rhythm Club" program to WABC in New York. Waller's career was on the upswing again.

The radio-show package even went on the road for a while, appearing in theaters. Big offers, including one from Paul Whiteman, came Waller's way now, but Fats had a new manager, a string of invitations to make guest radio appearances, and, best of all, a new contract with Victor Records. It was 1934, and he had visited the recording studios only three times—once with Jack Teagarden, again with Billy Banks, and for a single side with the Blue Rhythm Band—since his vocal performances for Columbia in 1931. (There has been some speculation that Waller may have spent part of those three years in jail, for he was still inclined to neglect his alimony payments.)

The first Victor session was characteristically Waller-like and pretty much like the rest of Fats's prodigious output for the same company over the next eight years. A few names within the group changed now and then, but the basic formula—a loose six-piece band jamming around Waller's tongue-in-cheek vocals—remained unchanged. It was almost as if Fats had picked up where *The Minor Drag* and *Harlem Fuss* had left off back in 1929. It was typical of Waller, too, to begin his first session in 1934 with a song written by two of his closest friends, James P. Johnson and Andy Razaf's *A Porter's Love-Song to a Chambermaid*. A few months afterward, he even put Mezz Mezzrow to work on one date—and greater loyalty than that has no man.

Amazingly, of more than four hundred Victor titles recorded for commercial distribution between 1934 and 1942, only fourteen are piano solos. There are, of course, many outstanding examples of Waller's own playing in the Rhythm series, but it is his rare solo performances that provide a more accurate measure of Fats's musical growth.

In November, 1934, the pianist recorded four original compositions, three of which are piano masterpieces. (The fourth, *Alligator Crawl*, is good but not extraordinary.) *Viper's Drag*, a logically constructed showpiece (in three themes, ABCA), sets a high standard of excellence. As written, *Viper's Drag* is a sixteen-bar minor blues followed by a twelve-bar minor blues, a four-bar modulation and a thirty-two-bar major "shout" section that finally returns to the blues pattern again. As he plays, Fats improvises on the structure as well as on the melodic units of the work. Thus his 1934 version moves from the initial sixteen-bar blues to an eight-bar section that forms a bridge to an eight-bar restatement of the opening blues theme. In short, he plays his opening thirty-two-bar minor blues section in a remarkably free manner, fitting four-bar, eight-bar, and sixteen-bar units into whatever order struck his fancy. (On a 1935 version, originally recorded for Muzak, Fats jumps from his first sixteen-bar blues directly to a modulation into the "shout" chorus, leaving out twelve bars of development altogether!)

Clothes Line Ballet is a virtual three-minute suite in a simple ABA form. The B strain, however, is far from the conventional ragtime-march trio, for it is a charming Romberg-like thirty-two-bar melody in F, contrasting with the opening twenty-four-bar theme in A-flat. *Clothes Line Ballet*, as performed by its composer, is a romantic piece, full of delicate pedal work and fascinating harmonies. Fats was highly skilled in the art of the gentle dissonance. He could make a left-hand tenth against a treble ninth sound wholly innocent.

African Ripples is a curious combination of rag and song. It is a good demonstration, too, of how much Waller had learned from Bach, in his unusual figured bass lines and in small details such as his avoidance of parallel fifths (not to be confused with the parallel *quarts* about which Mezzrow wrote). The left-hand work in *African Ripples* is a far cry from the "stride" *oom-pah* bass line many fans associate with Fats Waller.

The second group of piano solos, recorded in June, 1937, was of an entirely different nature. These performances are variations on standard songs—*Star Dust, Tea for Two,* Spencer Williams' *Basin Street Blues* and *I Ain't Got Nobody,* and Fats's own *Keepin' Out of Mischief Now.* The best is *I Ain't Got Nobody* (one of Fats's favorites), which sparkles with wit (rather than comedy), musical thought, whimsicality, and real tenderness. Fats's control of dynamics throughout is exemplary. Close behind is *Basin Street,* ennobled by intelligent understatement and discreet harmonic alterations. *Tea for Two,* a tune popular with jazz pianists from Willie Smith to Thelonious Monk is accorded a common New York treatment—rhapsodic opening followed by an increasingly taut set of variations. *Star Dust* is a trifle florid, perhaps, but well developed and slightly suggestive of Waller's organ style. A principal point of interest in *Keepin' Out of Mischief Now* is Fat's use of an unusually long concluding line, a scalar line not unlike those sometimes used many years later by saxophonist John Coltrane.

There is some evidence to support the notion that Waller did not regard many of his own popular songs very favorably. He was, of course, expected to perform them; but when the choice was his own, he frequently selected superior songs by other writers and only the very best of his own. Panassié was surprised to discover, upon requesting Waller to play *Sweet Savannah Sue* in 1932, that the pianist had completely forgotten it. Fats could write such songs as fast as he could notate, then promptly forget them; he had less trouble remembering his more complex and better pieces, such as *Viper's Drag* and *Clothes Line Ballet.*

Waller recorded a number of interesting solos for Muzak (the company that supplies recorded music to restaurants, etc.) in

1935 that were not issued until some twenty years later. As usual, the solos were dashed off without preparation, but several catch an aspect of Fats seldom preserved on records. *Hallelujah,* for example, is a fast romp in the most advanced jazz language of the time. Here one can glimpse the virtuosity and depth of musicianship only touched upon in Waller's ordinary commercial releases. The same qualities burst through in a later (1939) transcription record for radio use. The solo is built around *Poor Butterfly* in a dazzling rococo manner comparable to that of Art Tatum.

"Fats was really a truly great artist," Gene Sedric, who played saxophone with him on most of the hundreds of Victor titles, has said. "Only his very personal friends knew how much he could play. He could play all styles from modern on down. What is generally called the Waller style is more or less the style he became known by commercially. He had a much wider range than most people realize."

The new Victor small-band series was highly successful commercially, and Fats took to the road again with his piano, "jive" vocals, and a full orchestra directed by bass player Charlie Turner. From Turner's band, Fats selected the men who usually appeared on records with him—Al Casey (guitar), Herman Autry (trumpet), Gene Sedric (tenor saxophone and clarinet), Slick Jones (drums), and Turner himself. Later, Fats traveled with Don Donaldson's orchestra, frequently using trumpeter John Hamilton and bassist Cedric Wallace for his six-piece recording band. All were competent players, and trumpeter Autry a notch better than that, but most of the action came from Waller himself. Without him, it is doubtful that his spirited but wobbly little group would have held together at all.

The Rhythm recordings often glitter with gemlike piano solos, however. *Do Me a Favor, Oooh! Looka There Ain't She Pretty?, I'm Crazy 'Bout My Baby, Fractious Fingering, Honeysuckle Rose, Blue Turning Gray Over You, 'Tain't Nobody's Bizness If I Do* (a third version from 1940), and many others contain first-rate Waller, but the burden is upon the listener to sort them out from dozens of run-of-the-mill variations on pointless transient tunes.

Waller appeared in his first of several films in 1935 and climaxed this side of his career with some winning footage in *Stormy*

Weather, released in 1943. In 1938, he traveled to Britain and Europe, this time as a working musician at a good price. The idea came from Ed Kirkeby, who had recently been assigned by RCA Victor and the National Broadcasting Company to take over Fats's confused business affairs.

"Our first venture together was a flop," recalls Kirkeby. "It was when Fats tried fronting a big band on a Southern tour. I tried looking around for a new territory. Why not Europe? Fats's records had already made him famous there. We asked twenty-five hundred a week for an eight-week tour—big money in those days. But we came to London on those terms and, as you know, opened the Palladium in 1938."

It was in England that Fats must have decided he could use the organ again without jeopardizing his commercial position. He recorded in London on the Compton organ, performing both popular tunes and straight spirituals. On his first recording session back in the States that fall, Fats used the Hammond organ on two titles, *I'll Never Forgive Myself* and *Yacht Club Swing*. (The latter was a reference to the Fifty-second Street saloon where Waller worked for several months.) Though less satisfying than the pipe organ, the electric organ had the advantage of portability, and Fats became one of the Hammond firm's most effective traveling salesmen.

In 1939, Fats's economic position was still not what he and manager Kirkeby wished it to be. The RCA Victor company had shunted the pianist to their cheaper Bluebird label after his return from Europe, and this represented some loss of prestige as well. Again Fats and his manager went abroad, this time to Scandinavia and to England, only weeks before Great Britain went to war.

While in London in 1939, Fats improvised a set of six pieces called *The London Suite*. Each part was made up on the spot as Kirkeby described various sectors of the city—*Piccadilly, Chelsea, Soho, Bond Street, Limehouse,* and *Whitechapel*. Interestingly, only *Piccadilly* is in the Harlem "shout" tradition; the others are essentially reflective, low-key improvisations, superior as spontaneous motifs (the entire suite was completed within a single hour) but not up to what Waller might have done with this idea. The most original of the six is *Chelsea*, a charming, whimsical melody. *London Suite* was the second group of related pieces that Fats had attempted to write. His first, *Harlem Living Room Suite,* was composed in 1935 and consisted of *Functionizin', Corn Whiskey Cocktail,* and *Scrimmage.* Only *Functionizin'* was recorded, and it was issued only in England.

The songs RCA Victor encouraged Fats to record became worse and worse. In 1940, he tackled incredibly insipid pieces like *Eeep, Ipe, Wanna Piece of Pie, Little Curley Hair in a High Chair, My Mommie Sent Me to the Store,* and *Abercrombie Had a Zombie.* Whenever possible, Waller jeered and joshed his way into a bumptious burlesque of popular music, but too often the laughs were empty and the enthusiasm forced. One serious piano solo session in 1941 was all that Fats was allowed, and he made the best of it. Again Waller the artist came forth, demonstrating what he had accomplished since that last session back in 1937. The material consisted of two Hoagy Carmichael songs, *Georgia on My Mind* and *Rockin' Chair,* Duke Ellington's *Ring Dem Bells,* James P. Johnson's *Carolina Shout,* and Waller's *Honeysuckle Rose. Carolina Shout* is a faithful reading in the old Harlem tradition, but the other selections suggest that Fats, at 37, was evolving a sound and timeless piano style, only incidentally of Harlem ancestry, that would take its historical place alongside the finished accomplishments of Earl Hines, Teddy Wilson, Art Tatum, and Thelonious Monk. It was a sensitive and serious style, though laced with wit and fancy, and a logical outgrowth of Waller's own musical experience, from hymns, blues, and stomps to show tunes, ballads, and suites. It was, too, the style of a creative, two-fisted pianist, as much concerned with invention in the left as in the right hand.

If Waller's new contemplative solo style for the piano ever completely crystallized, it was not his good fortune to preserve it on records. That which he did leave behind, of course, was sufficient to assure his status as a major jazz figure, but to this day there hangs over his recorded work the uneasy air of the unfulfilled promise.

Fats maintained his strenuous schedule of touring, entertaining, composing, film assignments, and recording (now earning for him about $70,000 a year) well into 1942. His weight and physical irresponsibility, which had brought dire predictions from his doctors as early as 1940, were rapidly gaining on him, however, and he began to think about disbanding his group and settling into a calmer life of composing and playing as he pleased. In early 1942, he had presented a disastrous concert at Carnegie Hall that may have reminded the pianist how late it really was. Dave Dexter reviewed the affair in *Down Beat:*

> His fingers, throughout most of the concert, were shaky and unsure, and bad notes were too common. Several times, Waller started a melody, elaborated upon it, and then lost the original theme completely. And instead of dishing out such Waller gems as *Numb Fumblin'*, *Alligator Crawl*, *Handful of Keys*, *Black and Blue* and other revered Waller recorded classics, the Carnegie Hall Waller instead chose to mess with Gershwin and, incongruously enough, variations on a Tchaikovsky theme. That was the weakest portion of the entire program . . . his playing was unnatural. It wasn't the Fats Waller of Jazz. . . . His musical artistry was subordinated throughout.

So "unnatural" was Fats's behavior by this time that he even forgot to invite his old friend and teacher, James P. Johnson, to attend what was intended to be a high point in his musical life.

In the spring of 1943, with a musicians' union recording ban halting one aspect of his career, Fats broke up his band and went to work on the score of a new musical, *Early to Bed*. He hadn't lost the ability to throw melodies together easily, as he had shown a few months earlier with *Jitterbug Waltz*. (Waller's son, Maurice, remembers his father writing that one in about ten minutes flat.) However, his new tunes—*Slightly Less Than Wonderful*, *There's a Gal in My Life*, *Martinique*, *This Is So Nice It Must Be Illegal*—were rather ordinary, and one, *Martinique*, was merely a rehash of an earlier Waller piece called *Mamacita*. Nevertheless, *Early to Bed* was a success and undoubtedly a tonic for Fats in the final year of his life.

The end came on a train bearing Waller from Los Angeles to New York in December, 1943. Fats was suffering from influenza, and his remarkable constitution simply collapsed. He died in his sleep before a doctor could reach him.

It is rare for a brilliant jazz musician of conservative good taste to win public acclaim in America; when the artist happens to be, paradoxically, a riotous popular entertainer, as was Fats Waller, his musical gifts often are all but ignored. Despite this outgoing manner, Waller's best work was frequently delicate and tender.

The internal structures of his solos were the work of a contemplative, not a frivolous, musical mind. André Hodeir has commented
(in *Jazz: Its Evolution and Essence*) on the depth of thought re-
siding beneath Waller's casual veneer:

> *Keepin' Out [of Mischief Now]* is an excellent example of clear,
> well-directed thought serving a marvelously felicitous melodic
> simplicity. It has been said that the melodic continuity of this solo
> comes from the fact that Fats doesn't get very far away from the
> theme. This opinion won't stand up under analysis. Fats may make
> frequent allusions to the original melody of *Keepin' Out,* but most
> of the time he remains completely independent of it, treating what
> he is doing as, successively, an exposition-paraphrase, a paraphrase-
> chorus, and a free variation. On the other hand, the endless con-
> trasts he uses are not merely an easy way to avoid monotony. They
> are not arbitrary; they not only are joined to the creative musical
> thought, but are part of it. It would scarcely be paradoxical to write
> that continuity here springs from contrast.

Waller's own recommendations to aspiring jazz pianists, made
when he was 31, bear out Hodeir's view:

> First get a thorough bass. Make it more rhythmic than flashy, a
> pulsating bass. Know how to play first without pedals and then always
> use the pedals sparingly. Study harmony so you will know the chords.
> Play clean both in the right and left hand. This is one of the marks of
> the modern pianist, he plays much cleaner than the old school. There is
> also much more expression to modern playing, and it is necessary to
> know how to build climaxes, how to raise up and let down, to show
> sudden contrasts. Keep the right hand always subservient to the
> melody. Trying to do too much always detracts from the tune.

Lyricist Andy Razaf remembered Fats as something of an intellectual, despite his lack of schooling, who absorbed and discussed
Beethoven, Shakespeare, and Plato. It is not an untenable image,
for the finest Waller solos reflect musical planning and aesthetic
judgment as well as joyful spontaneity. Along with this concern
for content, however, went a deep regard for communicative
warmth, the quality that immediately set Fats's piano work apart
from that of his imitators. James P. Johnson himself could not
match his former pupil in sheer human expressiveness.

In reply to the perennial question, "What is swing?" Fats once said, "It's two-thirds rhythm and one-third soul." Then he added, touching his heart and holding up his outsize hands, "It's got to be in here first and then come out here."

Waller's influence over other pianists was more oblique than direct in most instances. His powerful but measured attack and perfect sense of time served as models for individual pianists such as Art Tatum, Joe Sullivan, Hank Duncan (who learned from Fats while traveling with him in the thirties), Billy Kyle, Count Basie, and even Teddy Wilson, who began as an Earl Hines disciple. His influence bounced back, too, on older men such as Eubie Blake, Willie "The Lion" Smith, Duke Ellington, and James P. Johnson, all jazzmen who kept in touch with new developments. (Johnson, in 1947, was one of the few old-timers to praise Dizzy Gillespie, and Blake went to school to study the modern Schillinger system of composition when he was 66!) A few younger pianists—Johnny Guarnieri, Ralph Sutton, Bobby Henderson, Dick Wellstood, Martha Davis, and Don Ewell are prime examples—have at one time or another borrowed the Waller style intact and made it their own. And occasional flashes of pure Waller can be heard in the work of Oscar Peterson, Nat Cole, Erroll Garner, George Shearing, and Dave Brubeck.

One of the reasons for the wide appeal of Fats's style to pianists was its appositeness to the physical layout of the keyboard. Waller could reach thirteenths, but he seldom exceeded the tenth; his harmonic voicings were calculated to draw the most sound from the fewest notes; Fats's left hand covered the entire bass range rather than operating solely within the middle register as did many others; similarly, the highest treble tones were used to good effect; his trills and tremolos, like his "stride" bass patterns, were executed flawlessly with hands straight and fingers close to the keys. These and other features of Waller's playing still cause pianists, novice and veteran, to listen to and learn from his recorded contributions.

The history of the jazz pipe organ virtually began and ended with Fats Waller. When he played the electric Hammond, it was not the same, although Fats was one of the first to explore the jazz potential of that instrument as well. Had he been permitted to record noncommercial ideas on the pipe organ in his later years,

Waller might well have left an impressive body of new and unusual music.

Thomas Waller's 39 years were crowded with good times, prosperity, and rewarding friendships; yet the frustation he experienced in his musical life must have weighed heavily upon him. Fats's son, Maurice, has told how his father played and composed, in the privacy of his home, ambitious works that no one but the family ever heard. A handful of serious solo recordings, so dwarfed by the mountain of recorded trivia that made Waller a "success" in the thirties, remains as an indictment of an unenlightened people who allowed a great talent to slip through its fingers, just for a laugh.

Recommended Reading

Blesh, Rudi, and Harriet Janis: *They All Played Ragtime,* Knopf, New York (1950).

Condon, Albert Edwin, and Richard Gehman: *Eddie Condon's Treasury of Jazz,* Dial, New York (1956).

Davies, John R. T.: *The Music of Thomas "Fats" Waller,* "Friends of Fats," London (1953).

Fox, Charles: *Fats Waller,* Barnes, New York (1961).

Hodeir, André: *Jazz: Its Evolution and Essence,* Grove, New York (1956).

McCarthy, Albert (ed.): *The PL Yearbook of Jazz,* Editions Poetry, London (1947).

Mezzrow, Mezz, and Bernard Wolfe: *Really the Blues,* Random House, New York (1946).

Shapiro, Nat, and Nat Hentoff (eds.): *Hear Me Talkin' to Ya,* Rinehart, New York (1955).

Shapiro, Nat, and Nat Hentoff (eds.): *The Jazz Makers,* Grove, New York (1958).

Smith, Willie, and George Hoefer: *Music on My Mind,* Doubleday, New York (1964).

Recommended Listening

James P. Johnson: Rare Solos (piano rolls), RIVERSIDE RLP 12-105.

James P. Johnson: Backwater Blues (piano rolls), RIVERSIDE RLP-151.

Luckey Roberts and Willie "The Lion" Smith, GOOD-TIME-JAZZ M 12035.

Piano Roll Discoveries (Waller and Johnson, one track each), RCA Victor LPM-2058.

Early and Rare (Waller, one track), Riverside RLP 12-134.

Young Fats Waller (piano rolls), Riverside 12-103.

Young Fats Waller, "X" LVA-3035 (deleted).

"Fats," RCA Victor LPT-6001 (deleted).

The Sound of Harlem, Columbia C3L-33.

James P. Johnson: Father of the Stride Piano, Columbia CL-1780.

James P. Johnson: Yamekraw, Folkways FJ-2842.

Willie "The Lion" Smith: A Legend, Mainstream 56027.

A String of Swingin' Pearls (Waller, two tracks), RCA Victor LPM-1373.

Fats Waller: Handful of Keys, RCA Victor LPM-1502.

Fats Waller: One Never Knows, Do One?, RCA Victor LPM-1503.

Fats Waller: Ain't Misbehavin', RCA Victor LPM-1246.

The Real Fats Waller, Camden CAL-473.

Fats Waller in London, Capitol T-10258.

The Amazing Mr. Waller, Riverside 12-109.

The Art of the Jazz Piano, Epic 3295.

JACK TEAGARDEN

JACK TEAGARDEN, who had a great deal to do with how the jazz trombone was played after 1930, made his basic contributions during the twenties. Trombonists have been trying to measure up to his accomplishments ever since, but surprisingly few have succeeded, for Jack had a running head start.

Around Vernon, Texas, in 1905, he was known as Weldon, first-born son of Helen and Charles Teagarden. Helen was a trained pianist and Charles a persistent, if less than gifted, trumpet player. Before Weldon reached school age, he was playing a horn himself and making blunt remarks about his father's musicianship.

"We had an old brass baritone horn around the house when I was about five years old," the trombonist once recalled. "I used to watch my dad practice the trumpet—he had a tin ear—and he used to make so many mistakes on this, every morning before he'd go to the cotton-oil company, well, I used to tell him which finger to push on the trumpet, because I had already discovered it on the baritone. And he used to get real hacked at me. He figured kids should be seen and not heard."

After a couple of years at the baritone horn, Weldon was given a trombone. It was a sensible choice, for the slide trombone is the most perfect brass instrument, permitting a sensitive player to differentiate between, say, C-sharp and D-flat. Young Teagarden, already exhibiting an almost painfully acute sense of perfect pitch ("Jack could call off the overtones of a thunderclap," sister Norma insists), was doubtless happy to graduate from his tempered baritone horn. He progressed rapidly enough to take a chair in the Vernon City Band while still too small to reach beyond the fourth slide position.

It was, in fact, Weldon's short reach that brought about some of his technical grace and flexibility. In the process of learning how to hit all the notes without using the outer positions, he developed a highly plastic embouchure and a fast, close-to-the-chest right arm. The town's bandsmen, who tried to laugh off the boy as a mere mascot, must have had some uncomfortable moments. "I used to irk those fellows, I guess, a little bit because I knew the fingers [for valve horns] and I knew both clefs and everything," Jack remembered many years later.

Helen Teagarden had started teaching piano by this time, and her son picked up valuable keyboard training along the way. (In later years, Teagarden carried piano-tuning equipment on jobs to prevent outrages on his delicate ear.) In 1914, Weldon, now 9, was taken to a trombone teacher in nearby Wichita Falls and told that he was playing wrong but getting fine results. The teacher prudently refused to interfere.

It was a strange and rather melancholy childhood for a robust Western kid. Weldon's friendships were few, and most of his waking hours had something to do with music, if only by way of observing his mother's students or his father's quiet musical frustrations. He played hymns for three years in church with his mother and was drafted into the Vernon High School band as a trombonist and drummer while still in the grades. He listened with interest to the gospel songs coming from revivalist tent meetings held near his home.

In 1918, Charles succumbed to influenza, and Helen, now with a brood of four, was faced with working out the family's economic problems alone. She joined her mother in Oklahoma City for a while, then moved on to Chappell, Nebraska. There she found work in a local movie house, where Weldon operated the projector (things mechanical had always run a close second to music in Teagarden's life) and sat in with his mother on the weekends. The going was difficult, however, and the Teagardens drifted back to Oklahoma City. At this point, Weldon decided he might best help his family's problem by leaving town, making one less mouth to feed. It was faulty adolescent reasoning—the family would have preferred his earning a little money at home—but the move served to make him an independent professional musician at 15.

After a discouraging turn accompanying his Uncle Joe's out-of-tune country fiddle in San Angelo, Texas, the young trombonist joined Cotton Bailey's band at the Horn Palace in San Antonio. There he met pianist Terry Shand and clarinetist George Hill, who represented what may have been his first enduring friendships. About this time, too, he arbitrarily selected the name Jack to replace the long-resented Weldon.

In the summer of 1921, Jack worked at the Youree Hotel in Shreveport, Louisiana, with a trio that included Shand. This was the hotel for which New Orleans musicians Tom and Vic Gaspard had organized the Maple Leaf Orchestra a year or two before. Whether in 1921 or at a later time (it could have been as late as 1925, when Jack played the Youree with Johnny Youngberg's orchestra), Teagarden filled in some gaps in his musical education under Vic Gaspard, one of New Orleans' finest reading trombonists and an associate of the highly regarded Tios, Pirons, Bigards *et al.* Eddie Sommers, another New Orleans trombonist just Teagarden's age, remembers taking lessons from Gaspard at the time Teagarden did. In any event, New Orleans music was enormously appealing to Teagarden, and engagements in neighboring Shreveport, Galveston, or Biloxi, Mississippi, put him in touch with many Crescent City musicians. On one trip to New Orleans, he heard Louis Armstrong play the cornet, an experience that left a deep and lasting impression on the novice from Texas.

That fall, Jack met and went to work for pianist Peck Kelley. Kelley, seven years Teagarden's senior and already a prominent musician around Houston, was to Jack a kind of combination father figure, musical hero, instructor, and understanding friend—then, as later, the trombonist's ego needed frequent shoring up. It was largely through Kelley that Teagarden acquired a deep regard for the blues and came in contact, if only through recordings at first, with blues performers like Bessie Smith. He stayed with Peck almost two years, well into 1923, and during this period developed most of the fundamentals of his strikingly unique style. Most of the band's engagements were in the Houston–San Antonio area, including an intriguing date at the Houston City Auditorium in late 1922 called, according to Teagarden chronicler Howard Waters (in *Jack Teagarden's Music*), the Musicians Jazz Festival—almost certainly the first jazz festival on the books.

Jack worked again with Kelley in 1924 at Sylvan Beach Park, near Houston, on a summer job that included Pee Wee Russell and New Orleans clarinetist Leon Roppolo. The Sylvan Beach band was, from all reports, one of the best jazz combinations of the period, but it was not recorded. Those who were there remember Teagarden's fleet trombone solos above all else, even the advanced playing of Kelley himself.

Russell has recalled his initial impression of the music Kelley and Teagarden were playing in 1924:

"When I first went from St. Louis to join Peck in Houston, I felt I was a big shot arriving in a hick town. Texas was like another country, and nobody down there had done any recording, as we had in St. Louis.

"I met Peck, listened to him play, and got scared. I had heard good musicians around home—Fate Marable, Charlie Creath, Pops Foster, Zutty Singleton—but this was a different thing. Peck not only played an awful lot of piano, he played so positive and clean. He had a 'this is mine' style, with plenty of authority. And he wasn't like other fast pianists up North, who didn't know the blues. Peck played real blues. He and I spent a lot of time that summer listening to Bessie Smith records. It was our way of going to church.

"Anyway, then Teagarden walked in, took his horn off a hook on the wall, and joined Kelley. That was it. 'Look,' I said, 'I'm a nice guy a thousand miles from home, and I'm out of my class. Just send me back to St. Louis in two weeks.'

"It worked out all right, though. Leon Roppolo was in the band, and I had at least heard him before. But why, I wondered, hadn't I ever heard about these other guys?"

Jack and Peck went separate ways after 1924, but until Teagarden's death remained almost mystically bound to each other. Attempts by Teagarden and others to lure the brilliant but diffident pianist into the limelight always failed. Kelley explained his position to a *Down Beat* reporter in 1940: ". . . the main reason I don't want to go with the big guys is because I couldn't live the way I want to. If I was working with a top band it would be rehearse, record, broadcast, play, rush, hurry, with no time to myself. I like to practice two or three hours every day; I like to read an hour or so; I like to be able to do what I want to, when I want to do it, and that's how I'm going to live if I can." Kelley never changed his mind.

After a short interval out of music (working in the oil fields), Jack became a featured attraction with R. J. Marin's Southern Trumpeters in 1923. Marin billed Teagarden as "The South's Greatest Sensational Trombone Wonder" and traveled through Texas (with occasional radio broadcasts), into Oklahoma, and finally to Mexico City, where the band broke up. Jack, at 18, was regarded with something like awe by other members of the band, most of whom could not read. He doubled on euphonium (and at times on musical saw) and had begun to sing with a mellow baritone drawl as well.

Word of Jack's abilities had spread across the Southwest, and he was seldom out of work. After the Southern Trumpeters dissolved in 1924, he enjoyed a string of jobs under colorful banners such as Will Robison's Deep River Orchestra (Kansas City), Doc Ross and His Jazz Bandits (or Ranger Ross and His Cowboys, depending upon the location), the Youngberg-Marin Peacocks, Joe Mannone and His Mocking Birds, and the New Orleans Rhythm Masters. The area covered by these groups was a wide one, from Missouri to Mexico and from Mississippi to California. While in Los Angeles, Jack became aware of a still wider variety of band styles, including that of the newly organized Ben Pollack outfit, featuring Benny Goodman on clarinet.

By October, 1927, Jack had become a seasoned bandsman and a major, though not yet nationally known, jazz trombonist. His love for the music of Louis Armstrong had grown with each record released by the Hot Five, and he had worked many trumpetlike ideas into his trombone style. He had, too, learned to play and sing the blues with real conviction and authority. It was time, he rightly believed, to play for bigger stakes. In November, Teagarden, Doc Ross, and a few other members of the foundering Ross band piled into two cars and drove from Houston to New York City.

Teagarden came closer to taking New York by storm than he could have dared dream. Although essentially a noncompetitive sort of man, Jack was far from reluctant to demonstrate what he could do with his unorthodox approach to the horn. He was an inveterate jam-session player, sitting in at any hour with any combination of instruments. As soon as he arrived in the big city, Jack contacted old friends Joe "Wingy" Mannone and Pee Wee Russell, both of whom had direct access to the innermost circle of favored New York jazzmen. Red Nichols, Glenn Miller, the Dorsey brothers, Vic Berton, Eddie Lang, and others were bowled over by their initial encounter with the young Texan. So was Miff Mole, the hitherto undisputed monarch of New York jazz trombonists. To understand the impact Teagarden made on this rather smug little community of jazzmen, we might review Mole's large contributions in the preceding years.

Mole, a native New Yorker, was born in 1898 and started on the violin at 11. When barely into his teens, he had also become skilled enough on the piano to play in local movie houses. He began teaching himself how to play the trombone around 1914, eventually transferring his improvising style on the violin over to the brass instrument. Like Teagarden, who strove for an approximation of the clean lines of the baritone horn, Mole thus evolved a fast, accurate, and unusual trombone technique quite unlike the bawdy glissando vernacular associated with most early jazz trombonists. Again, like Teagarden, he drew upon the sounds of New Orleans jazz (the Original Dixieland Jazz Band in particular) for inspiration. He was a co-founder of a successful small group, patterned after the Original Dixieland Jazz Band, called the Original Memphis Five. Many musicians bought Memphis Five records in the mid-twenties just to hear the clean, fleet trombone parts. (Saxophonist Joe Rushton recalled recently that "Miff's ensemble and solo lines were like compositions" and that, though the phrasing had become outmoded, "they were still musically sound creations, full of unusual passing tones and fills.")

Mole traveled to Chicago during this period and sat in with King Oliver's band, an event that enlarged his debt to New Orleans jazz. After trying California for a year or so, Miff returned to New York, where he became the most sought-after trombonist in town. He worked with Sam Lanin, Ray Miller, and Ross Gorman on records, in radio studios, and under stage lights. From 1925 on, he played and recorded extensively with Red Nichols, frequently matching the cornetist's rapid-fire outbursts note-for-note. Mole's was a modern, complex, technical style that, although somewhat lacking in expressive warmth, was *the* dominant influence over Eastern trombonists prior to 1928. (Tommy Dorsey, it is said, was one of many who wrote out and studied Miff's solos.) He was an excellent reader, and in late 1927, when Teagarden reached New York, Miff was the leading "hot" man in Roger Wolfe Kahn's highly rated orchestra.

Within a month of his arrival, Jack landed a record date with Johnny Johnson's orchestra. A little later, he recorded with his old boss, Willard Robison, who needed no convincing about

Teagarden's abilities. In March, 1928, came what must have been a most satisfying assignment for Jack—a record date with Roger Wolfe Kahn, substituting for Miff Mole. His full-chorus solo on *She's a Great, Great Girl,* though suggestive of Mole's approach and less positive than later Teagarden solos, is unmistakably the work of a mature jazz trombonist with ideas well in advance of those of most of his contemporaries. Furthermore, he sets forth these ideas in the warm blues dialect of the South rather than in the more stilted ragtime-based phraseology of the Northeast. The effect is stunning.

Another significant feature of Teagarden's style caused other trombonists—even the best of them—to despair of ever catching up to him. His use of the lip, rather than the slide, to play fast triplets and sixteenth-note clusters opened the way for a whole new set of possibilities in improvising. This basic device permitted a true legato line to be played as cleanly as if it were articulated by a valve instrument, obviating the necessity for tonguing each note, however lightly. (Obviously, an attempt to play conventional legato phrases without tonguing on the slide trombone would result in a single confused conglomeration of glissandi.) Combining this freedom from the tongue with his extraordinary command of false positions, Teagarden could execute rapidly without sacrificing the relaxed manner so important to good jazz playing. After Teagarden, Mole's rapid single-tongue ideas, though still impressive, seemed slightly stiff-jointed and stodgy. New York trombonists went to work on lip flexibility after 1927. And, although lip triplets are now commonplace, no trombonist has yet matched the crackling immaculacy of Teagarden's triplet figures.

Jack quickly became the darling of the jazz fraternity and everyone's personal discovery. The Chicagoans admired his virile blues playing, the Nichols-Miller-Dorsey gang respected his musicianship, the Harlem insiders welcomed his outgoing modern musical ideas, and Paul Whiteman's top jazz players (Beiderbecke, Trumbauer *et al.*) looked for ways to draft the 22-year-old "wonder" into their company. But the man who acted first was saxophonist Gil Rodin, the organizing mind behind Ben Pollack. Rodin told about it in *Down Beat* ten years later:

Bud [Freeman], Jimmy [McPartland] and I lived together in New
York and at this point, the great "Mr. T." came into my life. Bud,
Jimmy and I went to the Louisiana Apartments on 47th St. to hear
a "session." We had been told about a fellow from Texas, a trombone
player by the name of Teagarden who would be there. . . . The
session was under way when we arrived. Jack started playing and
listening to him provided me with one of my biggest musical thrills.
He played some hot tunes, then some beautiful melodic phrasing on
things like *Diane,* the like of which I had never heard on a trombone, and finished off with a demonstration of his astounding conception and talent with his "glass and half trombone" [Teagarden's
device of obtaining a muted effect by removing the bell of his horn
and playing the tubing into a water glass] on some blues. His playing that night was the first taste I had of real, genuine hot trombone, and we all went home talking to ourselves. . . .

I told Bennie Pollack all about him, in fact, I'm afraid I probably
became a little incoherent in trying to tell him how greatly Jack
impressed me. As a result, when the band left for Atlantic City
[July, 1928], and Glenn Miller decided to remain in New York, I
suggested that Jack be brought into the band. Jack agreed and
joined soon after. His rise in music was inevitable and the swing
world should be thankful that he came to New York when he did.

One of the most important New York trombonists to be affected
by Teagarden was Jimmy Harrison. At the time of Jack's arrival,
Harrison was also attempting to develop an individual trumpetlike approach while working with Fletcher Henderson's band. His
rhythmic single-tongue ideas were widely admired, and after
meeting Teagarden, Harrison reached his full maturity as an outstanding soloist. The coming together of these two superior trombonists has been charmingly recounted by saxophonist Coleman
Hawkins (on the record *Coleman Hawkins: A Documentary*):

> Jimmy [Harrison], I thought, was quite a trombone player. He was
> on the . . . order of Jack Teagarden though, I think. . . . The
> first time we ever heard Jack Teagarden was in Roseland [Ball-
> room]. This other band played the first set, so I went upstairs. . . .
> I'd heard about this Teagarden. . . . Jimmy and all the rest of
> them were downstairs, or I don't even know if they were in yet. I
> heard him playin', so I went downstairs to get Jimmy and the fel-
> lows to start kidding about it.

I says, "Man, there's a boy upstairs that plays an awful lot of trombone."

"Yeah, who's that, Hawk?"

I says, "He's a boy from New Orleans or Texas or somethin'. I don't know. What do they call him? Jack Teagarden or somethin'. Jimmy, you know him?"

"No, I'm not gonna know him . . . trombone player, ain't he? Plays like the rest of the trombones, that's all. I don't see *no* trombones. I say the trombone is a brass instrument; it should have that sound just like a trumpet. I don't want to hear trombone sound like a trombone. I can't see it."

I said, "Jimmy, he doesn't sound like those trombones. He plays up high; sounds a lot like a trumpet, too."

He says, "Oh, man, I ain't payin' that no mind."

Jimmy and Jack got to be the tightest of friends.

After this first night, I couldn't separate Jimmy and Jack Teagarden. So we used to come up to my house practically every night. . . . I don't know how they made it, because we'd sit up there and fool around 'til two, three, four o'clock in the afternoon—no sleep. And we were working every night. We used to sit there and drink all night and eat these cold cuts, cheese and crackers and stuff, and we'd do this and play—playin' all night. Jimmy and Jack both jivin' each other . . . trying to figure out what he lacks that he can get from the other one . . . and I dug what was going on. . . . I had the piano, and they could play all night. It didn't disturb anybody or nothin'. The house was all well draped and carpeted. . . . Both of them got their trombones, and I played piano for them. This used to go on all night long, listening to records and eating and talking and back to playing again—every night.

You couldn't keep Jack out of Harlem. . . . He made every house rent party. . . . Jack made himself right at home. And always had that horn. He must have never slept, playing horn night and day.

But that was a funny experience when Jack came up, 'cause Jimmy never heard anyone play trombone like that.

Teagarden began recording prolifically in late 1928, lending a touch of the real blues to dozens of performances by Ben Pollack's band and studio groups. For two years or more, the records rolled out under pseudonyms like the Big Aces, the Broadway Broadcasters, the Whoopee Makers, the Hotsy Totsy Gang, the Lumberjacks, the Dixie Daisies, Sunny Clapp and His Band o'

Sunshine, Mills' Musical Clowns, the Cotton Pickers, Louisville Rhythm Kings, Jimmy Bracken's Toe Ticklers, the Kentucky Grasshoppers, Southern Night Hawks, Ten Black Berries, the Dixie Jazz Band, Louisiana Rhythm Kings, the Knickerbockers, the Badgers, the New Orleans Ramblers, and the Columbia Photo Players. Most of these mysterious groups were actually Ben Pollack's men, circumventing contractual obligations, and their confusing outpouring of discs has caused jazz record collectors endless problems ever since.

There are, in effect, three Jack Teagardens on these early recordings—the perfunctory "hot" soloist, the earthy blues singer–instrumentalist, and the creative melodist. As a valuable improvising sideman with Pollack and various recording groups basically concerned with turning out commercial "hit" material, Jack maintained an extraordinarily high level of musical integrity and sincerity. Tunes like *Buy, Buy for Baby* and *In a Great Big Way* are hardly inspiring vehicles, but Teagarden makes the best of them with brief energetic improvisations of real quality.

As an interpreter of the blues, particularly the minor blues, Teagarden had few equals in New York in 1928. (Louis Armstrong was still in Chicago.) His specialty, as Rodin pointed out, was playing with only the slide and a water glass, with which he achieved a plaintive, edgy, "vocal" sound rather like that of a magnificent singer humming through a kazoo. He used this arresting technique with excellent results on *Whoopee Stomp, Tailspin Blues, Digga Digga Do, St. James Infirmary,* and his celebrated *Makin' Friends* (also called *Dirty Dog*), a fine traditional blues close to the spirit of the rural South. Jack's blues performances, though frequently embellished with dazzling breaks and gruppetti, are fundamentally very simple statements, delivered straight from the stomach without the slightest hint of condescension.

Teagarden was more than a technical innovator and blues player, however. He was also a foremost improviser, with an ear for melodic, rhythmic, and harmonic subtleties that few jazzmen could match. Like Bix Beiderbecke (whom Jack claimed he helped with the writing of the piano piece *In the Dark,* incidentally), Miff Mole, and Coleman Hawkins, he was able to demonstrate his harmonic ideas on the piano. (Most of the leading developers of

modern jazz more than a decade later worked out their concepts
at the keyboard first, and it is a curious fact that Teagarden, Mole,
and Hawkins were among the most accepting of the older men
when bebop broke through in the forties.) Perhaps the best examples of Teagarden's melodic inventiveness during his Pollack period appear on some of the recordings he turned out for Red
Nichols in 1929 and 1930.

Indiana, which Jack recorded in April, 1929, with Nichols,
Benny Goodman, Gene Krupa, and others, reveals Teagarden as
the propelling force and musical paterfamilias of the date. Two
takes were issued, showing clearly the seaching creativity of the
24-year-old trombonist at that time. On the first turn, each soloist,
Jack included, experiments with the simple harmonic patterns of
the tune. Teagarden characteristically plays a blues game, altering
his opening G chord to a G minor and introducing flowing blueslike phrases. On the second take, Jack retains his minor blues feeling but goes into the upper harmonic reaches for his melody
notes. Building a melodic line with sixths and diminished, major,
and minor sevenths and ninths, young Teagarden suggests some
of the notions propounded by Charlie Parker and others ten to
fifteen years later. Only a few other jazzmen (Beiderbecke,
Hawkins, Russell, and Freeman were leading examples) could
have attempted this and succeeded in 1929. Mole and Nichols
were aware of the possibilities of these harmonic explorations, but
most of their attempts along such lines were self-conscious experiments that failed to grow naturally out of the heat of spontaneous
improvisation. Teagarden, like Charlie Parker in later years,
played rhythmically propulsive, blues-touched, emotionally satisfying jazz *first,* then added the melodic and harmonic interest.

Teagarden's natural tendency to transform popular songs into
the blues worked better on some tunes than on others. By insert-
ing ambiguous diminished chords and substituting minor for
major chords, he could change the character of most tunes, but he
appeared to be more comfortable working with chord structures
that lent themselves to his designs. Thus *I'm Just Wild About
Harry,* with its built-in ninths (even in the melody) and minor
harmonies, was ideal raw material for his trombone, as was
Dinah, on which Jack toys provocatively with minor seventh and
augmented chords without losing the blues idea.

Other Nichols recordings are equally impressive. *Tea for Two,*
After You've Gone, China Boy, Peg o' My Heart, and *The Sheik of*
Araby all feature extraordinary solos marked by harmonic bold-
ness, thematic unity, melodic charm, and rhythmic excitement. *I*
Want to Be Happy, in addition to offering a highly unified statement punctuated by sixteenth-note triplets, contains a good exam-
ple of Jack's use of the trumpetlike "shout," which also appears in
On Revival Day. One of Teagarden's very best contributions is on
Rose of Washington Square, performed by a Nichols group that
includes Chicagoans Bud Freeman, Joe Sullivan, and Dave
Tough, as well as Pee Wee Russell. Here is Jack in his freest form,
piling swirling chromatic triplet figures on top of powerful melodic declarations with taste, intelligence, and supreme finesse.
Teagarden always performed best when supported sympatheti-
cally by his musical equals, and *Rose of Washington Square* was
one of the all too rare occasions when close to ideal conditions
prevailed.

Jack made more than one hundred recordings in 1929. Some
feature him with handpicked groups of friends, such as the Eddie
Condon Hot Shots date with Leonard Davis on trumpet, the
Louis Armstrong session with Eddie Lang and Joe Sullivan, and
a couple of Fats Waller *thés dansants* that include jazzmen Gene
Krupa, Albert Nicholas, Pops Foster, Red Allen, and Kaiser Marshall, among others. On these, Teagarden's playing is at a consist-
ently high level. The larger portion of his studio time that year,
however, was logged as a Ben Pollack sideman. The Pollack records cover a wide musical range, from a kicking small-band *Bugle*
Call Rag and a bluesy full-orchestra *My Kinda Love* to a cloying
popular trifle such as *I'd Like to Be a Gypsy* and a bit of transient
nonsense like *Keep Your Undershirt On.* Considering the nature
of much of the material, Teagarden performs very well indeed.

By 1930, record companies were feeling the economic pinch,
but Jack continued recording, frequently on a free-lance basis,
through most of 1931. He showed up on dates contracted by
Hoagy Carmichael, Red Nichols, Ted Lewis, Ozzie Nelson, Joe
Venuti, Sam Lanin, and, of course, Ben Pollack. He also saw his
name appear on a label for the first time, but it turned out to be a
mere cover-up for the usual Pollack fare, which had by now
grown rather tepid. A few months later, in January, 1931, the

Crown company used Jack's name again, this time a little more appropriately, on *Rockin' Chair* and *Loveless Love,* but both performances are disappointing.

More important to Jack was a "Gil Rodin" (again the Pollack gang) date that produced *Beale Street Blues* and *If I Could Be with You.* As these were good songs for Teagarden to sing and play, he took over the whole show, and *Beale Street* became one of his staples in later years. A few months later, he recorded *Beale Street* with Benny Goodman; a month afterward, he cut the tune a third time, with Ben Pollack; then again in 1931, with Joe Venuti and Eddie Lang. Each has been considered a classic performance (although not on the high order of Jack's work with Nichols), and all four helped to carry the Teagarden name to listeners beyond the uncommercial world in which jazz musicians lived. Similarly, *Basin Street Blues,* included in the 1931 Goodman date, became associated with Teagarden over the years. By the sixties, he had made more than a dozen recordings of *Basin Street* and probably had grown very weary of playing it, on or off records.

From all his recording dates, radio remotes, pit-band assignments, and engagements with Pollack, Teagarden was earning up to $500 a week in the best days of 1928 and 1929. He had no concern for the future and, except for music, gave little thought to the present. He was already on his way to a breakup of his second marriage and to the doubtful distinction of possessing perhaps the greatest capacity for liquor of any major musician in the East, Fats Waller excepted. After 1930, however, life became somewhat less prosperous. Pollack's men experienced long layoffs, and extended hotel engagements, once common, became rare events. There simply wasn't as much money around, although the band was still working fairly regularly. At one point, though, Jack returned to Oklahoma City to spend a couple of lay-off months with his family. During this time, he also played with the orchestras of Clarence Tackett and Paul Christensen and sat in with top territory bands like Bennie Moten's and Andy Kirk's.

Jack made no records at all in 1932. Most of that depressed year was spent out on the road or playing in Midwestern ballrooms and nightclubs. The Pollack band had by now become a camp of musical dissension and unrest. Only Gil Rodin had weathered all

the storms from the beginning, while stars like Benny Goodman,
Glenn Miller, Bud Freeman, and Charlie Teagarden (Jack's tal-
ented, trumpet-playing younger brother) had come and gone.
The 1932–1933 band was a good one, with jazzmen like Sterling
Bose (trumpet), Eddie Miller and Matty Matlock (reeds),
Nappy Lamare (guitar), and Ray Bauduc (drums), but Pollack's
commercial policies caused constant friction. Finally, in mid-1933,
Jack and Sterling Bose broke away from the band to take a job at
the Century of Progress Exposition in Chicago.

The new job didn't even last the season. After a short summer
at the Exposition, Teagarden joined Mal Hallett's orchestra back
East. It was a good outfit for 1933, with "hot" men like Gene
Krupa, trumpeter Lee Castle, and saxophonist Toots Mondello
featured from time to time. This one lasted until December, 1933.

Before leaving Chicago, Teagarden recorded four sides under
his own name. One, *I've Got "It,"* is of interest because it indicates
a new direction the trombonist had taken since his last trip to the
studios. His solo lines are less trumpetlike here and closer in construction to the agile clarinet figures of Benny Goodman. It was a
remarkable turn for a trombonist to take, and only a musician of
Teagarden's skill could have attempted it. With this development
went an appropriate softening of tone and almost total abandonment of the "shout" device. The effect is a solo style that seems
"cool" rather than "hot," yet remains virile and rooted in the
blues. A cogent description by Otis Ferguson of Teagarden's low-
key post-1933 style appeared a few years later in *The New Republic:*

> He will hit fuzzy ones sometimes, sometimes crowd his horn too
> much and often bring back the same variation for a supposedly dif-
> ferent theme, but taken at his best he has that clear construction in
> melodic lines, that insistent suggestion through complexity of the
> simple prime beat. And in both tonal and rhythmic attack there is
> that constant hint of conquest over an imposed resistance which is
> peculiar to jazz and therefore undefinable in other terms. Something
> like the difference between driving a spike cleanly into a solid oak
> block and the hollow victory of sinking it in lath and plaster.

The new lithe Teagarden style also encompassed a superb ballad approach that had been shaping up for a long time. It came

out in a series of late 1933 recordings made in New York during Jack's Mal Hallett stint. One session was Teagarden's own, and the sophisticated songs he selected to sing and play—*Love Me, Blue River, A Hundred Years from Today,* and *I Just Couldn't Take It Baby*—were vastly superior to much of the material he had endured for five years as a Pollack sideman and were typically Teagardenish.

Better known are those dates on which Benny Goodman, now on the brink of the most successful period of his career, was in command of sidemen like the Teagarden brothers, Joe Sullivan, and Gene Krupa. Again Jack responded to the happy, if semicommercial, setting with fine solos on *I Gotta Right to Sing the Blues, Ain't-cha Glad?, Dr. Heckle and Mr. Jibe,* a blues called *Texas Tea Party, Love Me or Leave Me, Why Couldn't It Be Poor Little Me?, Keep On Doin' What You're Doin',* and a couple of numbers featuring vocals by 18-year-old Billie Holiday.

As these recordings, which held so much promise for the years to come, were being made, Jack signed a five-year contract with Paul Whiteman. It was one of the most unfortunate decisions of his professonal life, but there was no way he could have known it then. Within two years, jazz made a dramatic comeback. Goodman struck pay dirt with his swing band, and the old Pollack gang was lining up a bright future as a cooperative unit under singer Bob Crosby. Both groups wanted Jack Teagarden. Nothing could be done about it, however, and Jack settled down in the brass section of the hippopotamic orchestra to serve out his five years. During 1934, there was a rewarding Columbia date with Goodman and Teddy Wilson, a pleasant engagement with Adrian Rollini for the new Decca company, and a good session, organized by Jack for the Brunswick label, in which brother Charlie, Goodman, pianist Terry Shand, and jazz harpist Casper Reardon participated, but the four years that followed these high spots were long and dreary. Between June, 1936, and February, 1938, peak years for the big swing bands fronted by his old friends, Teagarden recorded exactly one solo—eight bars of crisp jazz somewhere in a forest of thirty instrumentalists toiling over *Shall We Dance?*

In 1937, Otis Ferguson took note of Jack's plight in *The New Republic:* "Though still a fine musician, he seems tired and cynical, his creation a bit shopworn—which knowing gentlemen have not hesitated to remark or less knowing gentlemen to echo, which in itself is enough to embitter a fellow and make him listless."

The situation improved somewhat in 1938. Whiteman, finally unable to resist the swing tide, allowed Jack a few moments in the light with a "swing wing" of the orchestra and permitted several outside dates that helped to relieve the monotony of warmed-over Gershwin and pompous Roy Bargy "concert" arrangements. Most gratifying was a reunion with friends Bud Freeman, Pee Wee Russell, Jess Stacy, Eddie Condon, George Wettling, and Bobby Hackett in the studios of the new Commodore company. Jack sang and played the blues (*Serenade to a Shylock*), revived the tune with which he had impressed New York jazzmen so much ten years before (*Diane*), demonstrated his current ballad manner (*Embraceable You*), and jumped into a rousing ensemble romp, Chicago style (*Meet Me Tonight in Dreamland*). It was good therapy as well as good music; Jack began to gain back his confidence and his ability to *think* while playing.

Within weeks of his release from Whiteman in December, 1938, Teagarden formed his own orchestra and plunged into a full schedule of ballroom jobs, hotel engagements, recordings, motion picture work, and broadcasting. On the surface, all looked well, but by 1939 the swing craze was waning, and it required both good management and a natural business sense to survive. Jack had neither. Like other disillusioned soloists-turned-leaders (pianist Bob Zurke, trumpeter Bunny Berigan, trombonist Jack Jenny, and trumpeter Bobby Hackett were a few), he discovered that the band business in 1939 was a dangerous jungle of avarice, dishonesty, crass commercialism, and bone-racking travel conditions. Teagarden's ingenuous affability and lifelong disregard for the harsher realities of life (one example: through sheer neglect, Teagarden lost all his teeth before he was 40) did not equip him to deal effectively even with personal problems, let alone with a bandleader's tribulations. Within a year, he filed a voluntary petition of bankruptcy.

Later in 1940, the trombonist was back in business again, this time with a less expensive and less jazz-oriented band. The group went over well at college dances and landed a few good location jobs with radio hookups. Its recorded output is without much interest, except for an occasional trombone specialty like *The Blues*, a masterpiece of sustained upper-register virtuosity. More common are bubbles like *I Hear Bluebirds* or *Fatima's Drummer Boy*. In 1941, Jack boosted the band's popularity with his appearance in the film *Birth of the Blues*, took on arranger Phil Moore, and secured a new contract with Decca Records. He had just begun to turn out some fairly good performances for Decca when the war and a musicians' union ban on recording interfered. The Teagarden orchestra was not asked to make regular records again, except for a couple of full-orchestra performances released in 1946 on a label called Teagarden Presents.

From 1940 to 1947, however, the trombonist took part in a number of successful small-band recordings. One of the most satisfying is a 1940 Bud Freeman album of eight tunes associated with the Chicagoans. Teagarden is in optimum form, especially on the blues *Jack Hits the Road* and on the curiously modern-sounding *Prince of Wails*. Drummer Dave Tough is the driving force of this session. In December, 1940, Jack recorded with Tough, pianist Billy Kyle, and bassist Billy Taylor, along with Duke Ellington sidemen Barney Bigard, Ben Webster, and Rex Stewart. (Oddly, Teagarden was quoted by Leonard Feather seven years later as follows: "I never did like anything Ellington ever did. He never had a band all in tune, always had a bad tone quality and bad blend.") Though these performances carry some of the external trappings of 1940 swing (or, as it has come to be called, "mainstream" jazz), they are, ironically, not as advanced for the period as the so-called Dixieland recordings of Bud Freeman earlier in the year.

Jack's other New York recordings made at this time usually find him with old friends—a date with George Wettling that includes pianist Herman Chittison and Coleman Hawkins or a Commodore blowout with sister Norma on piano and Max Kaminsky on trumpet. Some of the most relaxed moments can be heard on a couple of Eddie Condon gatherings for Decca in 1944 and 1947 that feature members of the clan such as Pee Wee Russell, Ernie Caceres, Bobby Hackett, and singer Lee Wiley. On these, Jack blows with more conviction and thought than he displayed in front of his own orchestra during the same period.

Throughout the war years, Jack struggled to keep his organization together in the face of selective service, travel restrictions, lack of promotion or good management or recording contracts, and the general decline of big bands in America. To add to his woes, a third wife was collecting alimony and Jack's fourth marriage seemed to be sinking. The trombonist had many interesting ideas for improving his band—hiring pianist Art Tatum was one —yet they never seemed to work out. His last orchestra (1946) was a potentially good one that featured modern arrangements like Jerry Redmond's *Martian Madness*, but Jack's health finally started to crack late in that year, and the group broke up for good.

"Jack was a good musical leader," remembers Leon Radsliff, saxophonist and arranger with the last Teagarden band, "but he was no businessman. He seemed to be more interested in steam engines than publicity, and his managers played him for a sucker. But we had a hell of a band for a while—ten brass, including a French horn, and five reeds. And we had some interesting arrangements. Jack invented a slide-rule method of writing, and he scored some far-out brass-choir things," Radsliff recalls. "We used to sit up at night and play Tatum records, then slow them down to catch what was happening. Jack was completely open-minded about modern jazz and admired the really good players like Gillespie and Parker."

Teagarden elected to remain in the unclassifiable niche he had carved for himself; the proper foundation for exploring modern jazz was there, but Teagarden's approach was already as "modern" as it was traditional, and there was little reason for him to change it. As Teagarden biographer Jay Smith wrote: "Woe be to the critic who dares approach the maverick with branding iron in hand."

After 1946, Jack, now broke, drew into the protective noncompetitive shell he had kept handy for such emergencies since his boyhood in Texas. He worked in California with a small group for a couple of months, wandered to the East Coast, and picked up a sextet in New York for a run on Fifty-second Street. Some nights he sat behind the piano, with only his fast-moving slide visible to the audience. With old friends Dave Tough, Max Kaminsky, and others, Jack explored a few of the contemporary ideas that were being played along the Street in the mid-forties and built up his confidence again. (This phase is best documented by a 1947 RCA Victor recording called *Jam Session at Victor.*)

A few weeks later, Teagarden joined Louis Armstrong's All-Stars (the trumpeter had had *his* big-band problems, too), a high-tension packet of jazz talent (Earl Hines, Barney Bigard, Sidney Catlett, etc.) that somehow never quite amounted to very much as a going band. Still, it was a chance to play jazz with a longtime hero and to make good money as well. He stayed with Armstrong for four years.

It was about 1952 that Jack Teagarden finally took full command of his personal life. Now 47, he quit drinking, salvaged his fourth marriage, assessed and assumed his responsibility toward a newborn son, relegated business affairs to his wife, and took to the road again with a sextet. Good things began to happen at last, and the group met with modest but firm success in the mid-fifties. In 1958, the American State Department sent Teagarden and his band on a tour of Asia that brought the trombonist's chronically drooping self-esteem to an unprecedented height.

Teagarden's Dixieland-oriented group, featuring trumpeter Don Goldie, carried on into the sixties, playing clubs and festivals and turning out records. The trombonist nearly always played flawlessly, though seldom with the drive and daring of his early days. Only occasionally was a Teagarden sextet performance memorable, as in a Roulette recording of *I'm Getting Sentimental Over You.* Yet, even when Teagarden was coasting, he tossed off casual trombone passages that could send novices running back to their woodsheds.

Teagarden's horn and voice never lost their singular charm and warmth. One of his last recording sessions features a set of songs written by former employer and longtime friend Willard Robison. They are the sort of offbeat songs modern jazz-based singers enjoy, and in doing them, Teagarden again proved himself an undated, front-rank jazz ballad singer.

In late 1963, the trombonist was presented at the Monterey Jazz Festival in California, along with his family (pianist Norma, trumpeter Charlie, and Jack's mother, still active as a piano teacher) and old comrade Pee Wee Russell. It was a happy reunion, but the aging trombonist was ill, overweight, and no longer on the wagon. Following another separation from his wife-manager, he had pared his regular band down to an economical quartet (sparked by pianist Don Ewell); yet, there were still those unpleasant leader chores to perform. Teagarden was looking for his old shell to pull into again when, during a New Orleans engagement in early 1964, his heart suddenly stopped.

Seldom has the influence of a single jazzman been so demonstrably clear as was Jack Teagarden's. After the shock of his 1927 charge on New York wore off, most Eastern trombonists set about the task of reorganizing their concepts of what could be done with the horn. Jimmy Harrison's pre-Teagarden ideas were not exactly like those he played later; Tommy Dorsey and Glenn Miller, enormously impressed, simply bowed to Jack's preeminence and became "sweet" players; young Benny Morton came close to Teagarden's clean, flowing, high-register style; Brad Gowans used a valve trombone to capture some of Jack's agility and lightness; Jack Jenny elaborated upon the Texan's elegiac ballad style, clearing a path for Bill Harris and Urbie Green; Fred Beckett, whose work inspired J. J. Johnson, demonstrated a kind of lip flexibility that could only have developed through Teagarden; Keg Johnson and J. C. Higgenbotham, possessors of fine original styles in the early thirties, were indebted to Teagarden for their flexibility and trumpetlike melodic lines. And, of course, there were literally hundreds of players who simply worked out of Jack's style from the start: Lou McGarity, Joe Harris, Ted Vesely, Abe Lincoln, and others.

It may be that the jazz trombone would have evolved along similar lines without Teagarden. There were, to be sure, trombonists like Jimmy Harrison and Lawrence Brown about to discover some of the same principles of post-tailgate playing. It is unlikely, though, that all aspects of Teagarden's style could have been worked out by others in less than ten years, if at all. Advances come more quickly after a single man has proved their feasibility.

Because Teagarden retained a superb command of the trombone until his death, there is a still-glowing awareness of his skills among younger performers. Trombonists Bob Brookmeyer, Bill Russo, and Urbie Green, saxophonists Stan Getz, Al Cohn, and Johnny Dankworth, and pianists George Wallington and John Mehegan are some who have praised Teagarden highly. Although his general musical outlook was, by the late forties, no longer shared by the new generation, Jack's ability to execute phrases that no one could duplicate preserved something of the image of invincibility he first created in the twenties. Teagarden's accomplishments, well documented by recordings, will probably continue to be used by jazz trombonists as a measure of their own abilities for many years to come.

Recommended Reading

Shapiro, Nat, and Nat Hentoff (eds.): *Hear Me Talkin' to Ya*, Rinehart, New York (1955).

Shapiro, Nat, and Nat Hentoff (eds.): *The Jazz Makers*, Grove, New York (1958).

Smith, Jay D. and Len Guttridge: *Jack Teagarden*, Cassell, London (1960).

Waters, Howard J., Jr.: *Jack Teagarden's Music*, Walter C. Allen, Stanhope, N.J. (1960).

Recommended Listening

Jazz, Vols. 7 and 8, FOLKWAYS FJ-2807, FJ-2808.
The Red Nichols Story, BRUNSWICK BL-54008, BL-54047.
A String of Swingin' Pearls (four tracks), RCA VICTOR LPM-1373.
The Louis Armstrong Story, Vol. 4 (one track), COLUMBIA CL-854.
Chicago Style Jazz (one track), COLUMBIA CL-632.
Benny Goodman from 1927 to 1934, BRUNSWICK BL-54010.
Great Jazz Brass (two tracks), CAMDEN CAL-383.
The Vintage Goodman, COLUMBIA CL-821.
The Bessie Smith Story, Vol. 2, COLUMBIA CL-856.
The Big "T" Plays the Blues, ULTRAPHONIC 1656.
Jack Teagarden's Big Eight, RIVERSIDE RLP-141.
Bud Freeman: All-Star Jazz, HARMONY HL-7046.
The Jazz Greats (three tracks), EMARCY MG-36053.
Eddie Condon: Ivy League Jazz, DECCA DL-8282.
A Night at Eddie Condon's, DECCA DL-8281.
Town Hall Concert Plus, RCA VICTOR LPM-1443.
Satchmo' at Symphony Hall, Vols. 1 and 2, DECCA DL-8037, 8038.
Satchmo' in Pasadena, DECCA DL-8041.
Big T's Jazz, DECCA DL-8304.
This is Teagarden, CAPITOL T-721.

Bobby Hackett: Coast Concert, CAPITOL T-692.
Bobby Hackett: Jazz Ultimate, CAPITOL T-933.
Jack Teagarden: Shades of Night, CAPITOL T-1143.
Jack Teagarden: Mis'ry and the Blues, VERVE 8416.
Jack Teagarden: Think Well of Me, VERVE 8465.
Jack Teagarden: King of the Blues Trombone, EPIC SN-6044.
The Golden Horn of Jack Teagarden, DECCA DL-4540.
Tribute to Teagarden, CAPITOL T-2076.
A Portrait of Mr. T, ROULETTE R-25243.

FLETCHER HENDERSON AND
DON REDMAN

FEW MEN in the annals of jazz have given rise to as disorderly a lot of historical misconceptions as has Fletcher Henderson. Henderson was an accomplished pianist but an undistinguished jazz instrumentalist; he was a gifted arranger, but he began writing in earnest only after the best years of his own orchestra were past; he was not a particularly good businessman, yet in the twenties he built his band into a top attraction. These and other ambiguities in his history have left behind a blurred picture of triumphs and failures that, over the years, have tended to cancel one another and all but wipe Fletcher Henderson right off the books of some jazz historians.

The problem of finding Fletcher's rightful place in jazz can best be approached, perhaps, by regarding him as the focal point in a musical movement that involved a number of important allied contributors. Henderson's was the role of musical catalyst, patriarch, straight man, and sometime fall guy in the story of the evolution of big-band jazz.

Fletcher was born in 1898 at Cuthbert, Georgia, where his father taught school and governed his family with an iron hand. Henderson senior was a pianist, as was Fletcher's mother, who taught music. Inevitably, each Henderson child was encouraged to begin keyboard studies at an early age. Fletcher started at 6 and was forced to continue, like it or not, for seven years. Younger brother Horace recalls occasions when Fletcher was locked in a room and not released until his practicing was done. All three Henderson children (two boys and a girl, Irma) finally developed absolute pitch, the ability to read difficult music at sight, and a well-rounded education in harmony and piano technique. Fletcher did well by his demanding father, performing in small classical recitals and avoiding the "undesirable" influence of the blues. By 1912, however, he had begun to be exposed to a variety of musical styles through piano rolls.

Young Henderson did not plan a career in music. In 1916, he entered Atlanta University, where he majored in mathematics and chemistry. There he occasionally worked piano jobs but devoted most of his energies to science and sports. It was about this time that his baseball batting average, along with a singular manner of smacking his lips, earned for Fletcher the nickname "Smack," an appellation that stayed with him the rest of his life.

In 1920, Henderson traveled north to New York City, where he hoped to continue studying chemistry and to start earning money in his chosen field. He soon discovered that the prospects were poor for him as a fledgling chemist and that he could earn more as a skilled pianist. He took a job with the Pace and Handy publishing house, demonstrating and promoting songs like *Aunt Hager's Children* and *Long Gone*. W.C. Handy specialized in blues songs, but he was more concerned with "proper" readings of them than with earthy interpretations. Fletcher met the firm's requirements perfectly.

Shortly after Fletcher entered music on a full-time basis, Mamie Smith's record of *Crazy Blues,* a big commercial hit, launched a torrent of blues songs and suggested an enormous untapped market for blues recordings. Harry Pace saw the possibilities and started a record company called Black Swan, appointing Fletcher Henderson as musical director. The new firm signed up Ethel Waters and, in the fall of 1921, made big money with her *Down Home Blues*. The accompaniment, furnished by Cordy Williams' Jazz Masters, was unbending and leaden, in the then accepted style of many of New York's top "jazz" bands.

Clarinetist Garvin Bushell, who toured with Ethel Waters and Fletcher Henderson in 1922, has described (in the book *Jazz Panorama*) the better big bands, some of them fifty men strong, around New York at the time:

They played dance music at places like the New Star Casino on 107th Street and Lexington and at the Manhattan Casino, now Rockland Palace. There were sometimes 20 men playing bandolins, a combination of the banjo and violin that was plucked. Among the leading conductors were John C. Smith, Allie Ross (who later conducted *Blackbirds*), Happy Rhone, and Ford Dabney, who had been in it from the beginning and was much bigger than Jim Europe.

They played pop and show tunes. The saxophone was not very

prominent as a solo instrument, but the trumpet, clarinet and trombone were. The soloists, especially the trumpet players, improved, and those trumpet players used a whole series of buckets and cuspidors for effects. The bands played foxtrot rhythm and still adhered to the two-beat rhythmic feel. . . . New York "jazz" then was nearer the ragtime style and had less blues. There wasn't an Eastern performer who could really play the blues. We later absorbed how from the Southern musicians we heard, but it wasn't original with us. We didn't put that quarter-tone pitch in the music the way the Southerners did. Up North we leaned to ragtime conception—a lot of notes.

Henderson "leaned to ragtime conception," too, but his jobs with Pace and Handy and Black Swan had put him in touch with those New York musicians closest to the blues idiom. Bushell himself, for example, had been exposed to the New Orleans style of clarinetist Larry Shields in New York and had studied various regional jazz styles while on the road with Mamie Smith in 1921. When asked to put a group together to accompany Ethel Waters on tour, Fletcher selected Bushell and the Aikens brothers, trumpeter Gus and trombonist Buddy, to create as "hot" an impression as possible. (The Aikens were but two of many fine brass players who graduated from the widely known Jenkins Orphanage band in South Carolina.) Ethel herself encouraged Fletcher to acquire a more positive jazz feeling in his piano work, suggesting that he listen carefully to James P. Johnson. The troupe appeared in auditoriums and large theaters during the winter months of 1922–1923, then returned to New York and disbanded. Ethel resumed recording for Black Swan, this time with Fletcher Henderson participating directly in the sessions.

Cornetist Joe Smith was the favorite horn player of many blues singers in the twenties, and a number of Ethel's records now carried the name Joe Smith's Jazz Masters as well as the singer's own. The task of organizing and controlling the small band usually fell to Henderson, however.

"Fletcher didn't write out anything for Ethel's record dates," Bushell told writer Nat Hentoff in 1958. "You didn't have written music to back singers in those days. The piano player did have music, and the trumpet player would take the melody off the piano sheet. We couldn't use a bass drum, although sometimes we used the snare drum or a wood block. Also we didn't use a bass. Therefore, when there was no drum at all, the rhythm tended to get ragged. Then too we'd be in awkward positions and scattered all over the place, which would also make it hard to keep the rhythm together. We'd spend the greater part of the day making two numbers."

Henderson's recorded performances of this period were an improvement over Cordy Williams' efforts, but his band's music was still hampered by stiff blues playing and stilted, staccato phrasing only one step removed from orchestral ragtime. By 1923, the records of King Oliver, the New Orleans Rhythm Kings, the Original Dixieland Jazz Band (and its New York imitator, the Original Memphis Five), Jelly Roll Morton, Kid Ory, Clarence Williams (with Sidney Bechet), and Doc Cook (with Freddie Keppard and Jimmy Noone) had already helped to spread the New Orleans approach across the nation. Because Louisiana jazzmen seemed to possess a special feeling for the blues, alert musicians everywhere—with the possible exception of Harlem pianists, who had their own tradition to build upon—attempted to master this stimulating and now quite profitable musical outlook. Those who were most successful in New York usually found themselves, at one time or another, in a recording studio with Fletcher Henderson.

By mid-1923 Fletcher had become one of the busiest recording artists in New York. He accompanied Bessie Smith on the Columbia label and was turning out some piano solos for Black Swan and performing with a band on Paramount and Edison records. The band he used in the recording studios was basically the one violinist "Shrimp" Jones directed at Harlem's Club Bamville, a group that was soon to form the nucleus of Fletcher's own orchestra. Included in Jones's crew were trumpeter Howard Scott, bassist Bob Escudero, saxophonist Coleman Hawkins, pianist Leroy Tibbs, and drummer Kaiser Marshall. Eliminating Tibbs and adding trombonists Teddy Nixon or Charlie Green, trumpeter Elmer Chambers, banjoist Charlie Dixon, and reedman Don Redman, Henderson threw together his first regular band for a six-month engagement at New York's Club Alabam in early 1924. Allie Ross, formerly violinist and arranger for Ford Dabney, directed and trained the Club Alabam orchestra until Henderson was fully ready to take over himself. Most of the men had played together for a couple of years or more, if only in Henderson recording sessions, and the group shaped up quickly into one of the finest bands in the city.

Fletcher's recordings of 1923 and early 1924 reveal that he had borrowed from several sources to achieve his distinctive band sound. The influence of New Orleans jazz could be heard in the band's use of riffs (an old New Orleans device that Chicago bands had already been using for some time by 1923), in the King Oliver-like instrumentation (Hawkins frequently played bass sax, leaving a front line of two trumpets, clarinet, and trombone), and in the unrelenting four-to-the-bar pulse established by the rhythm section.

"New Orleans drummers kept a steady beat," recalls Jerome Pasquall, a Henderson sideman of a later era. "They played 2/4 and 4/4, but *steady*. Before that, drummers were a show. They threw their sticks up and often lost the time."

There were other influences as well. Art Hickman and Paul Whiteman had helped establish the use of the saxophone *section* in a dance band. Whiteman, whose early band had little to offer in the way of jazz, had by 1922 developed a rigid but syncopated jazzlike manner of section phrasing, including arranged "call and response" devices. These and other ideas of the day were incorporated into the Henderson book, largely through the efforts of arranger Don Redman. From 1923 to 1927, Fletcher relied upon Redman for most of his arrangements, and it is to this diminutive saxophonist from West Virginia that much of the credit must go for the initial success of the Henderson orchestra.

Redman, two years younger than Henderson, had been reared as a musical prodigy by musical parents. He had played cornet at 3, joined his father's marching band at 6, started piano lessons at 8, taken up trombone at 15, and dabbled with violin before completing high school. At Storer College in West Virginia, Redman studied theory, harmony, counterpoint, and orchestration. He was graduated about the same time that Fletcher Henderson was leaving Atlanta University, then joined a small band in Ohio. He picked up the alto saxophone in 1921, traveled to New York with Billy Paige's Broadway Syncopators (under the auspices of bandleader Paul Specht), and within a few weeks was working record dates with Henderson. Redman's rich background of musical experience and training was unusual in the popular field, even in New York, and he was soon scoring for Fletcher's nine-piece group as well as playing creditable clarinet along lines lying somewhere between the styles of Ted Lewis and Larry Shields.

Henderson's early band recordings were often mere elaborations on the Eastern Dixieland style as played by the Memphis Five and others around 1923. (*When You Walked Out* is one example of this approach.) Coleman Hawkins, still in his teens, demonstrated obvious skill with the tenor and bass saxophones, but at that time his slap-tongue phrasing was unattractive and his rhythmic ideas were still rooted in monotonous dotted-eighth- and sixteenth-note patterns. He had already achieved a big sound, however, as his recording of *Do Doodle Oom* proves. Hawkins may have picked up some ideas from Sidney Bechet at the time, for the two men demonstrated a comparable degree of urgency and authority in their playing styles, although Bechet was by far the more mature improviser during this period.

On numbers like *Potomac River Blues*, there seems to be a serious absence of blues feeling in the band, but one can almost sense that these young men were working on that problem, too. Some blueslike mannerisms of Fletcher's band were doubtless acquired from the popular New York trumpeter Johnny Dunn. Dunn played a powerful, sometimes downright nasty, horn, and many trumpeters followed his example until Louis Armstrong arrived in New York. (A prime example of the influence of Dunn's plunger style can be heard on Henderson's Janurary, 1924, recording of *Lots o' Mama*.)

Henderson and Redman were searching for more than a mere assemblage of good improvisers; they wanted a crack reading band capable of taking on untried written ideas as well as handling straight jazz and conventional orchestrations of the day. That they did *not* allow the improvised portions of their arrangements to wither away in the face of bigger and better scored passages is the key to the importance of their contributions to the evolution of big-band jazz. Had Henderson followed Whiteman's example, there would have been precious little space left for jazzmen to play in the band. "The day of the improvising jazzers is over," announced a Whiteman publicist in 1925, "and members of

Mr. Whiteman's orchestra deport themselves as do the members of any musical organization, playing from scores which are marvels of part writing and tonal contrast."

Fletcher Henderson and Don Redman proved Mr. Whiteman and his press agents wrong by combining imaginative arrangements with improvised jazz so adroitly that written and ad-lib passages flowed together without a break in musical manner of expression or intensity of mood. As the playing of each Henderson soloist matured and took on new harmonic, rhythmic, and melodic interest, so, too, did Redman's arrangements. Redman set out to enlarge upon and consign to paper what King Oliver and Louis Armstrong had already proved could be created by ear—thematic variations performed by two or more horns in close harmony without loss of rhythmic freedom, the sensation of spontaneity, or the satisfaction of the creative urge within each player. With Redman's arrangements, musicians could enjoy it both ways: improvised solos became integral parts of the whole score, and the score itself was challenging and provocative as a point of departure for the soloist.

The compelling sounds that came from his Club Alabam orchestra, on records and radio as well as across the dance floor, earned Fletcher a better job at New York's Roseland Ballroom in 1924. He played there at least several months of each year until 1931. The group had improved steadily in the early months of 1924, particularly when cornetist Joe Smith joined, swelling the trumpet section to three. Redman widened his scores accordingly and took note of Smith's sublime tone—a tone that retained its seductive purity even when a plunger mute was held over the bell. Just as Coleman Hawkins' dexterity on his horn invited fast saxophone-section figures, so Smith's passionate cornet suggested lyrical possibilities to Redman. Arrangements designed to set off Smith's tone resulted (those for *Mobile Blues* and *Meanest Kind of Blues*, for example). There were others that emphasized Smith's "hot" side, derived largely from Johnny Dunn's style. *The Gouge of Armour Avenue* (double-time introduction *à la* Dunn; trumpet solo backed by riffs, New Orleans style); *My Papa Doesn't Two Time No Time* (Smith sounding like a cross between Dunn and Beiderbecke; this record is also notable for a genial, raggy Henderson piano solo and a scat vocal, possibly the first on record); *War Horse Mama* (wa-wa plunger mute, in the Dunn–King Oliver tradition); *Muscle Shoals Blues* (more Dunn-like double-time effects).

The Wolverines, with Bix Beiderbecke, arrived in New York in late 1924, about the same time Louis Armstrong replaced Joe Smith in Henderson's brass section. Now there was simply no avoiding the influence of the New Orleans outlook. The Wolverines, who borrowed many of their tricks from the Original Dixieland Jazz Band and the New Orleans Rhythm Kings, were playing modern riffs, brief repeated rhythmic phrases (their *Tiger Rag* is the best recorded example), with more ease and rhythmic thrust than Henderson or Redman had yet been able to bring to their performances. Best of all, of course, Armstrong himself, whom Fletcher had been hoping to hire for more than two years, was on hand every night to show the New Yorkers just how it was done. Most of them learned fast.

With Armstrong came a new phase of development in the Henderson band. Hawkins' slap-tongue solos and Redman's whimpering alto passages began to drop away. The reed section was enlarged to three with the addition of ex-King Oliver clarinetist Buster Bailey. New Orleans trombonist Charlie Green was brought in, creating in the four brass a still more powerful ensemble sound. Most important, Redman's arrangements were beginning to swing more comfortably and convincingly. On *Go 'Long Mule*, the band seems to respond to Armstrong's lesson in the art of sustaining end-of-phrase tones rather than chopping them short in the old New York tradition. Redman furnished appropriate sustained saxophone "organ" chords under Louis on pieces like *Words*. *Copenhagen* has much of the bite and momentum of the Wolverine recorded version of a few months before as well as the broad impact of an eleven-man band under full steam. *Naughty Man*, recorded in November, 1924, demonstrates how quickly Redman had whipped the three saxophones into an integrated, relaxed section quite unlike the agitated saxophone duo on earlier Henderson recordings. The clarinet trio, too, was a favorite Redman touch and begins to appear on records made about this time, most impressively on *Alabamy Bound*. By January, 1925, the band had swung almost all the way over to Armstrong, even to providing New Orleans-like riffs and afterbeat cymbal explosions as extra support for soloists. (*Money Blues* contains good examples of these devices.) *Sugar Foot Stomp*, a reworking of the Oliver-Armstrong specialty *Dippermouth Blues*, represents the culmination of Henderson's early period and the completion of the task of catching up to the New Orleans-dominated bands in Chicago. Riffs, "organ" chords, a good grasp of the blues idiom, loose-jointed but precise ensemble playing, and first-rate solo power all come together in this performance to place the Fletcher Henderson band—and its chief arranger, Don Redman—ahead of all its competitors.

While finding success at the Roseland Ballroom, Fletcher continued to keep his hand in studio recording work. The combination of his own experience as an accompanist and his ready access to a fund of talented instrumentalists (including sought-after cornetist Joe Smith, who returned to the fold in 1925) meant that a singer could be sure of superior backing whenever Fletcher was in charge. The combinations were endless: Henderson and Coleman Hawkins; Henderson and Joe Smith; Henderson, Smith, and Buster Bailey; Henderson, Smith, and Charlie Green; Henderson's Hot Six. The singers' styles were nearly as varied; Fletcher worked with Ma Rainey, Bessie Smith, Ethel Waters, Alberta Hunter, Maggie Jones, Clara Smith, Trixie Smith, Ida Cox, and a dozen others between 1924 and 1926. Some of the best of these are Bessie Smith classics such as *Cake Walkin' Babies*, on which a seven-man contingent from the orchestra improvises in the New-Orleans collective manner with grace and zeal. Henderson's own piano contributions to these sessions are generally simple, correct, and undistinguished.

In 1925, Fletcher married Leora Meoux, a professional trumpet player who occasionally filled in for lead trumpeter Russell Smith in the Henderson band. Smith, cornetist Joe's brother, had formerly been married to Leora, in fact, and the social structure of the band began to resemble that of a large family. (At one point, a third Smith brother, Luke, joined Joe and Russell in the trumpet section for a brief stay.) Fletcher's father occasionally visited Roseland to point with pride, although his pointing had to be done from the side of the bandstand, since that was the only spot in the ballroom where Negroes were allowed. (Many years later, when Roseland was no longer able to exclude Negro patrons, the ballroom stopped hiring Negro musicians.) Another frequent visitor was brother Horace, who was organizing a band of his own at Wilberforce University in the mid-twenties.

By 1926, the Henderson organization had become a permanent fixture at Roseland, except for three or four summer months spent on the road each year. The personnel was relatively stabilized with Russell and Joe Smith and the New Orleans trumpeter Tommy Ladnier, as good a substitute for the departed Armstrong as one could hope for. Redman was turning out splendid arrangements now, and Fats Waller (who had become the main influence on Henderson's own piano style) contributed a number of original compositions for Don to work on. Impressive electrical recordings like *The Stampede, Henderson Stomp,* and *Hot Mustard,* released at this time, give evidence of steady improvement in the band and its soloists. Section parts are even more challenging in these, but Redman's complex melodic figurations never led Henderson's men away from natural jazz-oriented readings. It was largely the ensemble playing of this orchestra that caused jazzmen to evolve a reading method all their own. Eighth notes became dotted eighths, sixteenths became thirty-seconds. Section members learned to think in terms of rhythmic and melodic *patterns* rather than in separate measures. This system of interpretative reading was the key to Henderson's unique style, a style that magnified and intensified the spirit of the small jazz band. From 1926 on, every major big band that featured any "hot" tunes at all followed Henderson's example.

Fletcher was beginning to experience difficulties as a bandleader about this time. His men were loyal to him and his musical philosophy, but he was not a strong leader, either as an instrumentalist or as a personality. When Fats Waller sat in on piano on several 1926 record dates, the entire orchestra responded with noticeable extra enthusiasm to the new authority that came from the piano. "Fats played with us every now and then," Coleman Hawkins has recalled. "I didn't think Fletcher was taking advantage of it like he should have. If it had been me, I'd have hired Fats. Fletcher could have done it."

Other possibilities were overlooked and neglected as well. Despite the group's musicianship and *élan,* its recordings were often allowed to pass with sloppy section work and faulty dynamics, while competing bands took great care with execution and shading. As the decade wore on, Henderson made fewer and fewer recordings, while the orchestras of Duke Ellington and Paul Whiteman increased their recorded output. Radio had also become important, and Fletcher's chronic bad starts were not desirable in broadcast work. "[Fletcher] would be starting off, and half the band would be looking for their music," Hawkins remembers. "That used to happen regularly. All kinds of things like that. . . . The band was a bit like they didn't care—sloppy—but it had something else. It had a good sound, a good beat. It lacked a lot of precision. I think that's why the records were like they were. Where in Duke's band it was loaded with precision, they couldn't give you that good in-person sound," Hawkins recalls. "Maybe sometimes you can get too precise, and maybe you lose something when you get like that. You certainly don't on records. A good record *has* to be precise." But, as Hawkins put it, "when it got down to the core of the music, when it was supposed to be sounding good, everybody was together and everybody was playing like mad."

Redman continued exploring new scoring ideas in 1927. He was still fond of clarinet trios, but he also featured "pyramid" (arpeggiolike) chords, sectional counterpoint, advanced harmonies (Redman had been writing flatted fifths, for example, into his scores since early 1924), and sudden shifts in rhythm and key signature. One of his most involved works is *Whiteman Stomp,* which both Henderson and Whiteman recorded. Despite Whiteman's more exact reading, with Jimmy Dorsey's excellent alto saxophone playing, Henderson's is the more appealing version. Redman's skill in dealing with riffs is apparent in his outstanding treatment of *Hop Off,* recorded in November, 1927. For this, he scored a variety of riffs to build to a natural climax, avoiding the monotonous excesses that detracted from the worth of many swing bands a decade later. *Hop Off* also features the vigorous, churning sound of reeds in countermovement to brass, an advanced idea that arranger Bill Challis used often in Jean Goldkette's orchestra at the time.

Like Challis, Redman discovered that some of his writing, though a delight to musicians, was not always within the public's grasp. A 1927 issue of *Orchestra World* magazine, for example, complains that the Henderson band played too much "modern stuff."

Redman received $25 an arrangement from Henderson, in addition to his regular pay of about $80 a week as lead alto saxophonist. In mid-1927, he accepted an offer—there had been many before—to take over the musical direction of McKinney's Cotton Pickers in Detroit, one of several bands handled by Jean Goldkette's office. It was potentially a good group and had grown out of a band called the Synco Septette, originally fronted by ex-circus drummer William McKinney. McKinney had hired the survivors of a Springfield, Ohio, outfit called Scott's Symphonic Syncopators, which had broken up in 1924. From that original Springfield group came trombonist Claude Jones, pianist Todd Rhodes, saxophonist Milton Senior, and banjoist Dave Wilborn. Before 1927, McKinney had turned over the drums to the talented Cuba Austin and had hired saxophonist-vocalist George Thomas and trumpeter-arranger John Nesbitt.

With Nesbitt's help, Redman built the McKinney band's book into one of the finest in the country. He added his own alto saxophone to those of Senior, Thomas, and Prince Robinson (a long-underrated tenor saxophonist) to form a four-man reed section. Together with the change to three brass (from Henderson's five), this new balance in instrumentation resulted in a fresh Redman sound, quite unlike his previous efforts. Don drilled his men and even gave them lessons in reading and interpretation. By mid-1928, he had created a first-class orchestra rivaling Henderson's.

Redman's saxophone section was without equal, and Don took advantage of all four voices, writing bravura passages that attracted wide attention from other arrangers. Nesbitt, whose jazz outlook was deeply affected by the work of cornetist Bix Beiderbecke and arranger Bill Challis, also began to contribute superior scores to the band's library. With records like *Stop Kidding, Milenberg Joys, Shim-Me-Sha-Wabble,* and *Cherry,* McKinney's Cotton Pickers was quickly established in 1928 as a leading dance orchestra and an important modern "hot" band. Redman settled into Detroit's Greystone Ballroom for a long and profitable stay.

Henderson never completely filled the enormous gap left by Redman's departure. Jerome Pasquall, who moved into the lead alto chair at this time, recalls that the band was full of "flaws" and lacked the rhythmic freedom of Fletcher's 1936 band, of which Pasquall was also a member. One problem may have been the absence of bassist Bob Escudero, who was now with Redman in Mc-Kinney's Cotton Pickers. Another was the old matter, grown even more serious without Redman, of lack of discipline. Still another, of course, was the loss of a highly skilled arranger within the band to write material suited to its individual soloists. With Redman, too, went some of the earthy quality that had characterized much of the band's work until 1927.

"[Fletcher] was exchanging arrangements with other bands," Coleman Hawkins has observed of this period. "He kept on and on, and finally the band, to me, got to the place where it sounded just like other bands, which is no good. We used to play numbers that sounded just like the Casa Loma band at times, because we had gangs of their arrangements. You see, what it was, for one thing, in the earlier band when he had Don Redman, Don used to do . . . some very good gutbucket arrangements."

For some time, the band got by on borrowed scores (some came from Goldkette's orchestra, others from Mel Stitzel, a few from Ellington, and some even from John Nesbitt), loose pieces tied together by Henderson himself (D Natural Blues, Oh Baby), "head" arrangements comprising riffs and fills elaborated by sidemen in the orchestra (King Porter Stomp), and old Redman specialties like Hop Off. Recording dates were rather rare events now, although the band was still an excellent one. Only about two dozen selections were turned out in the more than three years between October, 1927, and February, 1931, and a number of those carried the pseudonym Dixie Stompers in place of Henderson's own name.

During this slack recording period, Fletcher's soloists were expanding their abilities and reputations to new levels. By 1928, trombonist Jimmy Harrison, who had joined the year before, was heavily featured at Roseland, as was Hawkins, who now had no peers on the tenor saxophone. (Two good examples of his drive and technique are the 1928 recordings Oh Baby and I'm Feelin' Devilish.) Joe Smith, always a personal favorite of Fletcher's, had been in and out of the trumpet section again by the summer of 1928. Rex Stewart and the brilliant Bobby Stark were now the jazz soloists, while Russell Smith continued to handle most of the lead work. Then Fletcher hired altoist-arranger Benny Carter, formerly a member of Horace Henderson's Wilberforce band, who came closer to filling Don Redman's spot than anyone before or after him. Carter had a superb alto style—original, though touched by Frank Trumbauer—and wrote particularly handsome section figures for saxophones. The group responded to his command of modern voicings with spirited readings of *Come On, Baby, Easy Money, Blazin'*, and *Wang Wang Blues*. (The last features trumpeter Cootie Williams, who spent a brief period with Henderson in 1929 before joining Duke Ellington.)

While Redman worked out the principles of the four-man saxophone section in Detroit, Henderson was establishing the use of five brass—three trumpets, two trombones—in the East. Together, their respective orchestras anticipated the classic proportions of the thirteen-piece swing band in the thirties—five brass, four reeds, four rhythm.

From the spring of 1929 to the fall of 1930, the Henderson orchestra did not cut a single record. Fletcher played more one-night engagements than ever now, although Roseland was still home. "Every April we would pile into our assorted Packards, Buicks, and Caddies and hit the coalfields of Pennsylvania until September," Rex Stewart has recalled, "and each year we went further afield."

The rise of show bands and novelty attractions had left wholly musical organizations like Fletcher's behind. Henderson's main commercial card was trombonist Jimmy Harrison, who contributed comedy turns, Bert Williams impressions, and "preacher" routines. Ellington had his "jungle" style plus a visually effective, sleek presentation of his wares. Armstrong was an unbeatable showman who swept up his audiences in staged displays of high-note virtuosity and frivolity. Cab Calloway featured his own frenzied singing and band to match. The public was, in short, buying a show; that the music was often superior had significance mainly to other musicians and a very small portion of the listening audience.

Redman appraised the situation and laced many of his arrangements with moody themes suitable to the early Depression days (*Blues Sure Have Got Me*) and clever vocal routines, carried out by himself, saxophonist George Thomas, and banjoist Dave Wilborn (*If I Could Be with You One Hour, Rocky Road, Just a Shade Corn*). Most important, he dropped some of his more ambitious ideas and began to write simple, spare, melodic section lines that held appeal for musicians and nondiscerning listeners alike (*Baby Won't You Please Come Home?, Travellin' All Alone*). Together with a number of very commercial pieces, these generally excellent records brought unprecedented success to McKinney's Cotton Pickers. While Henderson's recording work dropped off, Redman's increased substantially in 1929 and 1930. Fletcher's morale might well have hit bottom when cornetist Joe Smith joined Redman, then returned East with Don to help select Henderson's best men for McKinney's Cotton Pickers recording dates. (The results, featuring Coleman Hawkins, Benny Carter and Kaiser Marshall, can be heard on *Plain Dirt, Gee Ain't I Good to You?, I'd Love It, The Way I Feel Today, Miss Hannah, Peggy,* and *Wherever There's a Will, Baby.*)

In 1931, Fletcher and his band, for some reason, became active in the recording studios again. (Henderson's slow recovery from a severe automobile accident in the late twenties might well have been a factor in the erratic course of his career about this time.) Their performances, now sparked by magnificent bravura flights of Hawkins and mature trombone statements of Jimmy Harrison, were better than ever. The impressive trombonist Claude Jones had by now come over to Henderson from Redman, and the rhythm section had profited by the arrivals of drummer Walter Johnson, banjoist-guitarist Clarence Holiday (Billie Holiday's father), and bassist John Kirby. The change, not yet complete, from banjo and tuba to guitar and bass was a significant one; a light but firm four-to-the-bar beat was now possible, opening the way for more supple, intelligently modulated arrangements. It meant, for example, that Coleman Hawkins could rhapsodize breathily on a slow ballad without fear of a flagging, top-heavy rhythm section and without losing the more subtle flourishes in his solos. This light, airy rhythm was also the perfect backdrop against which to play simple, insinuating riffs of the sort Don Redman had been writing for the Cotton Pickers.

Fletcher continued to pick up arrangements wherever he could. John Nesbitt contributed *Chinatown, My Chinatown,* Nat Leslie scored *Radio Rhythm,* and Benny Carter continued to turn out effective pieces like *Somebody Loves Me* and *Sweet and Hot*. The band used publishers' stock arrangements as well, often doctored here and there to permit more freedom for soloists. (*My Gal Sal* is a good lesson in the art of swinging a stock orchestration.) Others came from the old Jean Goldkette book (*My Pretty Girl*), publishing-house arranger Archie Bleyer (*Business in F*), Casa Loma's Gene Gifford (*Casa Loma Stomp*), and young Horace Henderson, who had by 1931 blossomed into a promising—if not yet original—arranger and a good jazz pianist. Horace's *Hot and Anxious* and *Comin' and Goin'* have themes borrowed from Ellington and others, but they point up the new soft saxophone blend that was replacing the old shouting, gutbucket sound at this time. The rhythmic figures thus played seem to melt into the rhythm section itself, creating a unified ensemble effect at once easygoing and surging with potential power.

In this leashed energy lay much of the appeal of this approach to big-band jazz. Arrangers, section men, and soloists all took part in the game of building, holding back, and releasing tensions, and this technique was proving to be more electrifying than the all-out stomp tactics of a few years before. Duke Ellington was probably the first major bandleader to make intelligent use of this more subtle method of big-band playing.

It was about this time—1931—that Fletcher himself took a greater interest in writing arrangements for the band. At first, he simply exercised his sharp ear by transcribing passages from old jazz records and scoring them for a full orchestra. Thus the Bix Beiderbecke–Frank Trumbauer 1927 versions of *Clarinet Marmalade* and *Singin' the Blues* became part of Henderson's library four years later. Fletcher's *Just Blues* suggests that he still had a good deal of catching up to do, for the arrangement itself, calling for a return to old banjo-tuba figures, has its roots in the King Oliver style of four or five years before.

Gradually, Henderson came out of this experimental phase as he grew more familiar with arranging techniques. His 1932 scores of *Honeysuckle Rose* and *Blue Moments* reveal considerable progress and a new understanding of tonal colors not unlike Ellington's. *Honeysuckle Rose* even carries implications of an original Henderson style, which the band needed badly if it was to survive the competition of many highly stylized orchestras in the popular-music field. Built on a resourceful manipulation of tuneful riffs in the Redman tradition, this style was soon to establish a whole new identity for the troubled 34-year-old bandleader.

Henderson learned from his own sidemen as well. It was indeed a remarkable band, not merely as a gathering of outstanding soloists but as a musical unit possessed of a rare and unique collective spirit. Some of Henderson's best numbers—*King Porter Stomp* is one—were head arrangements worked out by the players themselves. Made possible by the riff approach to ensemble playing, head arrangements were to be a significant but often overlooked characteristic of big-band music in the thirties. The process of developing a head arrangement often appears, like the collective creations of New Orleans bands, to be an easy matter. It requires, however, sensitive and experienced musicians to bring it off properly. A single sideman thinks of a new idea, plays it, and suddenly all his section mates join him with their appropriate harmonic parts. A player in a different part of the orchestra thinks of a logical answering phrase and is joined by *his* section. The third horn section adds its part in the same manner, and the entire orchestra is under way. The rhythm players add to the total effect by supporting the specific rhythmic figures devised by each section. When one set of riffs begin to wear thin, the entire process may repeat itself with new ideas, usually marked by an increase in tension.

Many excellent swing arrangements came from this practice, which found its finest expression in the Fletcher Henderson band. Fletcher's 1933 organization, which included saxophonists Hawkins and Hilton Jefferson, trombonist Dickie Wells, and trumpeter Red Allen, was particularly skilled in creating head arrangements.

Despite the quality of its work, the band continued to suffer from Fletcher's failure to establish a code of discipline. Several men drank too much, missed rehearsals (even fell off the stand occasionally), and sometimes had trouble keeping up with the music. Although Fletcher's arrangements often sounded elementary enough, many were written in unusual keys. Clarinetist Darnell Howard, who once substituted for Buster Bailey, remembers facing the task of sight-reading a score in the key of E (concert). When Howard suggested to Henderson that it might be a bit rough the first time around, Fletcher snapped, "You have a union card, don't you?"

"Everybody got juiced up when they wanted to," trombonist J. C. Higginbotham, who put in better than a year with the band in 1931 and 1932, has recalled. "You had a lot of fun."

Coleman Hawkins, the star performer and an important commercial asset to the band, finally departed in 1934, just as Fletcher's arranging talents had reached maturity. Hawkins had been heavily featured on a number of 1933 recordings (*Queer Notions, Its the Talk of the Town, I've Got to Sing a Torch Song*) made for release in England. The brilliant tenor saxophonist followed his fame to England and Europe, remaining there about five years. By the fall, Fletcher had found Ben Webster as a replacement and at last added a fourth saxophone to form still another first-rate band. In addition to arrangements by Benny Carter and Horace Henderson, Fletcher's own were now an important part of his book.

A new Decca contract in 1934 provided needed encouragement, and in two memorable sessions during September, Fletcher recorded his *Wrappin' It Up, Down South Camp Meeting, Shanghai Shuffle*, and the excellent *Big John Special*. Each piece is a masterpiece of intelligent, jazz-based writing. The four saxophones are blended to sound light yet muscular; despite challenging double-time figures and treacherous syncopations, ensemble passages appear to float effortlessly over the light but firm rhythm; each arrangement seems to swing virtually by itself, requiring only a few good soloists here and there to make up a completely satisfying performance, in jazz terms, from first measure to last. With these recordings, Fletcher set the high standards to which most other big bands aspired for the next five or six years. He also demonstrated in no uncertain terms that his creative strength now lay in arranging rather than piano playing or even leading a band.

As good as they were, the records did not save the Henderson band. Writing in *Swing* magazine in 1940, Duke Ellington recalled how and why the group broke up:

Smack's band was beginning to find the going a little tough around '32 and '33. Work was scarce, but the band was so fine, and the guys so attached to it, that nobody had the heart to quit. It was exceptional the way everybody stuck, hoping for a break. Almost each individual musician had money coming to him and yet nothing ever happened. Finally when they couldn't hold out any longer, the whole band got together, and everybody turned in their notice at the same time. That was the break-up of the Fletcher Henderson band. Maybe it was an appropriate finale for one of the greatest dance bands anybody ever heard.

That was in 1934 and the men in the band were: Pops Smith, Red Allen, and Mouse Randolph, Claude Jones, and Keg Johnson, Benny Webster (Hawk had already left for Europe), Procope, and Jeff, Walter Johnson, Lucie, Kirby, and Horace. Things had been so bad with Smack, the boys were working one-nighters for $50 a week. And yet some of them like Claude Jones, who had $400 coming to him, were refusing offers from Calloway and others, to stick till the end.

Incidentally, that was probably one of the partyingest bands that ever was. They used to travel on the road in cars, instead of buses. As soon as they'd arrive at their destination they'd start in having a ball. When they got through at night, they'd pick up where they left off. They'd wait till the last possible moment before leaving for the next town, and they'd have to hold a steady seventy on the road to arrive on schedule (which half of them never did).

In early 1935, temporarily without a band at all for the first time in a dozen years, Fletcher became chief arranger for Benny Goodman, who now stood on the threshold of unparalleled success in the band business. The enthusiasm of Goodman and his players for Henderson's arrangements had much to do with this success. Goodman himself told of this period in his book, *The Kingdom of Swing:*

> It was then that we made one of the most important discoveries of all—that Fletcher Henderson, in addition to writing big arrangements such as the ones I have just mentioned [*King Porter Stomp*, etc.], could also do a wonderful job on melodic tunes such as *Can't We Be Friends?*, *Sleepy Time Down South*, *Blue Skies*, *I Can't Give You Anything But Love* and above all *Sometimes I'm Happy*. He had to be convinced of it himself, but once he started he did marvelous work. These were the things, with their wonderful easy style and great background figures, that really set the style of the band.

Up to that time the only kind of arrangements that the public had paid much attention to, so far as knowing who was responsible for them was concerned, were the elaborate ones such as Ferde Grofe's for Whiteman. But the art of making an arrangement a band can play with swing—and I am convinced it is an art—one that really helps a solo player to get off, and gives him the right background to work against—that's something that very few musicians can do.

The whole idea is that the ensemble passages, where the whole band is playing together or one section has the lead, have to be written in more or less the same style that a soloist would use if he were improvising. That is, what Fletcher really could do so wonderfully was to take a tune like *Sometimes I'm Happy* and really improvise on it himself, with the exception of certain parts of the various choruses which would be marked solo trumpet or solo tenor or solo clarinet. Even here the background for the rest of the band would be in the same consistent vein, so that the whole thing really hung together and sounded unified. Then, too, the arranger's choice of the different key changes is very important, and the order in which the solos are placed, so that the arrangement works up to a climax. In all these respects, Fletcher's ideas were far ahead of anybody else's at the time, partly because of all the experience he had with the great soloists in his different bands, and partly because he was such an outstanding musician himself. Without Fletcher I probably would have had a pretty good band, but it would have been something quite different from what it eventually turned out to be.

British writer G. F. Gray Clarke unwittingly added an appropriate footnote to Goodman's remarks in an essay titled "Deep Henderson":

I have heard a band of good stout Nazis in Berlin playing one of those Henderson-Goodman arrangements and, in spite of themselves, producing lift, drive and guttiness: you can't go terribly far wrong by just reading accurately whatever Henderson happens to write. The internal evidence of his scores is that he knows what a man can play on a man-made instrument, and never tries to guess what an archangel with musical leanings might produce in a moment of inspirational ecstasy from Jehovah's own silver trumpets. Too many modern orchestrators, both straight and jazz, make these impossible demands of flesh, blood and brass. . . .

Some of the dozens of arrangements that Fletcher wrote for Goodman in the next fifteen years line up almost like a capsule history of Benny's bands: *When Buddha Smiles, Get Happy, Christopher Columbus, Star Dust, Sugar Foot Stomp, Stealin' Apples, Beyond the Moon, Opus Local 802, Crazy Rhythm, Chicago, South of the Border,* and *Wolverine Blues.*

Don Redman had had his share of hard times by the mid-thirties, too. In 1931, he had taken over Horace Henderson's orchestra and made an impressive start as a leader with records like *I Heard* and *Chant of the Weed.* However, he soon ran into problems of poor management and lack of public acceptance, except for the vocals of Harlan Lattimore. In 1936, Don fronted a different and still excellent orchestra that included clarinetist-arranger Ed Inge, trombonist Benny Morton, and a trumpet section composed of Renauld Jones, Shirley Clay, and Sidney deParis, but the cards seemed stacked against him. He struggled on until 1940, then disbanded and took up a more predictable life as a busy freelance arranger. His scores found their way into groups as diverse as those of Harry James, Ella Fitzgerald, Jimmy Dorsey, Jimmie Lunceford, Charlie Barnet, Fred Waring, and Count Basie. Except for brief flings as a leader or musical consultant (including a stint directing Jay McShann's 1942 band), Redman has remained an independent arranger ever since and has often worked with singer-comedienne Pearl Bailey in recent years.

McKinney's Cotton Pickers lasted a couple of years after Redman left but reached the end of the rocky road in 1934. When last heard from, William McKinney himself was working as a bellhop in a Detroit hotel.

Fletcher, encouraged by public support of his Goodman scores, was back in the band business in 1936, again with a crack outfit. Buster Bailey returned, as did John Kirby. Joe Thomas, Dick Vance, and Roy Eldridge were the trumpeters. Jerome Pasquall and Chu Berry graced the saxophone section. Sid Catlett joined on drums for a while, then was replaced by Walter Johnson. The band's first record, *Christopher Columbus,* was a hit (musicians still speak of "Smack's Christopher Columbus band") and landed Fletcher in top locations again, notably the Grand Terrace in Chicago. The glory was relatively short-lived, however, and Henderson's failure to produce another hit started the downward slide once more. In 1938, he placed twenty-fifth in a music-magazine poll of favorite swing bands. (Mal Hallett, Jan Savitt, Skeets Tolbert, and Dean Hudson were among the names ahead of Fletcher's!) The battle-weary Henderson began to realize that the "swing craze" of the late thirties was little more than another manifestation of the public demand for novelty and not at all a musical awakening.

Whether or not the current tremendous public interest in jazz will die out and be replaced by a new popular idea [Fletcher wrote in the 1939 *Yearbook of Swing*] need not concern either intelligent musicians or honest admirers. It is encouraging to find that among a few persons a genuine understanding of jazz has at last flourished and promises to stimulate a wider interest and appreciation on the part of others who are able, through a knowledge of music generally, to interpret the aims and efforts of composers long neglected. The demand for old recordings of music in the hot style is persistent. If the small group, which really finds in this music an element of art to which it feels a definite response, can be looked to for moral support, then we can anticipate the evolution of an even finer jazz, brought about by composers, arrangers, and musicans fired with a new ambition.

The outstanding drawback to the development of jazz, as everyone knows, is the unfortunate commercialism which always turns a deaf ear to unconventional progress [obviously, a reference to his own plight]. Worthy organizations and individuals find it difficult to reconcile their art with their daily sustenance, and huge booking agencies have little regard for artistic sensibilities. Public reaction is always uppermost in importance, and many a worthy musician must suffer furious, if silent, indignation at the nature of "request numbers" from patrons. The average popular song is anathema to the musical taste of the orchestra characterized by talent and originality. It not only offends the taste, but, what is far more important, dulls the creative spirit and demoralizes real jazz music far more than jazz will ever—even with the assistance of professional reformers—demoralize the youth of this great nation.

In 1939, Henderson dropped his bandleading career a second time and joined Goodman's orchestra for a few months, playing piano and turning out more arrangements. After an abortive third try at maintaining a big band in 1941, he finally gave up the idea altogether, except for specific jobs that came up occasionally during the next few years. (A fifteen-month run at the DeLisa in Chicago around 1945 was the best of these.) In the late forties, he toured as arranger and pianist with Ethel Waters, much as he had done a quarter century before.

Fletcher's health began to fail in 1949, but in 1950 he was back at work in New York's Café Society with a sextet. The job was cut short by a paralyzing stroke in December. The famed arranger lost heart, retired for a while to his birthplace in Cuthbert, Georgia, then returned to New York City to await death. It came a few days after his fifty-fourth birthday, in December, 1952.

Without Fletcher Henderson, it is likely that big-band jazz would have developed differently. A big-band style, if it had come at all, might well have been dominated by pompous extensions of the Paul Whiteman–Ferde Grofe idea. It was largely through Henderson's outlook and Redman's talent that the free-swinging, blues-oriented music of New Orleans was combined successfully with the sophisticated harmonies and ambitious arrangements of the popular dance band. The basic rules of big-band jazz (and Fletcher saw to it that his remained primarily a *jazz* band) were first set up, carried out, and refined to a fine art in Henderson's groups.

By way of Henderson and Redman came the fundamental instrumentation of big bands in the thirties—three trumpets, two trombones, four saxophones, and four rhythm. Although these components were enlarged in later years, the relationship of each section to the other three has not changed to this day.

To the men in Fletcher's bands, as well as to Redman, must go much of the credit for the system of interpreting conventional music notation that has made possible the rise of hundreds of jazz-grounded orchestras in the last four decades. It was this departure from "legitimate" reading techniques that won for big bands the sort of relaxed swing found almost exclusively in small improvising combinations before Henderson.

Without Henderson, it is questionable whether head arrangements could have developed to any significant extent. The true head arrangement, seldom caught in full cry on records, is a marvel of collective improvisation and a logical extension of the best contrapuntal efforts of small New Orleans jazz bands. Among the post-Henderson orchestras, those of Count Basie, Cab Calloway, Woody Herman (c. 1945), and, of course, Duke Ellington made extensive and impressive use of this method of creating new orchestral literature.

Henderson deserves special credit, too, for helping to build the skills and reputations of his sidemen. Louis Armstrong, Joe Smith, Coleman Hawkins, Jimmy Harrison, Don Redman, and many others were featured in specialty numbers that drew attention to their individual talents as artists, not merely as entertainers. Fletcher himself benefitted from this when he was with Benny Goodman, who, following Henderson's example, felt that sidemen *and* arrangers should receive proper recognition, even on record labels. For all its faults, the star system has been essential to the rapid growth and broad acceptance of jazz around the world since 1930.

Finally, there is the influence of Henderson the arranger. Had he made no other contribution, Fletcher's place in jazz would be assured by his role in the spread of jazz through Benny Goodman's orchestra. That it was not Fletcher's own organization that caught the brass ring is a strange piece of irony that would require a volume of psychological, sociological, and economic essays to explain. Goodman happened to be the symbol of the age, but this came about, at least in large part, as a result of the artistry and craftmanship, born of twelve hard years of musical experience, that Fletcher Henderson brought to him at just the right moment in history.

Recommended Reading

Feather, Leonard: *The Encyclopedia of Jazz,* Horizon, New York (1960).

Goodman, Benny, and Irving Kolodin: *The Kingdom of Swing,* Stackpole, Harrisburg, Pa. (1939).

Shapiro, Nat, and Nat Hentoff (eds.): *Hear Me Talkin' to Ya,* Rinehart, New York (1955).

Shapiro, Nat, and Nat Hentoff (eds.): *The Jazz Makers,* Grove, New York (1958).

Recommended Listening

The Birth of Big Band Jazz, RIVERSIDE RLP 12-129.
The Fletcher Henderson Story, COLUMBIA C4L-19.
Young Louis Armstrong (one track), RIVERSIDE RLP 12-101.
The Bessie Smith Story, Vol. 3, COLUMBIA CL-857.
Jazz: Big Bands (1924–1934), Vol. 8, FOLKWAYS FP 69.
Guide to Jazz (one track), RCA VICTOR LPM-1393.
The Encyclopedia of Jazz on Records, Vol. 2 (one track), DECCA DL 8399.
This Is Benny Goodman, RCA VICTOR LPM-1239.
The Golden Age of Swing, RCA VICTOR LPT-6703.
Benny Goodman Presents Fletcher Henderson Arrangements, COLUMBIA CL-524.
Swing with Benny Goodman, HARMONY HL 7190.

BESSIE SMITH

ONLY ONE WOMAN contributed significantly to the development of jazz in the twenties. She was an aggressive singer from Chattanooga, Tennessee, christened, unprepossessingly, Elizabeth Smith. Everyone called her Bessie.

It is not known just when Bessie was born, but most educated guessers place the time around 1898. She was one of five children —Tinnie, Viola, Lulu, and Clarence were the others. A natural entertainer, Bessie appeared in school plays and even earned $8 for a single appearance in a Chattanooga theater when she was only 9. There was a period, too, when she sang in a choir that gave performances in other parts of Tennessee. Her early experience in church groups must have made a lasting impression, for, as veteran promoter Perry Bradford has observed, Bessie's vocal style had "that spiritual touch" throughout her career. As she grew into a tall young woman, Bessie gradually assumed a bearing that has frequently been described as regal, to match her increasingly powerful and authoritative voice.

When she was about 14, Bessie met Gertrude "Ma" Rainey, a splendid blues singer from Columbus, Georgia, whose big somber voice was already well known throughout the South. Ma, some twelve years Bessie's senior, and Ma's husband, Will, heard the youngster sing and took her as a kind of protégé into their traveling troupe, called the Rabbit Foot Minstrels. During the next critical couple of years, Bessie learned all about show business as practiced in the big tents up, down, and across the Deep South. She learned to project her impressive voice over spirited gatherings without a megaphone (there were, of course, no electric microphones at that time); she discovered how to take advantage of her outgoing personality and handsome features; most important, she came to know the ways of a wide segment of the Southern public, particularly its boundless affection for the blues.

The word "blues" as an expression of melancholy had been in common use throughout the country—even as far north as Vermont—for many years. But by the end of the nineteenth century, a definite musical and vocal form by that name had found its way into the realm of Southern folk and popular music. It is a simple form, its lyrics usually comprising two identical four-bar statements and a third four-bar "punch line" to conclude the chorus.

For example:

Don't the moon look lonesome rising through the pine?
Don't the moon look lonesome rising through the pine?
Don't a woman look lonesome when her man leaves her behind?

Blues songs, however, were not always sung in twelve-bar cycles; formal eight-bar and sixteen-bar patterns were common, and self-accompanied folk singers often stretched or compressed these songs to unusual dimensions. Bessie, like Ma Rainey, drew largely upon the vast reservoir of anonymously created blues melodies and verses that were public domain, adding a few notions of her own as she went along. Possessed of a more flexible and vibrant voice than her mentor, Bessie eventually became the better all-around singer of the two, but neither she nor anyone else ever sang a *blues* more convincingly than Ma Rainey.

By about 1914, Bessie had left the Rainey tent show to try her luck in theaters as a singer and a dancer. Perry Bradford saw her in Atlanta at this time: "She was playing at the Dixie Theater, and I was playing at Charlie Bailey's Theater [the "81"] on Decatur Street. But she was doing an act at the time with a partner, Buzzin' Burton, and they were featuring a dance called *Buzzin' Around*. [She was] a whopping good flat-foot dancer."

In succeeding years, Bessie worked countless jobs in theaters, tents, dance halls, and cabarets throughout most of the South-eastern states, returning frequently to the TOBA (Theater Own-ers' Booking Agency) circuit, which included Atlanta's well-known "81." There was a minstrel show called the *Florida Cotton Blossoms,* trio acts, dance routines, comedy—in short, any kind of entertainment that would pay. All this time, Bessie was becoming a blues singer of extraordinary musical quality and unsurpassed communicative power. "When you went to see Bessie and she came out, that was it," New Orleans guitarist Danny Barker re-called years later. "If you had any church background, like people who came from the South as I did, you would recognize a similarity between what she was doing and what those preachers and evangelists from there did, and how they moved people. . . . Bessie did the same thing onstage."

She had built a fairly good reputation in clubs and theaters by 1919. Northern musicians visiting Atlanta heard her there in places like the "91" (just up the street from the "81"), where she worked with two other entertainers in an act called the Liberty Belles. The money was good—$75 a week plus tips. In 1920, an offer came to join the revue at the Paradise in Atlantic City.

Frankie "Half Pint" Jaxon, a popular entertainer-producer-man-about-show-business (and a former partner of the aforementioned Buzzin' Burton), also worked the Paradise that season. Jaxon's description (in *Australian Jazz Quartely #3*) of a typical Paradise show, probably much like the one in which Bessie participated, reveals the level at which even gifted performers had to operate if they were to keep working in the twenties:

Then the finale. All who had been on came out on the big wide floor. The band struck up a tune called "I Ain't Gonna Give You None of My Jelly Roll." Each had an imitation of a real Jelly Roll. They'd do a walk all around inside of the floor, showing their Jelly Roll, with their costumes as dresses made to look like grass skirts, and short, holding the skirts up to thighs and stomachs. Then I'd come out from and thru the band stand, strutting around each female, while the band played a vamp. I'd pick up and start singing the tune, pointing my finger at each gal. The band kept the tune going on. I went to the right of the girls all around the ring. The band kept the tune going all the time. I stopped, and called the first girl. (They were all different shapes, you know, each typed by the type of tune that she sang.) I did the pantomime of holding a conversation with her, she still shaking and twirling her body every way. I stood still and just looked at her shake and twirl. Then, when she'd put on a heck of a shake and stand shimmying her body, my eyes would go here and there around her body, but I'd make believe I was touching her, and I'd lean close to her and whisper in her ear. She'd step back and shake her head, and I'd signal as if asking how much she wanted. She put up 5 fingers. I looked, and put up 2 of my fingers. She shook her head, and put up 7 fingers. I shook my head, put up 3 fingers. She made a quick twirl, stood before me just turning every muscle in her body; I was twirling and looking in every one of my pockets, searching for my money. When

I found it, I stepped back and made a long slide into her. She tried to keep going on in a pretending manner. I put my arms around her hips, she put hers around my neck. She tried not to faint, but I gave a high bounce up in the air, and danced in front of her. She held me again, and I made a twirl. She jerked from me, and as I twirled and twirled 3 or 4 times, 2 girls walked out of the lines and caught her behind the back parts of her shoulders and dragged her off the floor, as I am supposed to have made her faint.

The music kept the tune going, but loud, and the customers just fainted and shouted laughing, and most everybody wanted to pour water on her. The waitresses did.

While Bessie was appearing in Atlantic City, a singer named Mamie Smith (no relation) opened the door to a vast market for blues recordings with her hit *Crazy Blues*. It was now but a matter of time until someone "discovered" Bessie Smith.

Following an engagement at a theater in Detroit, probably in early 1921, Bessie was guided by Perry Bradford to Emerson Records in New York, where she made a test. Curiously, the company failed to follow up this opportunity (Bradford claims it had to do with his prior managerial commitments to Mamie Smith and the Okeh company), and Bessie went off to a successful Philadelphia engagement and a swing through the South again.

During a stay in Washington, D. C., Bessie met saxophonist Sidney Bechet at the home of blues singer Virginia Liston. Bechet helped secure a part for Bessie in the show *How Come*, and their friendship deepened into a fitful romance as they toured together. The two cut a test record for Okeh, but that firm already had as many blues singers as it could handle, and Bessie remained unsigned. It was, in fact, the third company to turn her down, for Black Swan Records had judged her too rough for their taste.

"Bessie was a hell of a fine woman [Bechet recalled in his last years]. A fine farmer, too; she had a place of her own in New Jersey and was doing well growing things. Another thing about Bessie, she could be plenty tough; she could really handle her own. She always drank plenty, and she could hold it, but sometimes, after she'd been drinking a while, she'd get like there was no pleasing her. There were times you had to know just how to handle her right.

"She had this trouble in her, this thing that wouldn't let her rest sometimes, a meanness that came and took her over. But what she had was alive; she'd been through the whole book. And you can say that one way and you can say it another. If you understand it, it's there, and if you don't understand it, it's not for you. Bessie, she was great. She was the greatest."

Frank Walker of Columbia Records, who had heard Bessie sing several years before, finally sent for her, and in February, 1923, the first of many successful sessions for that label took place. *Down Hearted Blues* and *Gulf Coast Blues* were instant hits, launching one of the most profitable careers in the history of the recording industry. She was billed as a "comedienne," but Southern listeners, including many who had resettled in the North, knew that Bessie was the real article—a woman steeped in authentic blues lore who sang the familiar old words as if she really meant them. Over the next six years, Bessie's admirers purchased about six million of her records, and about two million of them were sold in the first ten months of her Columbia contract.

Some "respectable" families winced at the popularity of the earthy songs Bessie sang. Singer Juanita Hall, who has come about as close to re-creating the Smith style as anyone, remembers the effect Bessie's first record had upon her: "I'll never forget it. I was on my way home one day, and out of this house came the sound of a record playing, and I heard Bessie Smith singing *Down Hearted Blues*. Well, I went home singing it at the top of my voice, and my grandmother said to me, 'Wherever did you hear a thing like that? You should know that is very, very bad music!' But I never forgot the tune—it was one of her greatest ever."

Bessie's winning style, made beautiful by a sonorous, deep-chested, but perfectly controlled voice, came straight from Ma Rainey. Like Ma, she worked around strong "center tones" in an ingenious variety of ways. Bessie's most powerful, ringing tones were F, F-sharp (or G-flat), G, A-flat, and A. Within this interval of a third, she invariably selected a single note to serve as her center tone, working this note into her rendition as often as possible. When singing in C, as in *Down Hearted Blues*, she usually built her melody around G, the fifth of the tonic chord. Upon changing to the inevitable F chord, she was only a step away from a strong root note, while the customary G-seventh change could be accommodated with either the F or the G. Thus, it was actually possible to sing an entire twelve-bar blues song on only two notes, although Bessie never carried the idea quite that far. Her constant return to, elongation of, and emphasis upon these strong center tones tended to create the illusion of a kind of modern plainsong with almost spiritual intimations. Under this attack, the most trite popular song could be transformed into a fine blues as Bessie reshaped its melodic, harmonic, and rhythmic configurations to match her simple but moving style.

In Bessie's case, this center-tone approach, probably born of the necessity for projecting the voice, without benefit of microphone, to the last row in tents and theaters, did not lead to monotony. On the contrary, it was an effective means of finding new harmonic possibilities in old materials merely by changing key, which automatically changed the relationship of Bessie's strongest notes to the tonic tone. Thus *'Tain't Nobody's Bizness If I do,* sung in D, has an F-sharp center tone, or the third, while *Graveyard Dream Blues,* in B-flat, emphasizes F, or the fifth. On *Cemetery Blues,* she achieves a more somber mood by dwelling upon the minor third (G-flat) in the key of E-flat. When skilled pianists such as Fletcher Henderson or James P. Johnson were on hand to accompany, Bessie tried more adventurous keys that might have confounded most instrumental groups. *Any Woman's Blues,* for example, is in B, and the singer's center tone here is the fifth, or F-sharp. Occasionally, too, she selected unusual harmonic positions from which to work, as in *Yellow Dog Blues,* where A-flat (the fourth to the root) becomes the center tone. In *Nashville Woman's Blues,* sung in B-flat, she uses her strong notes F and G (the fifth and sixth, respectively) with almost equal emphasis to create a slightly different effect. A singer with less imagination or skill in bending and stretching notes to fit her expressive needs might have run into trouble with this system.

Bessie had a good range, nearly two octaves, from low F to high E, but worked most creatively within the single octave in which her strong middle F was just about dead center. On *Ticket Agent, Ease Your Window Down, Cold in Hand Blues,* and *You've Been a Good Old Wagon,* she even manages to perform convincingly while staying almost entirely within the range of a fifth. Like the best instrumentalists, Bessie could fashion a compelling solo from an absolute minimum of musical raw material and, again like most jazzmen, was frequently forced to do just that.

Many of Bessie's songs were "composed" by her accompanists, notably Clarence Williams and Fletcher Henderson, or by New York songwriters looking for a fast dollar. These men usually tacked together a series of familiar public-domain lines, tossed in a few Tin Pan Alley clichés, and fit the result to a stock twelve-bar or sixteen-bar melody pattern. Lyrics were mined from seemingly inexhaustible folk sources as fast as Bessie and dozens of other blues singers could record them. This would have been an acceptable procedure if the songs always told a logical story, but often they did not.

Clarence Williams' *Jail House Blues,* for example, goes like this:

> Thirty days in jail with my back turned to the wall,
> Thirty days in jail with my back turned to the wall.
> Look here, Mr. Jailkeeper, put another gal in my stall.
>
> I don't mind being in jail, but I've got to stay there so long;
> I don't mind being in jail, but I've got to stay there so long,
> When every friend I have is done shook hands and gone.
>
> You better stop your man from tickling me under my chin,
> You better stop your man from tickling me under my chin,
> Because if he keeps on tickling, I'm sure gonna take him on in.
>
> Good mornin', blues; blues, how do you do?
> Good mornin', blues; blues, how do you do?
> Say, I just came here to have a few words with you.

Jail House Blues is a good example of Williams' disregard for the meaning of the blues. His first stanza and opening lines of the second stanza are pure folk blues, close to the final lines of *I Don't Mind Bein' in Jail,* collected in the Southeast by Odum and Johnson:

> I laid in jail, back turned to the wall;
> Told the jailer to put new man in my stall.
> I don't mind bein' in jail,
> If I didn't have to stay so long.

The third stanza seems jarringly inappropriate and may be the work of Williams himself. It is totally out of place and detracts from the song. The final stanza is a powerful folk blues declaration but somehow fails to conclude the thoughts put forth at the beginning of the song.

Despite these flaws, Bessie sings each stanza with authority and conviction, revealing her skill as a seasoned performer as well as her ability as a singer. At that, *Jail House Blues* was one of the better blues handed to her and rates as one of her finest recordings. Curiously, the pianist for this date was not Clarence Williams but Irving Johns.

Many of Bessie's recordings were not blues at all, but cabaret favorites, torch songs, and robust vaudeville tunes: among Columbia's early Smith releases are *Baby, Won't You Please Come Home?*, *Beale Street Mama*, *Oh Daddy Blues*, *Yodeling Blues*, *If You Don't, I Know Who Will*, *St. Louis Gal*, and *Aggravatin' Papa*. She sometimes recorded blues or blues songs written by other singers as well, including *Down Hearted Blues*, by Alberta Hunter; *Graveyard Dream Blues*, by Ida Cox; and *Moonshine Blues*, by Ma Rainey.

Bessie's 1924 version of *Boweavil Blues*, a piece which was first recorded by Ma Rainey in 1923, points up a fault in the younger woman's work that usually went unnoticed behind the awesome strength of her voice and the wonder of her dramatic delivery. Though she made the most of the lyrics as she sang them, her poetic sense was less acute than Ma Rainey's. Compare her two final stanzas of *Boweavil Blues* with Ma's later recording *New Boweavil Blues:*

Bessie Smith:

> I went downtown, I bought myself a hat.
> I brought it back home, I laid it on the shelf.
> I looked in my bed, I'm tired sleepin' by myself.
> I'm tired sleepin' by myself.

Ma Rainey:

> Lord, I went downtown and bought me a hat.
> I brought it back home and laid it on the shelf.
> Looked at my bed—I'm gettin' tired
> Sleepin' by myself.

Ma Rainey's artfully paced stanza leads gracefully and inevitably to her final stark summation of loneliness—"sleepin' by myself." Bessie, barely avoiding disaster from excessive use of the same personal pronoun, throws her finish line away on a weak phrase and can finally do no more than repeat the words to fill the remaining time.

Yet Bessie's very determination to do things her own way was the real basis for her influence over many jazzmen. In her work, instrumentalists recognized the sort of individuality they sought to express on their own horns and strings. Jazzmen heard, too, a thoughtful blend of precomposed song structures and Southern blues feeling, a blend close to their own ideas about how good jazz should sound. Pure folk blues, as in the music of Blind Lemon Jefferson, was once removed from jazz: it lacked the urbane so- phistication that had marked jazz music from its earliest New Or- leans days. Bessie Smith bridged the gap; she was both *from* country blues and *of* big-city ways at the same time. Unlike Ma Rainey, she repeatedly demonstrated her desire to become a musician-singer as well as merely an interpreter of the blues.

Composer-arranger Don Redman once declared that he and many other musicians around New York learned much from Bessie Smith. Because she and her records were in New York at least eighteen months before the arrival of Louis Armstrong, Bessie functioned as a first contact with full-blown blues expres- sion for countless Easterners. Like Armstrong, she drew out each tone to its fullest value, projecting strength and excitement over a deep foundation of inner repose. The effect was electric, causing jazzmen like Redman to ponder the less profound aspects of their own "hot" styles, many of which were rooted in mere agitation rather than in human expressiveness.

In 1924, Bessie began to use leading jazz musicians for her ac- companying band, often those associated with Fletcher Hender- son's young orchestra. Her favorite was trumpeter Joe Smith (no relation), whose poignant tone and simple ideas contrasted per- fectly with Bessie's effusive style. From this time to the end of 1926, the popular singer hit the peak of her popularity and her highest consistent performing level. Record after record proved to be an enduring classic, a definitive lesson in the art of blues singing. *Weeping Willow Blues*, Bessie's first recording with Joe Smith, is one such performance, described enthusiastically by writer Abbe Niles twenty-five years afterward (in *A Treasury of the Blues*):

[Weeping Willow Blues] had never been published, and on comparing the original manuscript with Bessie's record, it became evident that, starting out with a good tune and idea, she and her accompanists had done a most extraordinary job of interpretation and embellishment in the best New Orleans jazz vein.

The instrumental lead, in general, is the trumpet's; the trombone [Charlie Green] coming in with occasional baleful growls, and the piano [Fletcher Henderson], in its typical subordinate New Orleans role, following lazily along with this finger and that—but in this record the timing, the touch and the feeling, in every instance, were about perfect. (Not that the accompaniment is emotional—the poor girl's tale of woe is, to these musicians, no more than a pleasant path along which to trifle, observing meanwhile the flowers and the birds.) Keep in mind that the trio played slowly, quietly, in exquisite time and, in the "riff" accompaniment to the patter, with the spring and light-footedness of a cat on hot rocks.

In this recording, without doubt, the entire introduction, accompaniment, and the two interludes were wholly *improvised*—as are some of the words and much of the vocal line.

It is open to question whether *Weeping Willow* was *wholly* improvised or not (the riffs, the repeated instrumental figures, were probably worked out carefully in advance by Henderson), but Niles was quite right about the emotional detachment of the musicians. Bessie had good reason to prefer it that way; it was *her* date and *her* voice occupying the center stage, not the improvisations of the musicians. In this light, it is reasonable to assume that Bessie was not altogether pleased by Louis Armstrong's highly charged cornet playing on a couple of 1925 recording sessions, despite her own fine work on those occasions. For one thing, Armstrong already knew the fine points of blues expression, as most New York musicians did not, and his matching of Bessie's lowered or raised pitch for a given melody note tended to destroy the shock value of her alteration as it collided with the "legitimate" pitch.

Ironically, however, Bessie's recordings with Armstrong are among her very best. Perhaps she was attempting to outperform Armstrong by leaning a bit harder into her "blue" minor thirds and sevenths; whatever the motivation, Bessie came out of these sessions victorious.

Referring to these Smith-Armstrong sessions, Winthrop Sargeant has written (in *Jazz: Hot and Hybrid*):

> Her treatment of conventional tunes is exceedingly free, in the sense that she pays very little attention to the notes, or even the words, of the printed version. As in the case of all true "hot" soloists, the rigid conventional lines of the standard tune on which her improvisation is based often become almost unrecognizable in what she produces. Her freedom of treatment, however, is not the freedom of elaboration. She does not add florid elements to the original tune. She rather subtracts its superfluous elements, pruning it down and simplifying its phraseology; making it, in fact, more truly "primitive."
>
> Most of her songs are based on a single tetrachordal grouping, either the upper or lower, and strayings beyond the four-note limits of this grouping are infrequent.

Sargeant regarded the "cool freedom with which European conceptions of melody are disregarded" by Bessie "both amazing and refreshing":

> Where *You've Been a Good Old Wagon* occupies exclusively the lower tetrachordal grouping of tones, the *Cold in Hand Blues* is sung entirely in the grouping associated with the upper tetrachord. Whether the singer herself was conscious of this change of orientation in relation to the tonic may be questioned, although she uses her scalar material somewhat differently in the new surroundings. The actual pitches of her tones may, of course, be the same in both recordings, and the change may be brought about by a shift in the key of the accompaniment.

Though he underestimated the fairly wide range of Bessie's voice, Sargeant was intrigued by the singer's ability to flatten out the contours of written melodies to suit her blues style. (This simplifying process was a function of the center-tone approach, discussed above, although Sargeant did not carry his analysis through to that conclusion.) The critic went on to describe Bessie's treatment of *St. Louis Blues:*

> Bessie Smith's version of the famous *St. Louis Blues* is governed more by complicated harmonic considerations than either of the above mentioned recordings. Handy's composition contains a section

in the minor scale—an unusual feature in the simpler type of blues—and there are other factors of a chordic nature that tend to force the singer into more sophisticated scalar treatment. Nevertheless it is interesting to note that the vocal interpretation tends always to simplify rather than to complicate Handy's original melody.

In so doing, Bessie followed the same pattern used by preachers and rural blues singers all over the South. Small wonder that her music had more meaning for Southern audiences than for sophisticated Northerners.

"When I was a little girl," singer Mahalia Jackson remembers, "I felt she [Bessie] was having troubles like me. That's why it was such a comfort for the people of the South to hear her. She expressed something they couldn't put into words.

"All you could hear was Bessie. The houses were thin; the phonographs were loud. You could hear her for blocks."

The theaters were generally packed on Bessie's Southern tours. Her Columbia records had become so identified with the singer that, for a time, part of her act was devoted to re-creating a studio recording session. Plenty of money was coming in, but Bessie had other problems. She had purchased a home in Philadelphia for herself and her husband, a policeman named Jack Gee, whom Sidney Bechet once summed up as "a mean man, really a mean man." With money came a horde of new opportunistic friends and parasites, most of them unconcerned with her growing drinking problem. And by 1926, whether Bessie sensed it or not, the rage for elemental blues had begun to wane. A new era of popular music, shaped in part by the introduction of the electric microphone, was just around the corner.

The microphone, along with improved radio broadcasting, put the shouters and the crooners on an equal footing, the size of the hall notwithstanding. Established popular singers—Irving Kaufman, say—suddenly finding themselves shouting unnecessarily into the sensitive new instruments, changed to a softer, more intimate style. For Bessie, whose singing style was as natural as breathing to her, it was not so simple. Her blues depended on a full-bodied voice. And hadn't her fans made it clear that that was exactly what they wanted?

But a new record market was growing for the sort of singers long favored in small urban cabarets, singers such as Ethel Waters. "For years they had been used to Bessie Smith and Ma Rainey," Ethel wrote in her autobiography. "They loved them and all the other shouters. I could always riff and jam and growl, but I never had that loud approach."

Ethel had had considerable success in clubs and on records, particularly her Black Swan recordings of 1921–1923, but with electrical recording methods, she became still more popular. To make matters more uncomfortable for Bessie, Ethel began recording for Columbia in 1925, often with the same accompanying musicians Bessie used. This was tough competition, and it became more difficult for Bessie to ignore than the run-of-the-mill releases of blues shouters such as Clara Smith, Chippie Hill, Sara Martin, and Bessie Tucker. (There were, incidentally, about a dozen singing Smith girls, none related to Bessie.)

The momentum of Bessie's enormous popularity carried her easily into 1927, but in her soberest moments she must have noticed that as her recorded output was going down, Ethel Waters' career was on the upswing. Having already experimented with the Tin Pan Alley type of song in 1925 (*At the Christmas Ball*) and 1926 (her own composition *Baby Doll*), Bessie tackled more such non-blues material in 1927, including *After You've Gone, There'll Be a Hot Time in Old Town Tonight, Muddy Water, Alexander's Ragtime Band, Lock and Key, A Good Man Is Hard to Find,* and *Them's Graveyard Words.* Her attempts at big-city sophistication in diction and delivery probably succeeded only in cutting off some of her remaining Southern support without winning over wise urbanites at all. She was soon back to the blues format again, singing magnificently on numbers like *Mean Old Bed Bug Blues, Foolish Man Blues,* and *Dyin' by the Hour.* About this time, she recorded her superb *Back Water Blues* and the even better *Preachin' the Blues,* with James P. Johnson providing the most virile piano accompaniment Bessie had ever had.

Throughout 1927, the still popular singer kept busy with shows and revues, including her own *Harlem Frolics,* with a company of forty dancing girls. She toured the South as usual, but also found a receptive audience in Chicago, where many Southerners had settled since the war. With her visits to Chicago from 1924 to

1928, Bessie left a solid impression on a whole generation of apprentice jazzmen there.

"There she is," pianist Art Hodes reminisced in his magazine *Jazz Record*. "Resplendent is the word, the only one that can describe her. Of course, she ain't beautiful, although she is to me. A white, shimmering evening gown, a great big woman and she completely dominates the stage and the whole house when she sings the *Yellow Dog Blues*. Ah! I don't know, she just reaches out and grabs and holds me. There's no explainin' her singing, her voice. She don't need a mike; she don't use one. I ain't sure if them damn nuisances had put in their appearance in that year. Everybody can hear her." Hodes noted, "As she sings she walks slowly around the stage. Her head, sort of bowed. From where I'm sittin' I'm not sure whether she even has her eyes open. On and on, number after number, the same hush, the great performance, the deafening applause. We won't let her stop. What a woman."

"Every note that woman wailed vibrated on the tight strings of my nervous system," Mezz Mezzrow wrote many years later. "Every word she sang answered a question I was asking."

". . . the New Orleans Rhythm Kings, who planted the seed, and then Joe Oliver, Louis Armstrong, Bix, Jimmy Noone . . . and Bessie Smith," said Bud Freeman. "Our style, 'Chicago style,' came from all of that."

"That spring Bessie Smith also came to town," remembers Eddie Condon. "We went to hear her at the Paradise, a battered joint with the buttons off at Thirty-fifth and Calumet. The first night Bix turned his pockets inside out and put all his dough on the table to keep her singing. We had been raised on her records; we knew she was the greatest of all the blues singers; but she was better than any of us could possibly have anticipated."

In 1928, Bessie broke with her manager, Frank Walker, who had long taken a sincere interest in the singer's welfare. She still made trips to the Columbia recording studios, although some of the singing seemed mechanical and the material she worked with was frequently inferior. The voice was still full and strong, but the words were often contrived, sometimes bordering on the pornographic, and Bessie seemed more caught up in theatrical Northern ways (the popular ways of Ethel Waters and of the recently deceased Florence Mills) than she ever had been. Nevertheless, she could still knock out a deep blues at will, as she did on *Wash-woman's Blues*, recorded in August, 1928. Her last recording that year—the next session was not to be until more than eight months later—was, appropriately, *Me and My Gin*.

It was mostly downhill now. Bessie flopped at New York's Connie's Inn, a key location on the sophisticated nightclub circuit. The few recordings she turned out in 1929 are dominated by trashy songs like *I'm Wild About That Thing, I Got What It Takes*, and *You've Got to Give Me Some*. Most of these are tossed off with disdainful expediency, but two—*Nobody Knows You When You're Down and Out* and *Kitchen Man*—leave no doubt that the great voice was still as true and strong as ever. There were even intimations that Bessie had discovered how she might adapt to the new environment of show tunes, cabaret dramatics, and piquant balladry without sacrificing her leading assets— power, projection, tone, and feeling. As of 1929, she had become several times removed from the folk sources of her earlier blues songs.

In October, she recorded a typical transient popular song, *Don't Cry, Baby*, with James P. Johnson. Though not particularly successful, this performance suggests where Bessie might have traveled had her luck held out. *Don't Cry, Baby* is performed with what Winthrop Sargeant might have called "the European conception of melody" rather than with Bessie's old center-tone Ma Rainey-like technique. In effect, she was coming around to Ethel Waters' outlook on jazz singing—to treat the melody as an instrumentalist would. Unhappily, this change failed to alter Bessie's fortunes, and the downward slide continued.

In 1929, Bessie made her only film appearance, in a two-reel short called *St. Louis Blues*, which also features a band under James P. Johnson's direction and a large choir. The sound track is crude and the scenario hopelessly offensive, but Bessie was allowed to let her voice all the way out, with fine results. "It's too bad that we didn't make a feature picture out of this," an executive of RCA Photophone remarked to W. C. Handy at the time. The film soon disappeared, rarely to be seen again in the United States until long after Bessie's death.

A new kind of blues market bloomed in 1928 and 1929, but it

failed to help Bessie very much. These were the best years for the big-city blues players and singers, especially the boogie-woogie pianists. Into the spotlight stepped performers like Cow Cow Davenport, Will Ezell, Cripple Clarence Lofton, Romeo Nelson, Pine Top Smith, Montana Taylor, and Rufus "Speckled Red" Perryman, whose masculine, optimistic blues styles replaced the moaning and wailing blues of the Smith girls and all their imitators. A rugged amalgam of hokum, stomps, country blues, old dance rhythms, and urban party games, the music now called boogie-woogie (piano) and skiffle (add jugs, washboards, and kazoos) had been gathering force since 1925, particularly in Chicago. Bessie was, of course, aware of this group of players (especially one of the most creative of them, Jimmy Yancey, at whose home she sometimes stayed while in Chicago), but she did not identify her stage act with their back-room informality. She used only "high class" musicians—trained instrumentalists of the jazz world—for her shows.

Another trouper caught in a kind of middle ground similar to Bessie's was guitarist-singer Lonnie Johnson. Johnson was a superior jazz guitar player but earned most of his money as a singer of blues, many of them salacious. Like Bessie, he recorded blues extensively but preferred to regard himself an all-around musician, as authoritative with ballads and jazz pieces as with twelve-bar Freudian imagery. The two singers toured in Southern theaters together several times in 1929. "Nobody I know could sing better than Bessie," Johnson has recalled. "She didn't mind shouting over a crowd to wake them up and make them listen to her sing. She didn't need a microphone, either. Bessie was lively and full of fun," he added, "but nobody could push her around."

Perhaps she had felt Frank Walker was "pushing her around," but without his guidance (which included putting her on an allowance), Bessie was soon burning up money much faster than it was coming in, even after she separated from Gee and moved to a modest home in New York. (Gee had managed Bessie's own show, called the *The Midnight Steppers*, just before the breakup, with unimpressive results.) She could ill afford layoffs; yet in 1930, as clarinetist Edmond Hall remembers it, Bessie "wasn't doing anything. . . . It was a long time before I even found out that Bessie Smith was living in the apartment next to mine," Hall recalls. "She was just about on her way out then."

In 1930, Bessie recorded just eight tunes, none of them deep blues of the sort she had once been famous for. Her voice was not responding with consistency now. There is a touch of strain in her performances of *New Orleans Hop Scop Blues* and *See If I'll Care*, although *On Revival Day* and *Hustlin' Dan*, recorded a few weeks later, show her in fine form. In fact, on the day that she turned out *On Revival Day* and *Moan You Moaners* (June 9, 1930), both rendered in a pseudogospel style, Bessie sang from a resonant low A-flat to a strong high E, a very respectable range. And in these recordings is still more evidence of Bessie's changing outlook on her own role in show business at that time; she was definitely trying to achieve a tuneful quality in a substantial portion of her work, eschewing the blues chants of her early career.

Another year passed. Two more recording sessions were held in 1931, ending her long association with the Columbia company. These dates seemed to be deliberate attempts to go back to the old shouting blues style of 1924. Bessie plays her part well, singing *Long Old Road* effectively (around a center tone on the fifth interval of the tonic), but the tongue-in-cheek antics of her musicians give the secret away. Trumpeter Louis Bacon and trombonist Charlie Green obviously did *not* feel this was the way jazz should be played in 1931. Though still in command of her marvelous voice, Bessie began to have some breathing problems about this time, most noticeably on *Safety Mama* (a dreary set of coarse metaphors), where she seems unable to complete normal cadences without bobbing up for more air.

Following the last six years of Bessie Smith's life is not unlike attempting to chronicle the death throes of a whale. Occasionally the subject surfaces to register its agony, but most of the process takes place below and out of sight. Bessie put in well-remembered appearances now and then, but much of her remaining time was spent knocking about the South, playing theaters or anyplace that would have her. Professional jazz fan John Hammond arranged for and supervised her final recording date, in 1933, an occasion that found her in good spirits and quite acceptable voice. The band, which included trumpeter Frankie Newton, tenor saxophonist Chu Berry, Jack Teagarden, and Benny Goodman, was probably the best studio group she ever had. On the four tunes recorded that day (*Do Your Duty, I'm Down in the Dumps, Gimme a Pigfoot,* and *Take Me for a Buggy Ride*), Bessie returns to her mid-twenties shout, clinging to tonic tones and thirds most of the way, with happy, if not distinguished, results. It was as good a note on which to end her recorded career as any, considering the hard times that were yet to come.

She surfaced again in early 1936 to sing on Fifty-second Street in a blues and jazz concert. Carl Van Vechten, leader of a group of New York intellectuals who admired Bessie's music, told (in *Jazz Record* magazine) of photographing the singer at that time: ". . . she came to see me between shows, cold sober and in a quiet, reflective mood. She could scarcely have been more amiable or co-operative."

With the worst of the Depression behind her and some fresh recognition, Bessie must have felt better about her future in early 1937. A run at Connie's Inn the season before, new shows, new tours, and some possibilities for film and recording work suggested that 1938 was to be her happiest year in a long, long time.

The blues men were making a comeback as the nation pulled out of its colossal slump, and Bessie asked Lonnie Johnson, about to record again after a five-year lapse, to join her new fall tour with a show called *Broadway Rastus.* Johnson felt a premonition of disaster and turned down the offer. Days later, Bessie Smith lay dead in Mississippi, the victim of a ghastly highway collision.

"Someways, you could almost have said beforehand that there was some kind of accident, some bad hurt, coming to her," Sidney Bechet observed in later years. "It was like she had that hurt inside her all the time, and she was just bound to find it."

Bessie Smith's magnificent voice and direct approach to the blues left their mark on almost every singer—including Ethel Waters—who ever heard her in person or on records. Jazz musicians were deeply affected by her work, too, largely because it contained the sort of fundamental order and integrity they strove to bring to their instrumental styles. Unlike the supper-club singers, Bessie was, in her best days, totally involved with but one goal—to sing the blues better than anyone else. She was completely successful in doing just that. Up to 1927, her singing was unmarred by affectations or phony diction. Jazzmen hailed Bessie's honesty and earthiness and winced as otherwise beguiling singers, such as Ethel Waters, fell into jarring mannerisms—the rolled "r" was one—alien to their natural speech.

Bessie brought dignity, even majesty, to the blues in much the same way that Louis Armstrong did. Her recordings were models of simple but eloquent expression for countless instrumentalists. And she accomplished this in the language of common folk, one- and two-syllable words that all could understand. Jazzmen, always interested in the most direct, unvarnished forms of self-expression, liked that, too.

Ethel Waters, unlike Bessie, borrowed many of her ideas from jazz musicians. Her voice was a fine instrument upon which she improvised, ran chord changes, and learned to swing in a most modern way. (Her *Sweet Georgia Brown*, recorded in 1925, was fifteen years ahead of its time, despite the stodgy accompaniment.) Ethel's outlook had even more influence than Bessie's, but only over other singers, not instrumentalists. From Ethel's easy-swinging, slightly cynical, and very worldly approach came the styles of the finest girl singers of the thirties—Lee Wiley, Mildred Bailey, Ella Fitzgerald, and Billie Holiday (compare Ethel's 1929 *Travellin' All Alone* with Billie's later recorded version).

Bessie was also deeply admired by all these singers, but none of them possessed the natural power to follow her example, even if it had been commercially feasible to do so. Billie Holiday, more than any other popular singer, preserved some of Bessie's chanting blues expression, but she put the idea to an altogether new use in her unique style. Probably the closest approximation of Bessie's sweeping vocal command and rafter-ringing projection is the voice of Mahalia Jackson, who is able to perform seriously in the musical idiom of the mid-twenties by dealing only in gospel songs.

"In New Orleans, where I lived as a child," Miss Jackson once told an interviewer, "I remember singing as I scrubbed the floors. It would make the work go easier. When the old people weren't home, I'd turn on a Bessie Smith record and play it over and over. *Careless Love*, that was the blues she sang."

No singer or musician who heard Bessie Smith sing, if only on a recording, ever forgot the experience.

Recommended Reading

Bechet, Sidney: *Treat It Gentle,* Hill and Wang, New York (1960).

Handy, W. C., and Abbe Niles: *A Treasury of the Blues,* Boni, New York (1949).

Oliver, Paul: *Bessie Smith,* Barnes, New York (1961).

Sargeant, Winthrop: *Jazz: Hot and Hybrid,* Dutton, New York (1946).

Shapiro, Nat, and Nat Hentoff (eds.): *Hear Me Talkin' to Ya,* Rinehart, New York (1955).

Shapiro, Nat, and Nat Hentoff (eds.): *The Jazz Makers,* Grove, New York (1958).

Waters, Ethel: *His Eye Is on the Sparrow,* Doubleday, New York (1951).

Recommended Listening

The Bessie Smith Story, Vols. 1, 2, 3, 4, COLUMBIA CL 855, CL 856, CL 857, CL 858.

The Jazz Makers (one track), COLUMBIA CL 1036.

Jazz, Vol. 2 (one track), FOLKWAYS FP 55.

Jazz, Vol. 4 (one track), FOLKWAYS FP 59.

The Perry Bradford Story (one track), CRISPUS-ATTUCKS PB 101.

Great Blues Singers, RIVERSIDE RLP 12-121.

Blues: Ma Rainey, RIVERSIDE RLP 12-108.

Ma Rainey: Broken Hearted Blues, RIVERSIDE RLP 12-137.

Juanita Hall Sings the Blues, COUNTERPOINT CPST 556.

EDDIE LANG

THE ONE major jazz figure of the twenties about whom relatively little has been written is guitarist Eddie Lang. Perhaps because there is general agreement among critics and musicians as to this man's singular influence over other jazz guitarists, or possibly owing to a lack of colorful extramusical digressions in his life story, Lang has never been considered particularly good copy. Nonetheless, it was this mild young man from Philadelphia who, as modern jazzman Barney Kessel expressed it, "first elevated the guitar and made it artistic" in jazz. Eddie Lang, working without precedent or predecessor, virtually wrote the book on jazz guitar in the twenties.

Lang was born Salvatore Massaro in 1904 (some jazz historians say 1902), the son of a South Philadelphia banjo and guitar maker. Sidestepping the instruments of his father's trade for a time, Eddie (whose professional name was apparently lifted from a boyhood basketball hero) devoted several years of his childhood to studying the violin. He shared his problems and triumphs during this time with another young violinist, Joe Venuti, who attended grammar and high school with Eddie and remained his closest friend until the guitarist's death. Eddie studied with Professors Changura and Luccantino and was almost certainly trained in solfeggio (sight singing) as well. (Venuti commenced *his* reading exercises when he was just four.)

"Solfeggio, of course," Venuti explained in *Down Beat* magazine years later, "that's the Italian system under which you don't bother much about any special instrument until you know all the fundamentals of music. It's the only way to learn music right."

Lang and Venuti worked a dance job with pianist Bert Estlow's quintet at Atlantic City's L'Aiglon restaurant in 1921 or 1922. Though Lang was still playing violin, he apparently picked up banjo (and probably guitar) at or shortly before this time, for the following season found him playing banjo with Charlie Kerr's orchestra. He experimented with the four-string banjo at first and later spent some time playing a six-string guitar-banjo, but the harsh sounds of these instruments obviously were not to his liking. Red Nichols remembers hearing Lang on guitar behind Venuti's violin in 1923, playing concert music at the Knickerbocker Hotel in Atlantic City. The two friends had been working up duets of one sort or another since childhood.

"We used to play a lot of mazurkas and polkas," Venuti has recalled. "Just for fun, we started to play them in 4/4. I guess we just like the rhythm of the guitar. Then we started to slip in some improvised passages. I'd slip something in, Eddie would pick it up with a variation. Then I'd come back with a variation. We'd just sit there and knock each other out."

In addition to Nichols, a number of soon-to-be-influential musicians played Atlantic City in the early twenties. Young players like the Dorsey brothers and Russ Morgan (all working with the Scranton Sirens) admired and relaxed with Lang and Venuti. Later, these friends were helpful in lining up lucrative jobs in top bands for the Philadelphia boys.

Eddie, back in Atantic City for the 1924 summer season after working winter jobs with the Scranton Sirens and others, met and sat in with a young novelty group from St. Louis, the Mound City Blue Blowers. This brash trio (Red McKenzie, comb; Dick Slevin, kazoo; Jack Bland, banjo) was riding high on its hit recording of *Arkansas Blues*, cut four or five months earlier that year. The Blue Blowers were booked into the Beaux Arts Café, a club owned by two Philadelphia entrepreneurs, Joe Moss and Nookie Johnson. In casual jam sessions, the uncommon sound of Lang's guitar added harmonic flesh and rhythmic bones to the rather rickety sound of the little group, and by August, Eddie was taken on as a regular member. He traveled to New York and a stint at the famed Palace Theater with the Blue Blowers; but for a while, Lang continued to play in Atlantic City, commuting to New York only when needed for theater or recording dates. From this time on, Eddie was never without plum jobs at the highest going rates—except when he wanted to be.

In the fall of 1924, the Blue Blowers played the Piccadilly Hotel in London and a short engagement in Limehouse at a place called Haggarty's Empire. England's reaction seems to have been rather mixed at best, for the quartet was back in New York before the end of the year. Mound City Blue Blowers recordings of late 1924 and early 1925 document the sound of Eddie Lang at this juncture.

A piece called *Deep Second Street Blues* reveals that Lang had already fixed several aspects of his personal style and was well on the way toward establishing the guitar as an important band instrument as well. For one thing, Eddie, like comb player McKenzie, knew how to get inside a blues and express himself convincingly in this essentially Southern idiom. *Deep Second Street,* for all its emphasis upon novelty effects, is performed with genuine blues feeling, a feeling Lang apparently acquired quite easily and was never to lose, even on very commercial assignments. *Deep Second Street* also has Lang playing rhythm in a manner that was highly personal and distinctly advanced for the time. His tendency was toward an even four-to-the-bar pulse, often with a new chord position, inversion, or alteration on every stroke of the strings. In contrast to the monotonous chopping of most banjoists of the day, Eddie's ensemble guitar sparkled with passing tones, chromatic sequences, and single-string fills. With all this went a firm, individual tone unlike the sound of any other instrument yet heard in jazz.

Another moody piece called *Play Me Slow* demonstrates many of these same qualities, as well as Lang's early mastery of varying vibratos (often adapted from violin techniques) and the startling sound of "artificial" harmonics—the technique, seldom used in jazz, of barely touching the string to achieve overtones an octave higher than normally sound in the given fret position.

For faster selections, such as *Tiger Rag* and *Gettin' Told,* Lang often reverts to straight 4/4 rhythm or to a "walking" line in 2/4 or 4/4 on his lowest string in the manner of a string-bass player.

The Mound City Blue Blowers' somewhat rustic library was hardly a challenge to Lang's advanced ear. Like most of the outstanding jazzmen of the twenties, the guitarist's most valuable asset was his ability to hear and grasp new material upon a single exposure to it. Lang had a photographic memory and a perfect sense of pitch. "He had the best ear of any musician I ever knew," wrote guitarist Jack Bland many years after working with Lang in the Blue Blowers. "He could go into another room and hit A and come back and play cards for fifteen minutes, and then tune his instrument perfectly. I've seen that happen."

In the summer of 1925, Lang and Venuti landed in Atlantic City again. The resort town was, as usual, full of live music. The Benson Orchestra was booked into the Million Dollar Pier, the Mason-Dixon Seven worked the Steel Pier, the California Night-hawks were at Evelyn Nesbitt's Silver Slipper, and the Dance-land Seven, with whom Venuti played for a while, appeared in a show called *The Wild Ways of 1925* at the Beaux Arts. The Mound City Blue Blowers, with Lang, also put in some time there that summer, and Venuti could often be found playing with them, with or without pay. Everyone sat in with everyone else from time to time.

Although the Mound City Blue Blowers continued to delight audiences in movie houses (". . . at a theater date in Minneapolis on a Friday night they had to take the picture off three times because the crowd was clapping so hard, especially for Lang," Bland has recalled), it was obvious that their peak of success had been passed and equally obvious that Lang could do much better elsewhere. From late 1925 on, the guitarist was more in demand than perhaps any other jazz musician in the country. He was especially valuable on recordings, where microphone balance could easily compensate for the guitar's lack of carrying power.

Singers in particular discovered that Lang's sensitive chording and striking single-string arpeggios added immeasurable class to their performances, many of which were at the outset rather grim affairs. A case in point is a recording by one Norman Clark, a pre-electric-microphone shouter of the lowest order. His painful versions of *Sleepy Time Gal* and *Lonesomest Gal in Town* are gilded with superlative guitar accompaniments, complete with ringing artificial harmonics and advanced single-string runs. Other highly forgettable singers to whom Lang gave his best were Charles Kaley, Harold Lem, Seger Ellis, Russell Douglas, Peggy English, Emmett Miller, Lee Morse, Ruth Etting, Sammy Fain, Cliff Edwards, and Vaughn de Leath.

By late 1925, Eddie was also recording with Ross Gorman's respected studio band (with members often drawn from Paul Whiteman's orchestra), along with other rising instrumental stars like Red Nichols, Miff Mole, and Jimmy Dorsey. On these dates, Lang's guitar was sometimes featured as a solo instrument only, while a conventional banjo played rhythm in the background.

Throughout this period, Eddie demonstrated constant improvement and deepening in his command of the guitar and in his concepts of the harmonic language of jazz. With Mole, Nichols, and Dorsey exploring new ideas alongside him, Lang began to hit his full stride. On one Gorman title, *No More Worryin'*, he tosses off a virile blues-touched solo, played partly with pick and partly with fingers. Other guitarists were amazed by Lang's ability to tuck the pick into his palm, play with his fingers, and suddenly bring the pick back again—all without disturbing the flow of his solo.

With Lang's arrival, arrangers began to recognize the potential of the guitar as a melody instrument. One of Gorman's scores, *Sleepy Time Gal*, called for the unheard-of duet combination of baritone saxophone and guitar in a surprisingly modern interlude. With electrical recording methods, Lang's solo guitar became a familiar sound to many record buyers. Often he was featured in "hot" passages along with Venuti's violin, for where one man went, the other usually followed.

Eddie was favored by demanding bandleaders, too, because he was, as jazzmen went, a reliable man to have on the job. He seldom drank and was by nature a rather retiring person. Only his passion for gambling games and an overwhelming urge to spend every summer fishing with Venuti in Atlantic City were allowed to intrude occasionally upon Lang's devotion to the guitar.

After a stint with the pit orchestra of *Earl Carroll's Vanities* (co-directed by Gorman and Don Voorhees), Eddie began in 1926 to be heard in arrangements by outstanding jazz-slanted bands such as Jean Goldkette's, Roger Wolfe Kahn's, and, eventually, Paul Whiteman's. Lang and Venuti were continually drafted into such organizations but frequently departed after short tenures. Sometimes it was the call of Atlantic City; often it was simply the lure of steady radio and recording work in New York.

In the fall of 1926, Venuti and Lang turned out their first duet record, *Stringin' the Blues* (a thinly camouflaged *Tiger Rag*) and *Black and Blue Bottom*. Venuti, displaying a good share of his bag of violin tricks, is clearly the featured performer, but Lang's clean four-to-the-bar pulse and pregnant chords are impressive. Most musicians had never heard a guitarist of this caliber before, except in classical and flamenco circles. Lang made many realize that for small jazz groups, the guitar could offer subtlety, dynamic response, and flexibility beyond what the banjo was capable of delivering. Some banjoists began studying the guitar in earnest.

An even wider audience of musicians and fans was reached with a series of 1926–1927 recordings by Red Nichols and the Five Pennies (also billed as the Redheads). Nichols' own work usually suffered from overconcern with precision ("King Oliver's records were full of mistakes," the cornetist once said. "So were ours, but *we* tried to correct them"), but his little recording group gleamed with new ideas and talent. He was given a relatively free hand to try unusual tunes, original arrangements, and daring instrumental effects. The gang Eddie worked with usually included Vic Berton, a trained and imaginative drummer who doubled on tympani; Jimmy Dorsey, already regarded as a virtuoso alto saxophonist and a very capable clarinetist; Arthur Schutt, a skilled pianist with a deep knowledge of harmony and arranging techniques; and Miff Mole, considered by New Yorkers in 1927 to be without equal on trombone.

Lang may have played his old six-string guitar-banjo on a few of these dates, but his important solo work was performed on the plectrum guitar. Using a precise, powerful attack derived from tight, high strings and a stout plectrum (pick), Eddie moved in close to the microphone to achieve on records a vibrant, personal sound as persuasive as the sounds of the horn players around him. Further, he seemed completely at ease in the frequently tense atmosphere of Nichols' more advanced sessions.

The attitude of the Five Pennies was, in a way, a reflection of the spirit of unrest and experimentation that marked much of the world's music in the twenties. Indeed, the Nichols-Mole-Schutt credo could be expressed by the comments of Heinrich Simon, an observer of European formal music in the twenties: "The triad is the symbol of bourgeois conformity in music . . . a bore too tenacious to be done away with, an undesirable to be ignored. The same may be said of form . . . freedom of form is the slogan of the day."

Hoagy Carmichael's *Washboard Blues* was such a departure from conventional song forms. It includes, even in Nichols' simplified version, an unorthodox sixteen-bar melody (originally written as seventeen bars) leading to curiously altered blues sequences, all heavily syncopated. Tommy Dorsey and Bix Beiderbecke had attempted to play the composition several years earlier in the Gennett studios, but, as Dorsey expressed it in later years, "We must have fooled with that piece for hours, but we never could get to play it right."

Nichols featured Berton's tympani in a semimelodic role on *Washboard Blues* and left room for Lang to improvise a splendid, unusual countermelody. It was to remain one of the more creative melodic solos of Eddie's career.

Another strange composition from this period is *That's No Bargain*, which jazz writer Richard DuPage has described well: "*That's No Bargain* broke nearly all the Tin Pan Alley rules of the twenties. . . . It has an even number of bars but it sounds uneven, yet with a good beat throughout. Hardly anyone could whistle it correctly, even after several hearings. . . ."

The eighteen-bar chorus allotted to Lang on *That's No Bargain* comes out as an intelligent, ordered, and understated solo played *against* the basic pulse, creating the same mood the tune itself had been designed to achieve.

These Nichols records range from noisy and contrived to prophetic and breathtakingly adventurous, but Lang seems forever unruffled, even complacent, on them all.

For at least one recording, Eddie apparently had his solo well formed in his mind before beginning to play. It is *Get a Load of This*, a Lang melody probably inspired in part by Bix Beiderbecke's ideas (the performance is full of flatted fifths, minor sevenths, parallel ninths, etc.) and played by a quartet made up of Eddie, Nichols, Schutt, and Berton. Lang later developed this piece into a guitar specialty called *Eddie's Twister*, without changing his solo very much.

There were more Nichols dates in 1927. Some, like *Cornfed*, reveal that Lang, for all his brilliance as a soloist, accompanist, and innovator, had unfortunate lapses as a rhythm player. Here there is a tendency to allow his strings to ring too long, blurring and casting a cloud of doubt over the exact location of each pulse. As guitarist and Lang student Marty Grosz once summed it up, Eddie's rhythm sometimes sounds "a bit lumpy, like a guy running with a pie in his pants."

Grosz explained: "The Chicago guys felt that Lang didn't really swing, and I'm inclined to go along to an extent. At least, he had trouble swinging in the way that some of the Chicagoans did and in the way his successors did. But I think we can overlook that for the nonce. In his way he did so much, and it sounds so damn natural and easy. And he was first; he had to think the whole thing out for himself," Grosz added. "It is always more difficult to lead the way. Hence modern bass players can play rings around Jimmy Blanton—but Blanton was first and had the soul. Same with Lang."

During 1927, Eddie appeared on many recordings in the company of Bix Beiderbecke and a variety of supporting players, usually mutual friends selected from the Goldkette or Whiteman ranks. (Bix and Lang were both members of the short-lived 1927 Adrian Rollini band as well.) The most famous of these recordings are *Singin' the Blues* and *I'm Comin' Virginia*, on which Bix went far toward establishing a robust ballad style in jazz. Lang seemed to grasp the significance of the date, for his support of Beiderbecke is in the arpeggio single-note style he usually reserved for singers rather than "hot" instrumentalists. Moreover, the rich chords, inversions, and alterations Lang selected were valuable to Bix, whose quick ear promptly put such provocative material to excellent use. For *I'm Comin' Virginia*, arranger Irving Riskin wrote an unorthodox guitar lead over a brace of supporting horns, emphasizing the string instrument's new independence, which came in with Lang and electric microphones.

In several instances, Lang took on the large task of providing nearly all the rhythmic thrust behind the horns as well as sharing the front-line spotlight with Beiderbecke and Frank Trumbauer. This occurs in *Riverboat Shuffle*, a band performance that succeeds in spite of drummer Chauncy Morehouse's halting contributions.

One of Eddie's finest recorded solos of this period appears in a trio version of *I'd Climb the Highest Mountain*, slightly altered and retitled *For No Reason at All in C*. Beiderbecke, playing piano, turns about and supports Lang's guitar with anticipatory modern chords, as Eddie had done for his cornet. The result is a highly creative guitar solo marked by an unusual degree of melodic continuity.

The influence of these outstanding Beiderbecke-Lang sessions could be heard in numerous bands, large and small, around 1927.

Jean Goldkette, for whom Eddie worked only as an added attraction, used the guitar to advantage on his recordings. Lang can be heard playing breaks and filling spaces in Bix's remarkable solo on Goldkette's *Clementine*. Paul Whiteman also added Lang for special assignments. When Eddie was unavailable, Whiteman sometimes called upon guitarists Gilbert Torres or Carl Kress to perform similar duties.

It was shortly before this time that Roger Wolfe Kahn, a wealthy young man who decided to lead a band just for the fun of it, bought out Arthur Lange's orchestra and began restocking its ranks with the best New York talent available. Eventually, he was able to secure Lang, Venuti, Arthur Schutt, Miff Mole, and Vic Berton because the band spent much time in New York—more than two years at the Hotel Biltmore—and the pay was generous. Best of all for the musicians, Kahn's working hours were 11 P.M. to 1 A.M., which meant plenty of outside recording, radio, and theater work.

"Joe and Eddie were presented as a special attraction by themselves," pianist Schutt recalled. "Roger paid one price for the pair. We averaged five to ten recordings a week and made a lot of money—$400 or $500 a week was usual, and in one seven-day period I made $1,250. No one worked for scale—that was an insult. We got double scale for casuals and $175 for one radio show. We lived it up."

Eddie often supplemented his already large income with winnings from cards and billiards, at which he excelled. He also picked up some pin money working in a successful broadway show called *Rain or Shine*.

In addition to countless commercial recordings during 1927 and 1928, Eddie and Joe stepped up their record output with duet, trio, and quartet performances and, for Lang, an impressive set of guitar solos. All these records combined amounted to a virtual textbook on plectrum guitar playing that, in some respects, remains valid and useful to guitarists to this day.

Lang's solo recordings range from a sensitive, rather formal rendering of *Prelude in C-sharp Minor* to strong blueslike statements, as in a piece called *Melody Man's Dream* (which begins with a series of chromatic thirteenths). For blues numbers, he frequently employed the "smear," a sliding across the fret that added to the tone something resembling a human cry. This device was probably picked up from folk blues guitarists. And by using downstrokes almost exclusively, Lang also approached the kind of ringing authority and positive cadences usually associated with horns rather than strings.

In passages such as his introductory cadenza to *April Kisses,* Lang tosses off sixteenth-note and thirty-second-note single-string runs with precision and ease. Sometimes he changed the angle of the pick or the position of the stroke in relation to the fingerboard to achieve special sounds.

Eddie's Twister, Lang's first recorded solo piece (and, as has been mentioned, previously titled *Get a Load of This*), offers a nearly complete kit of Eddie's ideas. Here can be found "dead string" chords (achieved by dampening certain strings to obtain desired chords without losing the impact of a full stroke), the changing of fingers on the same fret to get a fresh attack, interval jumps of a tenth to simulate the effect of a jazz pianist, parallel ninth chords, whole-tone scalar figures, "smears," unusual glissandi, artificial harmonics, harplike effects, consecutive augmented chords, and relaxed, hornlike phrasing.

So it goes, through selections like *Perfect, Rainbow Dreams, I'll Never Be the Same, Church Street Sobbin' Blues,* and *There'll Be Some Changes Made* (the last two issued under the name Blind Willie Dunn).

Of *Changes Made,* Marty Grosz has written:

. . . it is a journey from Naples to Lonnie Johnsonville (New Orleans, Natchez, South Side Chicago) in two and a half minutes. After a cadenza right out of the bagnios of old Italy and a few F. Scott Fitzgerald chords from pianist Signorelli, Lang proceeds to play a slower than expected *Changes* in the simplest and yet most eloquent manner . . . blue and melancholy as hell. It is a very difficult matter to play a lead as simply and directly as that and to make it come to life, especially on guitar. Here is the real genius of Sal Massaro. This is the honest bread stick. How Eddie Lang found out I don't know.

In addition to his roles as rhythm player, guitar soloist, "hot" man, and accompanist, Lang recorded as a blues specialist, usually under the Dunn pseudonym. Sometimes he worked with singers such as Bessie Smith, Victoria Spivey, or Texas Alexander, and

Lang was always careful to play elemental blues phrases rather than delicate arpeggios behind these artists. Occasionally, he appeared in sessions with instrumental groups that included older men like Joe Oliver and Clarence Williams. He recorded fine straight-faced blues solos with a couple of hokum clarinetists named Wilton Crawley and Boyd Senter. Best of all, he turned out a dozen duets with New Orleans jazzman Lonnie Johnson, one of the very few original guitar stylists (other than straight folk blues players) in the late twenties and, like Lang, an ex-violinist. "Eddie could lay down rhythm and bass parts just like a piano," Johnson recalls. "He was the finest guitarist I had ever heard in 1928 and 1929. I think he could play anything he felt like."

If Lang suffered from problems with rhythm, they are not conspicuous on his duets with Johnson. Together the two men charge through original blues and stomp pieces with titles such as *Two Tone Stomp, Bullfrog Moan*, and *Handful of Riffs*. One of the most stunning of these performances is a bustling number called *Hot Fingers*, where the two guitars sound like four.

By 1928, some of Lang's New York colleagues were turning toward more earthy blues-touched styles on certain record dates, and Eddie obliged by shifting to a matching mood. A pair of outstanding examples of this development are Jimmy Dorsey's *Praying the Blues* and Tommy Dorsey's trumpet recording of *It's Right Here for You*. Lang himself conducted one 1929 session in a similar humor, on which the Dorseys, Arthur Schutt *et al.* display obvious delight with their loose digressions from the old Red Nichols discipline. Two reasons for these bluesy performances (the Lang titles are *Bugle Call Rag, Walkin' the Dog, Freeze an' Melt*, and *Hot Heels*) were the arrivals in New York of Jack Teagarden and Louis Armstrong, whose Southern blues deliverances soon replaced the more ordered messages of Miff Mole and Bix Beiderbecke in the affections of Eastern musicians. In short, the gang had new heroes. For Eddie, it was easy; he already knew it all.

This shift of interest within the New York clique toward the blues—and Louis Armstrong's blues, in particular—is succinctly expressed in a single recording of a casual jam session involving Armstrong, Teagarden, Lang, and pianist Joe Sullivan, among others. Here these men play a simple and moving blues in a manner that almost seems to say, "If you can't play a real blues, don't bother to play jazz." The blues piece is called *Knockin' a Jug.* Eddie sets the mood of it and prudently stays out of Armstrong's path while the trumpeter brings the affair to its climax.

Some of Lang's best work of the 1927–1930 period can be heard on more than a score of records released under Joe Venuti's name. The earliest of these frequently reveal the influence of Beiderbecke, through choice of material and manner of improvisation. (Bass saxophonist Adrian Rollini, a convincing out-of-Bix soloist, appears on many Venuti records.) In a tune called *Sunshine,* made before Bix's classic *Singin' the Blues,* there are even intimations of the new style soon to come from Beiderbecke. Again, the famed cornetist's ideas seem to flow in and out of a selection called *Cheese and Crackers,* on which Venuti plays a pizzicato solo that sounds remarkably like Lang at the guitar.

One of the group's many "original" compositions is *Doin' Things,* which pianist Arthur Schutt developed from Debussy's *Maid with the Flaxen Hair.* Another is *A Mug of Ale* (actually *Limehouse Blues*), a good jazz vehicle that allows Lang to build a sixteen-bar spiral of ideas utilizing two-string chords and arpeggios dissolving into single-string melodic units. Some of the tunes borrow heavily from the perennial *Tiger Rag.* An unusual composition is *Pretty Trix,* a charming concert piece on which Lang achieves a Spanish–Latin American feeling while using his fingers instead of the customary plectrum.

The Venuti-Lang quartet performances represent a pioneer effort to present chamber jazz with a minimum of unmusical effects or superfluous vocals and without any pretense of its being anything but music for *listening.*

That Lang was still at odds with the ardent Chicago gang in matters of rhythm is dramatically demonstrated by a 1928 recording with Red McKenzie and banjoist Eddie Condon called *My Baby Came Home.* Condon, in the zealous Chicago manner, pushes to the top of the beat, while Lang remains coolly an eyewink or so behind him. Both are acceptable ways of setting out the rhythm, but not at the same time. Lang, however, was, unlike Condon, an important soloist, and his solo style derived much of its charm and impact from this penchant for "laying back." And, as it turned out, it was Lang's way (or, more directly, the ways of his successors) that triumphed in the thirties: the concept of an even, relaxed, flowing rhythm against which the soloist was free to build his own tension-and-release patterns rather than falling under the whip of a highly aggressive rhythm guitarist.

Paul Whiteman, who had been unable to hold on to Lang and Venuti more than a few weeks in 1927, hired the team once again in May, 1929. This time they stayed for a year. Lang is featured on many Whiteman recordings of this period, as well as in concerts, broadcasts, and the unsuccessful movie *The King of Jazz*. He appeared with Venuti in duets and frequently could be heard behind Whiteman's best vocalists, Mildred Bailey and Bing Crosby. Whiteman himself wrote about this period in *Down Beat* magazine a decade later:

> Eddie played with our band over a long period of time during which I had less trouble with rhythm than at any other time. . . . I don't even know whether he could read or not. It made no difference. . . . No matter how intricate the arrangement was, Eddie played it flawlessly the first time without ever having heard it before or looking at a sheet of music. It was as if his musically intuitive spirit had read the arranger's mind and knew in advance everything that was going to happen.

Frank Trumbauer remembered Lang carrying the entire Whiteman library in the form of cues written on the back of a small business card. Whatever the details, it seems safe to assume that Eddie played out his time with Whiteman almost entirely by ear.

Lang and Bing Crosby became fast friends during their stay with the orchestra. The guitarist married a close friend of Dixie Lee, Crosby's wife. Kitty Lang, a Ziegfeld Follies graduate, was Eddie's second wife, and their marriage remained lastingly successful.

About a month after Crosby's departure from Whiteman in the spring of 1930, Venuti and Lang also dropped out. The orchestra had been having trouble meeting its enormous payroll under Depression conditions, and with the coming of warm weather, Joe and Eddie doubtless turned their thoughts to Atlantic City.

In 1931, Lang became full-time accompanist to Crosby, who was beginning to build his fortune as a single performer. As Crosby's weekly income leaped toward five figures, Eddie dropped many of his independent activities to concentrate on four theater shows a day, Cremo Cigar broadcasts at night, and Crosby record dates in between. When Crosby closed a deal for five film assignments at $300,000, Lang went along to California. The guitarist even made a brief appearance in *The Big Broadcast of 1932.*

Most of Lang's record work behind Crosby consists in single-string fills and arpeggios, played as often with fingers as with pick. Some of his more impressive accompaniments are *How Long Will It Last?*, *Here Lies Love,* and *Please.*

For all his preoccupation with the genesis of the Crosby image, Eddie continued to find numerous extra recording jobs, jazz and otherwise. He worked frequently with the Boswell Sisters, a jazz-oriented vocal trio, displaying on pieces like *Mood Indigo, It's the Girl,* and *There'll Be Some Changes Made* a new feathery touch, combined with the steadfast 4/4 rhythmic flow, that was signaling the coming of swing music and the end of the "hot" era. There were, too, more dates with Venuti, notably four band selections under the name Venuti-Lang All-Star Orchestra.

The All-Star session, which included Benny Goodman, Jack Teagarden, and other contemporaries, was a curious mixture of stomp and swing; yet most of the participants seemed to be looking ahead to new developments of the thirties. Teagarden offers his traditional *Beale Street Blues,* and a nod to the past can be heard in *Farewell Blues,* but *Someday Sweetheart* and *After You've Gone* are harbingers of the sound of Benny Goodman, circa 1935. Lang displays on these numbers an evolving style of playing rhythm chords that would belong to the new decade. Along with a handful of other guitarists, most of whom had taken their inspiration from Lang, the quiet man from South Philadelphia had sealed the banjo's fate by 1932. (Duke Ellington's Fred Guy, one of the last to give up banjo for guitar, made the switch in 1933, a few weeks after Lang's death.)

Two guitar duets recorded with Carl Kress in 1932 document Lang's continuing search for new possibilities on his instrument. *Pickin' My Way* and *Feelin' My Way* are full of virtuoso tricks, such as the achievement of a gruppetto effect (several neighboring notes used as embellishment just before or after a melody note) with but a single stroke on the string. There is even a Hawaiian sliding device—used, of course, with taste and restraint. The two duets (and it should be mentioned that Kress, who used a unique tuning system and a rhythm approach different from Lang's, was a first-class performer) are the final chapters in Eddie Lang's text. There were other recordings, but nothing new was added to what had already been set out.

Eddie was still a young man of 28 in 1933, his last year, and was looking forward to continued personal prosperity with Bing Crosby. Crosby has given (in his autobiography *Call Me Lucky*) the facts of Lang's untimely death.

> He had a chronically inflamed sore throat and felt bad for a year or eighteen months before his death. He mistrusted doctors and medicine. Like many people who came from backgrounds similar to his and had no experience with doctors or hospitals, he had an aversion to them. But his throat was so bad and it affected his health to such a point that I finally talked him into seeing a doctor.
>
> Many times afterward I wished I hadn't.
>
> The doctor advised a tonsillectomy, and Eddie never came out from under the general anesthetic they gave him . . . [he] developed an embolism and died without regaining consciousness.

The legacy left by Lang to jazz guitarists was colossal. Almost alone he proved the desirability of the guitar as a band instrument, making life more interesting for rhythm players—as well as soloists—than ever before. Setting an example for all to follow, Eddie put to work technical devices, some established in formal music and others of his own invention, that had never been used in jazz before. More than thirty years after his death, guitarists are still impressed by Lang's command of his instrument. ("Artificial harmonics?" exclaimed guitarist Jim Hall in 1962. "I know about them, but the only man I've heard use them in jazz recently is Tal Farlow, who is probably the most technically advanced guitarist we have today.")

From Lang, guitarists Carl Kress and Dick McDonough evolved personal styles that in turn influenced many rhythm players in the thirties. Kress departed from Eddie's solo approach to combine chords and melody simultaneously. George Van Eps, also building on Lang's foundation, followed with a method of playing melody, chords, and intelligent bass lines at the same time. The Van Eps system was adopted or modified by many of the best rhythm guitarists—Freddie Greene of the Count Basie band was one—during the thirties. Musicians also learned from Lang that the guitar could be used to accompany singers as effectively as could the piano.

Part of the credit for the advent of the guitar solo in jazz must go to the electric microphone, but it was Lang who first put the microphone to work in a creative way. The guitarist did not merely play into the microphone, he *used* it to bring out his most subtle ideas. In this way, Lang's work presaged the arrival of the electric guitar, a development that followed his death by several years. With or without electrical amplification, however, Eddie's concept of hornlike single-string jazz solos was to remain the dominant mode of self-expression on the instrument, from the European Django Reinhardt to Tal Farlow. There were other men playing solo guitar in the twenties, musicians like Teddy Bunn, Lonnie Johnson, and blues man Blind Lemon Jefferson, but none approached Lang's finesse, technical command, resourcefulness, and expressive scope all at once.

Eddie Lang set another kind of example as well. Like Bix Beiderbecke, he was a serious musician who dug deep into jazz but also looked to formal music for inspiration. Despite Lang's reluctance to read music, other jazzmen saw in him the complete musician, a man who would handle any assignment, including a session with Bessie Smith, with authority and intelligence. He was one of the first to disprove the notion (still held in some quarters) that all-around musicianship and the spirit of jazz cannot go together.

Unlike some of his gifted friends, Lang neither dashed himself to pieces on the crags of self-indulgence nor shielded himself from everyday reality through perpetuated adolescence; yet he fared no better than the weakest of them at the end. In its way, his end may have held the deepest irony of all.

Recommended Reading

Ramsey, Frederic, and Charles Edward Smith: *Jazzmen*, Harcourt, Brace, New York (1939).

Shapiro, Nat, and Nat Hentoff (eds.): *Hear Me Talkin' to Ya*, Rinehart, New York (1955).

Recommended Listening

Thesaurus of Classic Jazz, COLUMBIA C4L-18.
The Bix Beiderbecke Story, Vols. 2 and 3, COLUMBIA CL-845, 846.
The Bix Beiderbecke Legend, RCA VICTOR LPM-2323.
Red Nichols: For Collectors Only, BRUNSWICK 54008.
Joe Venuti and Eddie Lang, "X" LVA-3036 (deleted).
The Louis Armstrong Story, Vol. 4 (one track), COLUMBIA CL-854.
Jazz, Vol. 7 (one track), FOLKWAYS FP 67.
The Encyclopedia of Jazz on Records, Vol. 1 (one track), DECCA 8383.
Lang and Venuti: Stringin' the Blues, COLUMBIA C2L-24.

INDEX

257

Other DA CAPO titles of interest